THE COMPLETE BOOK OF
BIBLE TRIVIA

THE COMPLE

Bible

J. STEPH

Tyndale House Publishers, Inc.

TE BOOK OF

Trivia

EN LANG

Wheaton, Illinois

Scripture quotations, unless otherwise noted, are
from the King James Version of the Bible

ISBN 0-8423-0421-5

To Mark Fackler,
who is a friend of the Bible
and who understands laughter

CONTENTS

INTRODUCTION

C an we speak of *the Bible* and *trivia* in the same breath? Can this inspired document that is pored over with great seriousness by pastors, seminarians, and lay people provide material for leisure and even laughter?

I think it can, and as I began writing this book, I became more and more convinced that the Bible, that divine book through which God's Truth shines, is an earthy, human collection of people and incidents that cannot help but amuse (as well as enlighten) a reader. I believe, as most Christians do, that the Bible has come down to us through God's initiative. I also believe that God chose to present his truth through stories, oracles, and letters that not only inspire us, but also captivate us as any good stories do. Even unbelievers have recognized for centuries that the Bible is a veritable treasure trove of stories, as attested to by the many poems, plays, novels, films, paintings, and sculptures that are based on the Scriptures.

The Bible throbs with human life. It is full of sublime teaching—and sometimes pathetic, sometimes amusing pictures of human failings. It evokes tears and laughter, repulsion and admiration. To probe its many characters and stories cannot be wrong. To ask questions about its content can, at the very least, provide innocent amusement. Even better, asking questions can lead us deeper into the content and make us appreciate and (it is hoped) study more deeply this fascinating treasury of stories.

This is not the first collection of questions and answers about the Bible, and it probably will not be the last. However, most previous books seem to have focused on the seriousness of the text, neglecting the possibilities of finding things to chuckle over and cry over. Too many of these volumes have been painfully dry, with questions arranged in neat Genesis-to-Revelation sequence.

I have tried to avoid dryness at all costs. The arrangement here is topical, with such topics as "Strange Ways to Die," "Hairy and Hairless" (yes, really), "All Kinds of Villains," "Women on the Throne," and so on. I hope the choice of topics will itself provide some chuckles. The category "Not to Be Taken Seriously" is just for laughs, and so is "Curious Quotations." (One can't include *every* subject in the book, of course, but the range is wide—supernatural fires, prostitutes, creepy animals, priests, violent men, earthquakes, prisoners, hugs and kisses, warriors, miracles, and many, many others.)

The topics are arranged under fourteen sections. However, despite the attempt at organization, the book is for browsing. It was made to fill up your time commuting on the train, the hour you spend waiting at the dentist's office, the few minutes before dinner is on the table, the hours on the freeway when you and the other two people in the back seat are in the mood for a game of "quiz me." In other words, the book is designed to be read randomly, anywhere, and with no preparation of any kind. It is designed to entertain the person who unashamedly likes to be entertained—and challenged. By the way, to avoid the hassle of having all the answers in one section at the back of the book, we've placed the answers in the most logical place—on the backs of the pages, behind the questions.

The author would like to hear from any person who is able to correctly (and without peeking at the answers on the back of each page) answer every question in this book. In doing the research for this book, the author himself learned quite a bit, but not enough to answer every question correctly—at least, not yet.

Happy reading! I hope you enjoy getting better acquainted with the divine—and very human—Book of books.

PART 1

A Cast of Thousands

◆The Naked Truth

1. What prophet walked around naked for three years?
2. Who went naked as a way of wailing over the fate of Jerusalem?
3. What king of Israel, struck with the power to prophesy, stripped off his clothes and lay naked for a whole day and night?
4. What father lay naked and intoxicated in his tent, which so disturbed his sons that they came and covered him?
5. In war, what persons were often humiliated by being stripped?
6. What prophet threatened to take away the flax that covered his wife's nakedness?
7. What disciple, busy at his daily work, was caught naked by Jesus?
8. Who embarrassed his wife by shamelessly exposing himself while dancing for joy?
9. Where did a follower of Jesus escape an angry mob by running away naked?
10. What prophet spoke of a woman (merely a symbol) who committed sexual sins while naked?

◆Laughers and Dancers

1. Whose entrancing dance proved fatal for John the Baptist?
2. Who held a feast with dancing when his son returned?
3. Who laughed at Nehemiah's plans to rebuild Jerusalem?
4. Who danced with all his might when the ark of the covenant was brought to Jerusalem?
5. Who laughed when she heard she would bear a son in her old age?
6. Who was snickered at for claiming that a dead girl was only asleep?

The Naked Truth (Answers)

1. Isaiah (20:3)
2. The prophet Micah (1:8)
3. Saul (1 Samuel 19:24)
4. Noah (Genesis 9:21-23)
5. Captives (2 Chronicles 28:15)
6. Hosea (2:3, 9)
7. Simon Peter (John 21:7)
8. King David (2 Samuel 6:20)
9. Gethsemane (Mark 14:51-52)
10. Ezekiel (23:10, 29)

Laughers and Dancers (Answers)

1. The daughter of Herodias (Matthew 14:6-8)
2. The father of the prodigal son (Luke 15:25)
3. Sanballat, Tobiah, and Geshem (Nehemiah 2:19)
4. David (2 Samuel 6:14)
5. Sarah (Genesis 18:10-12)
6. Jesus (Matthew 9:23-24)

7. What prophetess led the women of Israel in a victory dance?
8. Whose ill-fated daughter came out dancing after his victory over the Ammonites?
9. Who had his decree for a Passover celebration laughed at by the men of Israel?
10. What tribe took wives from among the dancers at Shiloh?
11. Who came out dancing after David killed Goliath?
12. What is the only book in the Bible to mention God laughing?
13. What epistle tells Christians to turn their laughter to mourning?
14. What old woman said, "God hath made me to laugh so that all who hear will laugh with me"?
15. Who told Job that God would certainly fill a righteous man with laughter?
16. According to Psalm 126, what caused laughter among the Jews?
17. What old man laughed at God's promise that he would father a child in his old age?
18. What group of people were busy dancing and partying when David caught up with them?
19. What graven image did the Israelites dance in front of?
20. What book says there is a time to weep and a time to laugh?
21. Who, in the Beatitudes, does Jesus promise laughter to?
22. What book says that laughter is foolishness?
23. What book says that even in laughter the heart is sorrowful?
24. Whom did Jesus speak of as dancing in the streets?
25. Who danced around the altar of their false god?
26. Whose wife despised him for dancing in the streets?
27. What instrument is usually associated with dance in the Bible?
28. What book says, "Our dance is turned into mourning"?
29. According to Job, whose children dance about and make music?
30. What Old Testament character's name means "laughter"?

7. Miriam (Exodus 15:20)
8. Jephthah's (Judges 11:34)
9. Hezekiah (2 Chronicles 30:5, 10)
10. Benjamin (Judges 21:20, 23)
11. The women of Israel (1 Samuel 18:6-7)
12. Psalms (2:4; 37:13; 59:8)
13. James (4:9)
14. Sarah (Genesis 21:6)
15. Bildad (Job 8:21)
16. Bringing the captives back to Jerusalem (Psalm 126:2)
17. Abraham (Genesis 17:17)
18. The Amalekites (1 Samuel 30:16-18)
19. The golden calf made by Aaron (Exodus 32:19)
20. Ecclesiastes (3:4)
21. Those who weep (Luke 6:21)
22. Ecclesiastes (2:2)
23. Proverbs (14:13)
24. Children (Luke 7:32)
25. The priests of Baal (1 Kings 18:26)
26. David's wife, Michal (1 Chronicles 15:29)
27. The timbrel, or tambourine (Exodus 15:20; Judges 11:34; Job 21:12; Psalm 150:4)
28. Lamentations (5:15)
29. The children of the wicked (Job 21:7-12)
30. Isaac (Genesis 21:3-6)

◆They Did It First

1. What king had the first birthday party in the Bible?
2. Where was the first beauty contest in the Bible, and who won?
3. Who was the first Christian martyr?
4. What is the first dream mentioned in the Bible?
5. What is the first war mentioned in the Bible?
6. Who was the first drunk?
7. Where was the first piggy bank?
8. Who was the first person to fall asleep during a sermon?
9. What is the first commandment in the Bible?
10. What is the first purchase of land in the Bible?
11. What was the first instance of book burning?
12. What was the first military coup in Israel?
13. Who used the first pseudonym?
14. Who built the first city?
15. Who was the first hunter?
16. Who was the first murderer?
17. What is the first book of the Bible named after a woman?
18. Who is the first prophet mentioned in the Bible?
19. Where did Jesus work his first miracle?
20. What was the first of the ten plagues of Egypt?
21. Who was the first king of Israel?
22. Who were the first foreign missionaries?
23. Who was the first shepherdess?
24. Who was the first single man to be exiled?
25. Who was the first judge of Israel?
26. Who was the first disciple chosen by Jesus?
27. Who wore the first bridal veil?
28. Who told the first lie?
29. Who was the first priest mentioned in Scripture?
30. Who wore the first ring?
31. What was the first city called?
32. What was the first animal out of the ark?
33. Where were the disciples first called Christians?
34. Who took the first census of the Hebrews?

They Did It First (Answers)

1. Pharaoh, at the time Joseph was in Egypt (Genesis 40:20)
2. The one at the court of Persian ruler Ahasuerus. The winner was Esther (Esther 2).
3. Stephen (Acts 6:7—8:2)
4. The dream of Abimelech, in which he was told to return Sarah to Abraham (Genesis 20:3-8)
5. The war of the kings of the north, led by Chedorlaomer, king of Elam (Genesis 14)
6. Noah, who planted a vineyard after leaving the ark (Genesis 9:21)
7. In the temple at Jerusalem. It was a chest, ordered by King Joash, who had a hole bored in the lid to keep priests from stealing funds (2 Kings 12)
8. Eutychus, who dozed off and fell out of a window during Paul's sermon (Acts 20:9)
9. "Be fruitful and multiply" (Genesis 1:28)
10. Abraham bought the Cave of Machpelah as a tomb for Sarah (Genesis 23:3-20)
11. Jeremiah's scroll, sent to King Jehoiakim, was burnt piece by piece as it was being read to the king (Jeremiah 36:21-23)
12. Absalom led an attempt to overthrow his father, David (2 Samuel 15—18)
13. Esther, whose real name was Hadassah (Esther 2:7)
14. Cain (Genesis 4:17)
15. Nimrod (Genesis 10:9)
16. Cain (Genesis 4:8)
17. Ruth
18. Abraham (Genesis 20:7)
19. Cana (John 2:1-11)
20. The river turns to blood (Exodus 7:14-24)
21. Saul (1 Samuel 10:1)
22. Paul and Barnabas (Acts 13)
23. Rachel (Genesis 29:9)
24. Cain (Genesis 4:12)
25. Othniel (Judges 3:9)
26. Simon Peter (John 1:42)
27. Rebekah (Genesis 24:65)
28. The serpent (Genesis 3:4)
29. Melchizedek (Genesis 14:18)
30. Pharaoh (Genesis 41:42)
31. Enoch, named after Cain's son (Genesis 4:17)
32. The raven (Genesis 8:7)
33. Antioch (Acts 11:26)
34. The priest Eleazar (Numbers 26:1-2)

35. Who was the first shepherd?
36. Who were the first exiles?
37. Who were the first twins?
38. Who constructed the first altar?
39. Who built the first Jerusalem temple?
40. Who planted the first garden?
41. Who was the first metal craftsman?
42. Who was the first farmer?
43. Who was the first polygamist?
44. What is the first commandment with a promise attached to it?
45. Who was the first apostle to be martyred?
46. Who was the first child mentioned in the Bible?
47. Who was the first daughter mentioned by name?
48. What is the first color mentioned in the Bible?
49. Who planted the first vineyard?

◆Second in Line

1. At 969 years, Methuselah was the longest-lived man. Who came in second at 962 years?
2. Saul was the first king of Israel. Who was the second? (Hint: It wasn't David.)
3. The first covenant God made with man was his covenant with Noah. With whom did he make the second covenant?
4. In John's Gospel, Jesus' first miracle is turning water into wine. What is the second miracle?
5. Stephen was the first Christian martyr. What apostle was the second?
6. Paul's first traveling companion was Barnabas. Who was the second?
7. The first plague in Egypt was the turning of the Nile waters to blood. What was the second plague?
8. Othniel was the first judge of Israel. Who was the second?
9. Jacob's firstborn was Reuben. Who was his second son?
10. David's first capital city was Hebron. What was his second, and more famous, capital?
11. The serpent in Eden was the first talking animal in the Bible. What was the second?

35. Abel (Genesis 4:2)
36. Adam and Eve, driven from the garden (Genesis 3:24)
37. Jacob and Esau (Genesis 25:23-26)
38. Noah (Genesis 8:20)
39. Solomon (1 Kings 6)
40. God (Genesis 2:8)
41. Tubal-cain (Genesis 4:22)
42. Cain (Genesis 4:2)
43. Lamech (Genesis 4:19)
44. "Honor your father and mother" (Deuteronomy 5:16; Ephesians 6:2-3) The promise is that the person will have a long life if he honors his parents.
45. James (Acts 12:1-2)
46. Cain (Genesis 4:1)
47. Naamah, daughter of Lamech (Genesis 4:22)
48. Green—"I have given every green herb" (Genesis 1:30)
49. Noah (Genesis 9:20)

Second in Line (Answers)

1. Jared (Genesis 5:20)
2. Ishbosheth (2 Samuel 2:8-10)
3. Abraham (Genesis 15–17)
4. Healing an official's son in Cana (John 4:43-54)
5. James, brother of John (Acts 12:1-2)
6. Silas (Acts 15:36-41)
7. Frogs (Exodus 8:1-8)
8. Ehud (Judges 3:15)
9. Simeon (Genesis 29:33)
10. Jerusalem (2 Samuel 5:6-10)
11. Balaam's donkey (Numbers 22:28-30)

12. Eve is the first woman in the Bible. Who is the second?
13. Solomon led the way in constructing the first temple in Jerusalem. Who led in the building of the second temple?
14. Esther is the first book in the Bible not to mention the name of God. What is the second book with this omission?

◆Kings, Pharaohs, and Other Rulers

1. What king hosted a banquet where a phantom hand left a message on the palace wall?
2. What king of Israel was murdered while he was drunk?
3. What king of Salem was also a priest of the Most High God?
4. What king of Gerar took Sarah away from Abraham?
5. What Hebrew captive interpreted the dreams of the Egyptian pharaoh?
6. What three kings listened to the prophet Elisha as he prophesied to the accompaniment of a harp?
7. What king attacked the Israelites on their way into Canaan, only to be completely destroyed later?
8. What king of Sidon gave his daughter Jezebel as a wife to Ahab?
9. What king of Bashan was famous for having an enormous iron bed?
10. Who was the last king of Judah?
11. What king of Hazor organized an alliance against Joshua?
12. What military man captured 31 kings?
13. What king of Moab sent the prophet Balaam to curse Israel?
14. What king of Mesopotamia was sent by God to conquer the faithless Israelites?
15. What Canaanite king of the time of the judges was noted for having nine hundred iron chariots?
16. What son of Gideon was proclaimed king in Shechem?
17. What king of the Amalekites was captured by Saul and cut into pieces by Samuel?

12. Cain's wife, who is not named (Genesis 4:17)
13. Zerubbabel and Joshua (Ezra 3)
14. Song of Solomon

Kings, Pharaohs, and Other Rulers (Answers)

1. Belshazzar (Daniel 5:1-9)
2. Elah (1 Kings 16:8-10)
3. Melchizedek (Genesis 14:18)
4. Abimelech (Genesis 20:2)
5. Joseph (Genesis 41:1-36)
6. Joram of Israel, Jehoshaphat of Judah, and the king of Edom (2 Kings 3:11-19)
7. The king of Arad (Numbers 21:1-3)
8. Ethbaal (1 Kings 16:31)
9. Og (Deuteronomy 3:11)
10. Zedekiah (2 Kings 25:1-7)
11. Jabin (Joshua 11:1-5)
12. Joshua (12:9-24)
13. Balak (Numbers 22:2-6)
14. Cushan-Rishathaim (Judges 3:8)
15. Jabin (Judges 4:2-3)
16. Abimelech (Judges 9:6)
17. Agag (1 Samuel 15:8, 32)

18. What much-married king is considered the author of the Song of Songs?
19. What Philistine king did David seek refuge with when he fled from Saul?
20. What shepherd boy, the youngest of eight sons, was anointed by Samuel in front of his brothers?
21. What king wanted to see miracles when the arrested Jesus was sent to him?
22. What king of Tyre sent cedar logs and craftsmen to King David?
23. What prophet had a vision of a time when the Lord would gather the kings of the earth together and put them all in a pit?
24. What man, David's oldest son, tried to make himself king of Israel?
25. What wise king made an alliance with Egypt when he married the pharaoh's daughter?
26. What Egyptian king gave refuge to Jeroboam when he fled from Solomon?
27. What king had a strange dream about an enormous, fruitful tree that was suddenly chopped down with only a dry stump left?
28. What man, one of Solomon's officials, had his reign over Israel foretold by the prophet Ahijah?
29. What king of Judah was constantly at war with King Jeroboam of Israel?
30. What king was confronted by the prophet Nathan because of his adulterous affair?
31. What king of Israel reigned only two years and was murdered while he was fighting against the Philistines?
32. What man violently protested having a king in Israel, though he himself anointed the first two kings?
33. What city did King Jeroboam use as his capital when the northern tribes split from the southern tribes?
34. What king of Israel reigned only seven days and killed himself by burning down his palace around him?
35. What king of Ethiopia was supposed to aid Hezekiah in breaking the power of the Assyrians?
36. What king led Israel into sin by allowing his evil wife to introduce Baal worship into the country?
37. Who was the last king of Israel?

18. Solomon (Song of Solomon 1:1)
19. Achish of Gath (1 Samuel 21:10)
20. David (1 Samuel 16:6-13)
21. Herod (Luke 23:8)
22. Hiram (2 Samuel 5:11)
23. Isaiah (24:21-22)
24. Adonijah (1 Kings 1:5-53)
25. Solomon (1 Kings 3:1)
26. Shishak (1 Kings 11:40)
27. Nebuchadnezzar (Daniel 4:10-18)
28. Jeroboam (1 Kings 11:26-40)
29. Abijam, or Abijah (1 Kings 15:6)
30. David (2 Samuel 12:1-15)
31. Nadab (1 Kings 15:26-27)
32. Samuel (1 Samuel 8-10)
33. Tirzah (1 Kings 14:17)
34. Zimri (1 Kings 16:15, 18)
35. Tirhakah (2 Kings 19:9)
36. Ahab (1 Kings 16:29-33)
37. Hoshea (2 Kings 17:4)

38. What king of the Amorites refused to let the Israelites pass through his kingdom?
39. What king called Elijah the worst troublemaker in Israel?
40. What king of Syria was Elijah told to anoint?
41. What evil king of Judah was humbled and repentant after being taken to Babylon in chains?
42. What king was told by the prophet Micaiah that his troops would fall in battle?
43. What saintly king had a fleet built to sail for gold, though the ships never sailed?
44. What king of Israel consulted the god Baalzebub after falling off his palace balcony?
45. What king of Moab was famous as a sheep farmer?
46. What king refused to let the Israelites pass through his country on their way to Canaan?
47. What king had the prophet Uriah murdered for opposing him?
48. Who became king of Syria after he smothered King Ben-Hadad with a wet cloth?
49. What king of Judah led the country into sin by marrying the daughter of the wicked Ahab?
50. Who is the only king in the Bible referred to as "the Mede"?

◆So Many Dreamers

1. Who told Pilate that a worrisome dream made it clear that Pilate was to have nothing to do with Jesus?
2. According to one Old Testament prophet, there will come a day when young men will see visions and old men will dream dreams. Which prophet?
3. Who repeats the words of this prophet in an early Christian sermon?
4. Joseph, Mary's husband, was warned in dreams to do four things. What?
5. In Nebuchadnezzar's famous tree dream, who is symbolized by the majestic tree that is cut down?
6. Daniel had a dream of four beasts rising out of the sea. What did they look like?

38. Sihon (Numbers 21:21-26)
39. Ahab (1 Kings 18:17)
40. Hazael (1 Kings 19:15)
41. Manasseh (2 Chronicles 33:10-13)
42. Ahab (1 Kings 22:17)
43. Jehoshaphat (1 Kings 22:48)
44. Ahaziah (2 Kings 1:2)
45. Mesha (2 Kings 3:4)
46. The king of Edom (Numbers 20:14-20)
47. Jehoiakim (Jeremiah 26:20-23)
48. Hazael (2 Kings 8:15)
49. Jehoram (2 Kings 8:16-18)
50. Darius (Daniel 5:31)

So Many Dreamers (Answers)

1. His wife (Matthew 27:19)
2. Joel (2:28)
3. Peter, at Pentecost (Acts 2:17)
4. Go ahead and marry Mary, take a different route out of Bethlehem, flee to Egypt, return from Egypt (Matthew 1:18–2:23)
5. Nebuchadnezzar (Daniel 4:5-17)
6. A lion, a bear, a leopard, and a monster with iron teeth (Daniel 7)

7. In Nebuchadnezzar's dream of the statue, what four metals are mentioned as composing the statue?
8. One of Gideon's soldiers dreamed of a Midianite tent being overturned by an unlikely object. What was it?
9. When God came to the young Solomon in a dream and asked him what he desired, what did Solomon ask for?
10. What three Egyptian officials did Joseph interpret dreams for?
11. God protected Jacob by sending a dream of warning that Jacob should not be pursued or harmed. Who received this dream?
12. Who irritated his brothers by telling them of his dreams?
13. Who slept on a stone pillow at Bethel and had a dream of a stairway to heaven?

✦Change of Life, Change of Name

What were the original names of these biblical characters?

1. Abraham and Sarah
2. Israel
3. Joshua
4. Solomon
5. Peter
6. Paul
7. Mara
8. Zaphnath-paaneah
9. Belteshazzar
10. Jehoiakim
11. Zedekiah

✦What's in a Name?

Most biblical names had specific meanings. Below are the meanings of the names of several biblical characters. Can you name the person in each case? (This isn't as hard as it

7. Gold, silver, brass, and iron (Daniel 2:31-35)
8. A cake of barley bread (Judges 7:13)
9. An understanding heart and good judgment (1 Kings 3:5-10)
10. The pharaoh, his baker, and his butler (Genesis 40–41)
11. Laban, Jacob's father-in-law (Genesis 31:29)
12. Joseph (Genesis 37:2-11)
13. Jacob (Genesis 28:10-15)

Change of Life, Change of Name (Answers)

1. Abram and Sarai (Genesis 17:5, 15)
2. Jacob (Genesis 32:28)
3. Oshea (Numbers 13:16)
4. Jedidiah (2 Samuel 12:24-25)
5. Simon, or Simeon (John 1:42)
6. Saul (Acts 13:9)
7. Naomi (Ruth 1:20)
8. Joseph (Genesis 41:45)
9. Daniel (1:6-7)
10. Eliakim (2 Kings 23:34)
11. Mattaniah (2 Kings 24:17)

looks. Except for 1, 2, 4, 6, 9-14, and 35, all the names are also the titles of books of the Bible. The other names are familiar.)

1. beloved
2. prosperous
3. God is strong
4. God is savior
5. help
6. great warrior
7. love's embrace
8. salvation of the Lord
9. God has helped
10. red earth
11. eagle
12. enlightened
13. the Lord sustains
14. the Lord is gracious
15. messenger
16. worshiper of the Lord
17. the Lord has consoled
18. star
19. something worth seeing
20. asked of God
21. exalted of God
22. dove
23. he that weeps
24. peace
25. honored of God
26. honorable
27. God is judge
28. the Lord is salvation
29. salvation
30. one with a burden
31. gift of the Lord
32. light-giving
33. rock
34. the Lord remembers
35. little
36. the Lord hides
37. the Lord has been gracious
38. praise of the Lord

What's in a Name? (Answers)

1. David
2. Festus
3. Ezekiel
4. Elisha
5. Ezra
6. Gideon
7. Habakkuk
8. Isaiah
9. Lazarus
10. Adam
11. Aquila
12. Aaron
13. Ahaz
14. Ananias
15. Malachi
16. Obadiah
17. Nehemiah
18. Esther
19. Ruth
20. Samuel
21. Jeremiah
22. Jonah
23. Job
24. Solomon
25. Timothy
26. Titus
27. Daniel
28. Joshua
29. Hosea
30. Amos
31. Matthew
32. Luke
33. Peter
34. Zechariah
35. Paul
36. Zephaniah
37. John
38. Jude

39. festive
40. who is like the Lord
41. compassionate
42. affectionate
43. the Lord is God
44. polite
45. supplanter

✦Names Made in Heaven

1. What did God change Jacob's name to?
2. Who was told by God to name his son Maher-shalal-hash-baz?
3. Who told Joseph what Jesus' name would be?
4. What prophet was told by God to name his son Lo-ammi?
5. Who told Hagar to name her son Ishmael?
6. What did God change Abram's name to?
7. Who was told by an angel that his son was to be named John?
8. What prophet told the priest Pashur that his new name was to be Magor-missabib?
9. What did God call his human creation?
10. What new name did Jesus give to Simon?
11. What was Hosea told to name his daughter?
12. What was Sarai's name changed to?
13. Who was told to name his son Solomon?
14. Who was told to name his firstborn son Jezreel?
15. Who told Mary that her son was to be named Jesus?

✦Hairy and Hairless

1. What prophet was a very hairy man?
2. Who is the only man mentioned in the Bible as being naturally bald?
3. What grief-stricken Old Testament man shaved his head after he learned his children had been destroyed?
4. What king of Babylon, driven from his palace, lived in the wilderness and let his hair grow long and shaggy?

39. Haggai
40. Micah
41. Nahum
42. Philemon
43. Joel
44. Mark
45. James

Names Made in Heaven (Answers)

1. Israel (Genesis 32:28)
2. Isaiah (8:3)
3. An angel (Matthew 1:20-21)
4. Hosea (1:9)
5. An angel (Genesis 16:11)
6. Abraham (Genesis 17:5)
7. Zacharias (Luke 1:13)
8. Jeremiah (20:3)
9. Adam (Genesis 5:2)
10. Peter (John 1:42)
11. Lo-ruhamah (Hosea 1:6)
12. Sarah (Genesis 17:15)
13. David (1 Chronicles 22:9)
14. Hosea (1:4)
15. The angel Gabriel (Luke 1:30-31)

Hairy and Hairless (Answers)

1. Elijah (2 Kings 1:8)
2. Elisha (2 Kings 2:23)
3. Job (1:20)
4. Nebuchadnezzar (Daniel 4:33)

5. Who is mentioned first in the Bible as being very hairy?
6. What prince had his hair cut only once a year?
7. What apostle purified himself, along with four other men, by shaving his head?
8. As a Nazarite, this judge of Israel never shaved or had a haircut until his mistress shaved his head. Who was he?
9. What leader plucked out his own hair and beard when he heard the Jews had intermarried with other races?
10. What smooth-skinned man had a hairy twin brother?
11. What sort of person had to shave all his hair twice, six days apart?
12. Who was forbidden to "round the corners of the head"?
13. What class of people could not shave their heads nor let their hair grow long?
14. What prophet did God tell to shave his head and beard?
15. Who was so incensed at the intermarriage of Jews with foreigners that he pulled out the hair of some men?
16. What prophet told the people of Jerusalem to cut off their hair as a sign the Lord had rejected them?
17. Who had to shave their whole bodies as part of the ceremony of consecrating themselves to the Lord?
18. If an Israelite man took a female prisoner of war as his wife, what did she have to do to her hair?
19. What group of consecrated men never cut their hair?
20. What Christian shaved his head at Cenchrea in connection with a vow?

✦The Runners

1. What bizarre person saw Jesus from far off and ran to worship him?
2. What belligerent man ran to meet his brother and kissed him after a long time of separation?
3. Who outran a team of horses?
4. What evangelist ran to meet a foreign official in his chariot?
5. What disciple outran Peter to Jesus' tomb?
6. Who ran to the priest Eli, thinking Eli had called him in the night, though it was actually God who called?

5. Esau (Genesis 27:11-23)
6. Absalom (2 Samuel 14:26)
7. Paul (Acts 21:23-26)
8. Samson (Judges 16:17)
9. Ezra (9:1-3)
10. Jacob, brother of Esau (Genesis 27:11-22)
11. A leper (Leviticus 14:7-9)
12. Jews (Leviticus 19:27)
13. Priests (Ezekiel 44:20)
14. Ezekiel (5:1-4)
15. Nehemiah (13:23-27)
16. Jeremiah (7:29)
17. The Levites (Numbers 8:5-7)
18. Shave it off (Deuteronomy 21:10-12)
19. The Nazarites (Numbers 6:5, 13, 18)
20. Paul (Acts 18:18)

The Runners (Answers)

1. The Gadarene demoniac (Mark 5:6)
2. Esau (Genesis 33:4)
3. Elijah (1 Kings 18:46)
4. Philip (Acts 8:30)
5. John (John 20:4)
6. Samuel (1 Samuel 3:4-5)

7. What cousin of Jacob's ran to tell her father when she found she and Jacob were related?
8. What boy ran into the Philistine camp to confront their best warrior?
9. What servant of the prophet Elisha ran to meet the woman of Shunem?
10. What short man ran to see Jesus but could not because of his height?
11. Who ran to meet the Lord in the plains of Mamre?
12. Who sent Cushi to run to David with the news of Absalom's death?
13. According to Isaiah, what sort of people can run and not be weary?
14. What prophet ran after another prophet to accept the appointment as his successor?
15. What usurper to the throne of Israel gathered up fifty men to run before him?
16. When the man of Benjamin saw the ark of the covenant captured by the Philistines, what Israelite did he run to tell?
17. What judge's mother ran to tell her husband Manoah that an angel had appeared to her?
18. What beautiful woman caused Abraham's servant to run to meet her?
19. What did a man at Jesus' crucifixion run to find for the dying Jesus?
20. Who ran into the midst of the Israelites carrying incense to stop a plague?
21. Who had a vision of one angel running to meet another?
22. What two women ran from Jesus' empty tomb to tell the disciples what had happened?
23. What man ran to meet Abraham's servant at the well?

◆Notable Women, and Some Less Notable (I)

1. The only female judge of Israel, she judged the tribes from under a palm tree. Her victory song is famous. Who was she?

7. Rachel (Genesis 29:12)
8. David (1 Samuel 17:48-49)
9. Gehazi (2 Kings 4:25-26)
10. Zacchaeus (Luke 19:4)
11. Abraham (Genesis 18:1-2)
12. Joab (2 Samuel 18:19-23)
13. They that wait upon the Lord (Isaiah 40:31)
14. Elisha (1 Kings 19:19-21)
15. Adonijah (1 Kings 1:5)
16. The priest Eli (1 Samuel 4:12-18)
17. Samson's (Judges 13:10)
18. Rebekah (Genesis 24:17)
19. A sponge (Matthew 27:46-48)
20. Aaron (Numbers 16:46-48)
21. Zechariah (2:3)
22. Mary and Mary Magdalene (Matthew 28:8)
23. Laban (Genesis 24:29)

Notable Women, and Some Less Notable (I) (Answers)
1. Deborah (Judges 4–5)

2. What widowed prophetess was eighty-four years old when she saw the young Jesus in the temple?
3. What wife of David had been married to Nabal, who died when she told him of the gifts she had given to David?
4. What elderly cousin of Mary became the mother of John the Baptist?
5. What prophetess, active during the reign of Josiah, consoled the king while chastising the people of Judah?
6. What scheming princess of Tyre married and manipulated the weak Ahab and imposed her pagan religion on Israel?
7. What Israelite woman aided the people by murdering the Canaanite captain Sisera in her tent?
8. What Jewish girl married a Persian emperor and helped save her exiled people from extermination?
9. What two sisters of Bethany had a brother named Lazarus and were close friends of Jesus?
10. What prophetess was the sister of two great leaders and was once afflicted with leprosy for being rebellious?
11. What harlot became a hero for saving the life of Joshua's spies and was so honored in later days that she is listed in the genealogy of Jesus?
12. What loving woman, a concubine of Saul, watched over the corpses of her slaughtered children, protecting them from birds and animals?
13. Though her profession was condemned by an official decree of King Saul, the king disguised himself in order to get help from her. Who was she?
14. What Persian queen upset the king and his counselor by refusing to appear before them at their drunken banquet?
15. What dancer so enchanted Herod that he offered her anything she wished?
16. Who was turned into a pillar of salt?
17. What king of Judah was Abi the wife of?
18. What sister of David had the same name as one of David's wives?
19. What woman was given as a wife after her future husband brought in two hundred Philistine foreskins as a gift to her father?
20. Who offered a bottle of milk to an enemy soldier and then killed him?
21. After Eve, who is the first woman mentioned in the Bible?

2. Anna (Luke 2:36-38)
3. Abigail (1 Samuel 25:18-20)
4. Elisabeth (Luke 1)
5. Huldah (2 Kings 22:14-20)
6. Jezebel (1 Kings 16—19)
7. Jael (Judges 4:17-22)
8. Esther
9. Mary and Martha (Luke 10:38-42; John 11)
10. Miriam (Exodus 15; Numbers 12)
11. Rahab (Joshua 2, 6)
12. Rizpah (2 Samuel 21:1-10)
13. The witch of Endor (1 Samuel 28)
14. Vashti (Esther 1)
15. The daughter of Herodias, known to us from the writings of Josephus as Salome, though her name does not appear in the Bible (Matthew 14:1-11)
16. Lot's wife (Genesis 19:26)
17. Ahaz (2 Kings 18:2)
18. Abigail (1 Chronicles 2:16-17)
19. Michal (1 Samuel 18:27)
20. Jael (Judges 4)
21. Adah (Genesis 4:19)

22. What Old Testament woman had children named Lo-ruhamah, Lo-ammi, and Jezreel?
23. What was Saul's wife's name?
24. What wife of David was also given as a wife to a man named Phalti?
25. What woman of Corinth had a household that Paul described as being full of strife among Christian leaders?
26. What woman was, in Ezekiel, used as a symbol of wicked Jerusalem?
27. What woman with a cumbersome name was the Hittite wife of Esau?
28. Who is the only woman mentioned in Paul's letter to Philemon?
29. What Egyptian woman was the wife of Joseph?
30. Who was the mother of the Levitical priesthood?
31. What king of Judah was the husband of Azubah?
32. What Hittite woman married Esau, causing grief to Isaac and Rebekah?
33. What handmaid of Rachel bore Jacob the sons Dan and Naphtali?
34. What daughter of a pharaoh married one of the descendants of Judah?
35. What woman was, in Ezekiel, used as a symbol of wicked Samaria?
36. What woman of Rome was mentioned by Paul as sending her greetings to Timothy?
37. What wife of David was the mother of the rebellious Adonijah?
38. What woman of Midian was killed by being run through with a javelin?
39. What woman of Athens became a Christian because of Paul's teaching?
40. What Egyptian woman was the mother of two of the tribes of Israel?
41. What two women of Philippi were asked by Paul to stop their quarreling?
42. Who were the first two women to be the wives of the same man?
43. What was Esther's Hebrew name?
44. What was the name of Sarah's Egyptian maid?
45. What did Naomi call herself after suffering great tragedy?

22. Gomer, wife of Hosea (Hosea 1)
23. Ahinoam (1 Samuel 14:50)
24. Michal (1 Samuel 25:44)
25. Chloe (1 Corinthians 1:11)
26. Aholibah (Ezekiel 23:4, 11)
27. Aholibamah (Genesis 36:2, 5)
28. Apphia, a Christian of Colossae (Philemon 2)
29. Asenath (Genesis 41:45)
30. Elisheba, wife of Aaron (Exodus 6:23)
31. Asa (1 Kings 22:41-42)
32. Bashemath (Genesis 26:34)
33. Bilhah (Genesis 29:29; 30:3-7; 35:22, 25; 37:2)
34. Bithiah (1 Chronicles 4:18)
35. Aholah (Ezekiel 23:4-5)
36. Claudia (2 Timothy 4:21)
37. Haggith (2 Samuel 3:4)
38. Cozbi (Numbers 25:15-18)
39. Damaris (Acts 17:34)
40. Asenath, mother of Manasseh and Ephraim (Genesis 46:20)
41. Euodia and Syntyche (Philippians 4:2)
42. Adah and Zillah, wives of Lamech (Genesis 4:19-24)
43. Hadassah (Esther 2:7)
44. Hagar (Genesis 16:1)
45. Mara (Ruth 1:20)

46. What Egyptian servant woman was insolent to Sarah?
47. What Midianite woman was slain by the priest Phinehas for marrying an Israelite?
48. Who was wife to godly King Josiah?
49. What queen of Judah was the wife of godly King Hezekiah and mother of evil King Manasseh?
50. What wife of Lamech was the mother of the founder of music?
51. What courageous woman was wife of the priest Jehoiada?
52. Who had a daughter named Jemima?
53. What daughter of a priest married a king who became a leper?
54. What evil woman is associated with the church of Thyatira?
55. What woman, the wife of a servant of Herod, was healed by Jesus?
56. What woman of the Roman church is commended by Paul for her hard work?
57. Who had a wife named Judith?
58. What church was Julia part of?
59. Who had a daughter named Keren-happuch?
60. Who was Abraham's wife after Sarah died?
61. What two Hebrew women did God make houses for?
62. What prophet had a daughter named Lo-ruhamah?
63. What wife of David was mother of the handsome—but rebellious—Absalom?
64. What daughter of Absalom married her cousin, King Rehoboam?
65. What servant woman was ordered out of the house by Sarah?
66. What wife of a palace official went to embalm the body of Jesus?
67. Who was Mehetabel?
68. What daughter of Saul was promised as a wife to David for slaying Goliath?
69. Who was the mother of Huz, Buz, and Pildash?
70. Who is the first daughter mentioned by name in the Bible?
71. What Ammonite woman, a wife of Solomon, became the mother of the royal dynasty of Judah?
72. What Israelite woman lived in Moab but returned to Israel after her husband's death?

46. Hagar (Genesis 16:3-5)
47. Cozbi (Numbers 25:15-18)
48. Hamutal (2 Kings 23:31)
49. Hephzibah (2 Kings 21:1)
50. Adah (Genesis 4:19-23)
51. Jehosheba (2 Kings 11:2)
52. Job (42:14)
53. Jerusha, wife of Uzziah (2 Kings 15:32-33)
54. Jezebel (Revelation 2:20)
55. Joanna (Luke 8:2-3)
56. Mary (Romans 16:6)
57. Esau (Genesis 26:34)
58. The church at Rome (Romans 16:15)
59. Job (42:14)
60. Keturah (Genesis 25:1)
61. Puah and Shiprah, the midwives (Exodus 1:20-21)
62. Hosea (1:6, 8)
63. Maacah (2 Samuel 3:3)
64. Maachah (1 Kings 15:2)
65. Hagar (Genesis 21:10-14)
66. Joanna (Luke 24:10)
67. Wife of Hadad, a king of Edom (Genesis 36:39)
68. Merab (1 Samuel 18:17-19)
69. Milcah (Genesis 22:20-22)
70. Naamah, daughter of Lamech (Genesis 4:22)
71. Naamah (1 Kings 14:21)
72. Naomi (Ruth 1)

73. What false prophetess made attempts to keep Nehemiah from rebuilding the walls of Jerusalem?
74. Who was Ruth's sister-in-law?
75. What church was the faithful Persis a part of?
76. Who were Puah and Shiprah?
77. What four women in the early church were described as prophetesses?
78. What servant girl in Jerusalem came to the door when Peter escaped from prison?
79. What Hebrew woman married an Egyptian and later saw their half-breed son stoned to death?
80. What man's daughters involved him in incestuous relations when they believed there were no other men around?

✦More Kings, Pharaohs, and Other Rulers

1. What king of Israel had a reputation as a fast and furious chariot driver?
2. What king did Esther marry?
3. What Syrian king besieged Samaria, causing great famine that led to cannibalism?
4. What Egyptian king fought against Judah and murdered King Josiah?
5. What king of Judah had to be hidden as a boy to protect him from the wrath of wicked Queen Athaliah?
6. Who set up golden bulls at Dan and Bethel so that his people would not go to Jerusalem to worship?
7. What good king of Judah was murdered by two of his court officials?
8. What king of Israel made Elisha angry by not striking the ground enough with his arrows?
9. What king of Judah showed mercy when he executed his father's murderers but spared their families?
10. What king ran a beauty contest to pick a bride and wound up marrying a Jewish girl?
11. What king of Judah was stricken with leprosy?
12. What king of Israel was assassinated by Shallum after a six month reign?

73. Noadiah (Nehemiah 6:14)
74. Orpah (Ruth 1:4)
75. Rome (Romans 16:12)
76. Hebrew midwives at the time of Moses' birth (Exodus 1:15)
77. The daughters of Philip (Acts 21:8-9)
78. Rhoda (Acts 12:13)
79. Shelomith (Leviticus 24:10-23)
80. Lot's (Genesis 19:30-38)

More Kings, Pharaohs, and Other Rulers (Answers)

1. Jehu (2 Kings 9:20)
2. Ahasuerus, also known as Xerxes (Esther 1:1)
3. Ben-Hadad (2 Kings 6:24-30)
4. Neco (2 Kings 23:29)
5. Joash (2 Kings 11:2)
6. Jeroboam (1 Kings 12:26-31)
7. Joash (2 Kings 12:20-21)
8. Jehoash (2 Kings 13:18-19)
9. Amaziah (2 Kings 14:5-6)
10. Ahasuerus, or Xerxes (Esther 2:1-18)
11. Uzziah, also called Azariah (2 Kings 15:5)
12. Zechariah (2 Kings 15:8-10)

13. What cruel king of Israel assassinated King Shallum and ripped open the pregnant women of Tappuah?
14. What king of Egypt received an appeal for help from Hoshea of Israel, who wanted to throw off the Assyrian yoke?
15. What king of Israel had much of his territory taken away by the Assyrian king?
16. What evil king of Judah sacrificed his son as a burnt offering and built a Syrian-style altar in Jerusalem?
17. What king of Israel experienced a long famine and drought during his reign?
18. What Assyrian king brought about the fall of Samaria and the deportation of the Israelites to other countries?
19. What godly king of Judah tore down the idols in the country and broke the power of the Philistines?
20. What king of Gezer opposed Joshua's army and was totally defeated, with no soldiers left alive?
21. What Assyrian king was killed by his sons while worshiping in the temple of his god Nisroch?
22. What king was criticized by the prophet Isaiah for showing Judah's treasure to Babylonian ambassadors?
23. What king of Syria joined the king of Israel in attacking Judah?
24. What Assyrian king received thirty-eight tons of silver as tribute money from Menahem of Israel?
25. What king of Assyria had his army of 185,000 soldiers destroyed by the angel of the Lord?
26. What cruel king lied to the wise men about his desire to worship the infant Jesus?
27. What king of Judah had the worst reputation for killing innocent people?
28. What king of Judah reigned for only two years and was murdered by his court officials?
29. What godly king began his reign at age eight and led a major reform movement in Judah?
30. Who had a dream about a statue composed of different materials?
31. What king reinstituted the celebration of Passover in Judah and invited the people of Israel to participate?
32. What king of Judah was killed at the Battle of Megiddo by the forces of Egypt?

13. Menahem (2 Kings 15:16)
14. So (2 Kings 17:4)
15. Pekah (2 Kings 15:29)
16. Ahaz (2 Kings 16:3, 10)
17. Ahab (1 Kings 18:1-2)
18. Shalmaneser (2 Kings 17:3-6)
19. Hezekiah (2 Kings 18:1-8)
20. Horam (Joshua 10:33)
21. Sennacherib (2 Kings 19:36-37)
22. Hezekiah (2 Kings 20:12-18)
23. Rezin (2 Kings 16:5)
24. Tiglath-Pileser (2 Kings 16:7-8)
25. Sennacherib (2 Kings 19:35)
26. Herod (Matthew 2:7-8)
27. Manasseh (2 Kings 21:16)
28. Amon (2 Kings 21:19-23)
29. Josiah (2 Kings 22–23)
30. Nebuchadnezzar (Daniel 2)
31. Hezekiah (2 Chronicles 30:1-12)
32. Josiah (2 Kings 23:29-30)

33. What king repented because of the preaching of the prophet Jonah?
34. What king of Israel tricked the worshipers of Baal by gathering them together in a temple and slaughtering all of them?
35. What king of Israel built the city of Samaria and made it his capital?
36. What Babylonian king sent his ambassadors to the court of Hezekiah, where they were shown all his treasures?
37. What son of Josiah was taken prisoner by Pharaoh Neco and never left Egypt?
38. Who reigned in Jerusalem when the Babylonian king's forces first attacked Judah?
39. Who was reigning in Judah when the Babylonians besieged Jerusalem and carried the nobles of the city away to Babylon?
40. What king of Judah saw the country threatened by the Assyrian army of Sennacherib?
41. What king of Babylon burned down the temple, palace, and city walls of Jerusalem?
42. What king of Judah was blinded and taken away in chains to Babylon?
43. Who was taken prisoner to Babylon, though he came to enjoy the favor of the Babylonian king?
44. What Babylonian king gave the deposed king of Judah a place of great honor in Babylon?
45. What king burned in his fireplace the letter sent to him by the prophet Jeremiah?
46. What king ordered Jezebel's servants to toss her out of a window?
47. What king of Persia issued the decree that the people of Judah could rebuild their temple?
48. What king of Assyria had sent foreigners to settle in Israel after the Israelites had been taken away?
49. What Persian king received a letter complaining about the Jews rebuilding their temple in Jerusalem?
50. What soldier was anointed king of Israel by one of Elisha's followers?

33. The king of Nineveh (Jonah 3:6)
34. Jehu (2 Kings 10:18-27)
35. Omri (1 Kings 16:24)
36. Merodach-Baladan (2 Kings 20:12-13)
37. Joahaz, or Jehoahaz (2 Kings 23:33-34)
38. Jehoiakim (2 Kings 24:1)
39. Jehoiachin (2 Kings 24:15-16)
40. Hezekiah (2 Kings 18:13)
41. Nebuchadnezzar (2 Kings 25:8-11)
42. Zedekiah (2 Kings 25:7)
43. Jehoiachin (2 Kings 25:27-30)
44. Evilmerodach (2 Kings 25:27-30)
45. Jehoiakim (Jeremiah 36:23)
46. Jehu (2 Kings 9:31-33)
47. Cyrus (Ezra 1:1-4)
48. Esarhaddon (Ezra 4:2)
49. Artaxerxes (Ezra (4:6-7)
50. Jehu (2 Kings 9:1-10)

✦Women on the Throne

1. Who plotted the execution of John the Baptist?
2. Bernice was the consort of what ruler?
3. The Ethiopian eunuch that Philip witnessed to was the servant of what queen?
4. Whose wife brought Daniel's gift of prophecy to her husband's attention?
5. What Jewish girl became queen of Persia?
6. Who defied her royal husband and was replaced by a foreign woman?
7. What daughter of Ahab tried to destroy the entire royal line of Judah?
8. Who was removed from her position as queen mother because she had made an idol?
9. What Baal-worshiping princess led Ahab into idolatry?
10. During the reigns of David and Solomon, Tahpenes was the queen of what country?
11. What queen traveled far to meet Solomon face to face?
12. What wife of the soldier Uriah became David's wife and bore him Solomon?
13. Rizpah was the wife of what king of Israel?
14. Who became David's wife after her husband, Nabal, died?
15. Who nagged at David for dancing in the streets?

✦Most Mentioned Men

1. What man, as if you didn't know, is the most mentioned man in the Bible?
2. What king, mentioned 1118 times in the Bible, is the second most mentioned man?
3. What leader, with 740 mentions, ranks third?
4. What priest ranks fourth with a total of 339 references?
5. What king has one less reference than the answer to Question 4 and ranks fifth?
6. What patriarch, with 306 mentions, ranks seventh?
7. What wise king ranks eighth with his 295 mentions?

Women on the Throne (Answers)

1. Herodias, wife of Herod (Matthew 14:3-8)
2. King Agrippa (Acts 25:13)
3. Candace (Acts 8:27-38)
4. Belshazzar's (Daniel 5:10)
5. Esther (Esther 2:17)
6. Vashti (Esther 1:11)
7. Athaliah (2 Chronicles 22:10)
8. Maacah (2 Chronicles 15:16)
9. Jezebel (1 Kings 16:31)
10. Egypt (1 Kings 11:19)
11. The queen of Sheba (1 Kings 10:1)
12. Bathsheba (2 Samuel 11–12)
13. Saul (2 Samuel 3:7)
14. Abigail (1 Samuel 25:39)
15. Michal (1 Samuel 18:20; 2 Samuel 6:16)

Most Mentioned Men (Answers)

1. Jesus
2. David
3. Moses
4. Aaron
5. Saul
6. Abraham
7. Solomon

8. What man would, if his famous nickname were considered a real personal name, outrank all the others in this list? (As it stands, using his usual name, he ranks ninth with 270 mentions.)
9. What government leader in a foreign land ranks tenth with 208 references?
10. What military man ranks eleventh with 197 references?
11. What apostle ranks twelfth with 185 references?
12. What apostle ranks thirteenth with 166 references?
13. What military commander in the reign of David ranks fourteenth with 137 mentions?
14. What prophet ranks fifteenth and has only one less mention than the answer to Question 13?
15. What prophet and judge has only one less reference than the person in Question 14 and ranks sixteenth?
16. What patriarch, though he is mentioned much less than his father or son, ranks seventeenth with 127 mentions?
17. What kinsman of Jesus ranks eighteenth with 86 references?
18. What government official is, with 56 references, the most mentioned unbeliever in the New Testament?
19. How many times is Adam mentioned in the Bible?
20. After Peter and Paul, which apostle is mentioned the most times (35 references)?

✦Most Mentioned Women

1. What Old Testament woman bore a child at age 90 and is the most mentioned woman in the Bible (56 mentions)?
2. What wife of a patriarch ranks second with 47 mentions?
3. What relative of Number 2 ranks third with 34 mentions?
4. What mother of twins ranks fourth with 31 mentions?
5. What evil woman ranks fifth with 23 mentions?
6. What New Testament woman ranks sixth with 19 mentions?
7. What wife of both Nabal and David ranks seventh with 15 mentions?
8. What sister of a famous leader ties with Number 7?
9. What follower of Jesus is mentioned 14 times?

8. Jacob, whose name Israel occurs more than any other name in this list. However, the name is almost always used of the nation, not the man.
9. Joseph
10. Joshua
11. Paul
12. Peter
13. Joab
14. Jeremiah
15. Samuel
16. Isaac
17. John the Baptist
18. Pilate
19. Only 30
20. John

Most Mentioned Women (Answers)

1. Sarah
2. Rachel
3. Leah
4. Rebekah
5. Jezebel
6. Mary, Jesus' mother
7. Abigail
8. Miriam
9. Mary Magdalene

10. What servant woman is also mentioned 14 times?
11. How many times is Eve, the first woman, mentioned?

✦Still More Kings, Pharaohs, and Other Rulers

1. Who built pagan temples to please all his foreign wives?
2. Which Gospel claims that Pilate had the plaque "The King of the Jews" fastened on Jesus' cross?
3. What Persian king was embarrassed by his disobedient wife?
4. What king of Judah was murdered after he fled to Lachish?
5. What king had a sinister prime minister named Haman?
6. What king is supposed to have written Ecclesiastes?
7. What two kings are mentioned as the authors of Proverbs?
8. What future king of Israel was out hunting his donkeys when Samuel came to anoint him?
9. What much-loved and much-quoted prophet was active in the reigns of Uzziah, Jotham, Ahaz, and Hezekiah, and, according to tradition, was executed by Manasseh?
10. What king had the apostle James executed with a sword and had Peter arrested?
11. What fat king of Moab was murdered by the judge Ehud?
12. What king of Babylon went insane and lived in the fields, where he ate grass and let his hair and fingernails grow long?
13. What king made a famous judgment about a baby that two women claimed was theirs?
14. What king ordered Daniel thrown into the lions' den?
15. What king of Judah tore down the pagan shrines and stamped out child sacrifice in Judah?
16. What king of Judah sacrificed his sons in the fire but later became repentant?
17. What cruel king had the infant boys of Bethlehem slaughtered?
18. What king broke his own law when he called on a spiritualist to bring up the ghost of Samuel?

10. Hagar
11. Only four

Still More Kings, Pharaohs, and Other Rulers
(Answers)

1. Solomon (1 Kings 11:1-13)
2. John (19:21)
3. Ahasuerus, or Xerxes (Esther 1:10-12)
4. Amaziah (2 Kings 14:19)
5. Ahasuerus, or Xerxes (Esther 3:1)
6. Solomon (Ecclesiastes 1:1)
7. Solomon and Lemuel (Proverbs 1:1; 31:1)
8. Saul (1 Samuel 9:15—10:1)
9. Isaiah (1:1)
10. Herod Agrippa (Acts 12:1-3)
11. Eglon (Judges 3:15-30)
12. Nebuchadnezzar (Daniel 4:33)
13. Solomon (1 Kings 3:16-28)
14. Darius (Daniel 6)
15. Josiah (2 Kings 23:10-14)
16. Manasseh (2 Chronicles 33:1-17)
17. Herod (Matthew 2:16)
18. Saul (1 Samuel 28:3-19)

19. Who was the only king of Israel to kill both a king of Judah and a king of Israel?
20. What king was referred to by Jesus as "that fox"?
21. What son of Saul was made king of Israel by Abner?
22. What king executed John the Baptist after his wife's daughter asked for the head of John on a platter?
23. What Assyrian king attacked the Philistines, leading Isaiah to walk around naked for three years?
24. What king, dressed in royal finery, was hailed as a god but then struck down by the angel of the Lord?
25. What king did Paul tell the story of his conversion to?
26. What king gave his daughter as a wife for David?
27. What Hebrew was given the daughter of the pharaoh as a wife?
28. According to Luke's Gospel, what Roman ruler ordered a census in the empire?
29. Who was the first king to reign at Jerusalem?
30. What saintly king of Judah was crippled with a foot disease in his old age?
31. What king was reprimanded by his military commander for weeping too long over his dead son?
32. What son of David tried to make himself king after David's death?
33. Who was king of Judah when the long-lost Book of the Law was found in the temple?
34. Who received a visit from the Queen of Sheba, whom he impressed with his wisdom?
35. Who is the only king who is said to have neither mother nor father?
36. What king of Judah became king at age seven and was aided in his reign by the saintly priest Jehoiada?
37. What king had the misfortune of his worst enemy being his son-in-law and the best friend of his son?
38. What king is considered to be the author of seventy-three of the Psalms?
39. What king built the first temple in Jerusalem?
40. What army commander made Saul's son Ishbosheth king over Israel?
41. What evil king of Israel pouted when he couldn't get a man to sell his plot of land?

19. Jehu, who killed Jehoram and Ahaziah (2 Kings 9:24, 27)
20. Herod (Luke 13:31)
21. Ishbosheth (2 Samuel 2:10)
22. Herod (Mark 6:14-28)
23. Sargon (Isaiah 20)
24. Herod Agrippa (Acts 12:21-23)
25. Agrippa (Acts 26)
26. Saul (1 Samuel 18:28)
27. Joseph (Genesis 41:45-46)
28. Caesar Augustus (Luke 2:1)
29. David (2 Samuel 5:9)
30. Asa (1 Kings 15:23)
31. David (2 Samuel 19:1-8)
32. Adonijah (1 Kings 1:5-53)
33. Josiah (2 Kings 22:8-10)
34. Solomon (1 Kings 10:1-13)
35. Melchizedek, king of Salem (Hebrews 7:3)
36. Joash (2 Kings 12:1-3)
37. Saul (1 Samuel 18:1, 28)
38. David
39. Solomon (2 Chronicles 2:1)
40. Abner (2 Samuel 2:8-10)
41. Ahab (1 Kings 21:1-5)

42. What psalm is supposed to be David's expression of guilt after his affair with Bathsheba?
43. What king suffered from an almost fatal illness but was promised fifteen more years of life by Isaiah?
44. Which of the ten plagues finally convinced the Egyptian pharaoh to let the Israelites leave?
45. Who reigned in Persia when Nehemiah heard the sad news about the walls of Jerusalem?
46. What king of Judah purified the temple and rededicated it to God?
47. What apostle fled the soldiers of King Aretas in Damascus?
48. What king of Israel was told by the prophet Jehu that the royal family would be wiped out because of its destruction of Jeroboam's dynasty?
49. What son of Solomon caused the kingdom to split when he threatened the people of Israel?
50. What king sent his son to David with expensive presents that David decided to use in worship?

✦A Herd of Prophets

1. This bald prophet was the performer of many miracles and the successor to another great prophet.
2. This court prophet confronted King David with his adultery.
3. This young prophet had a vision of a statue composed of different metals.
4. This prophet, put into a hole in the ground for being too outspoken, was often called the "weeping prophet."
5. This king of Israel was, early in his career, associated with a group of prophets.
6. This wilderness man confronted the prophets of Baal in a famous contest. He was taken to heaven in a chariot of fire.
7. This prophet, famous for his vision of the dry bones, was with the exiles in Babylon.

42. Psalm 51
43. Hezekiah (2 Kings 20:1-6)
44. The death of the firstborn (Exodus 12:30-32)
45. Artaxerxes (Nehemiah 1:1)
46. Hezekiah (2 Chronicles 29)
47. Paul (2 Corinthians 11:32)
48. Baasha (1 Kings 16:1-4)
49. Rehoboam (1 Kings 12:1-17)
50. Toi, king of Hamath (2 Samuel 8:9-12)

A Herd of Prophets (Answers)

1. Elisha (1–2 Kings)
2. Nathan (2 Samuel, 1 Kings)
3. Daniel
4. Jeremiah
5. Saul (1 Samuel 10:1-13)
6. Elijah (1-2 Kings)
7. Ezekiel

8. This prophet's work is quoted in the New Testament more than any other's. He is famous for his vision of God in the temple.
9. This kinsman of Jesus ate locusts, preached repentance, and baptized penitents in the Jordan.
10. This Christian prophesied a famine in the land.
11. This New Testament character prophesied the destruction of Jerusalem.
12. This woman was sent for when the long-neglected book of the law was found during Josiah's reign.
13. These four young women, daughters of a Christian evangelist, were considered prophetesses.
14. This elderly woman recognized the infant Jesus as being the Messiah.
15. This man, who anointed the first two kings of Israel, was considered both a judge and a prophet.
16. This prophet of Moab had a confrontation with his talking donkey.
17. This Old Testament patriarch was revealed as a prophet to King Abimelech.
18. This Egytian-born Hebrew leader predicted the coming of a prophet like himself.
19. This prophet took David to task for numbering the people of Israel.
20. This prophet predicted that Jeroboam would be king over ten tribes of Israel.
21. This reluctant prophet was thrown overboard in a storm.
22. This man of Tekoa was a simple laborer who had the audacity to confront the king's priest at his shrine.
23. This man prophesied against Nineveh.
24. This prophet was famous for his marriage to a prostitute.
25. This prophet predicted the outpouring of God's Spirit upon all people.
26. This man wrote a brief book against Edom.
27. This sister of a Hebrew leader was herself a prophetess. For a time she was afflicted with leprosy.
28. The only female judge of Israel, this woman was considered a prophetess.
29. This apostle of Jesus recorded his visions of the world's end times.

8. Isaiah
9. John the Baptist
10. Agabus (Acts 11:27-28; 21:10-11)
11. Jesus
12. Huldah (2 Kings 22)
13. The daughters of Philip (Acts 21:8-9)
14. Anna (Luke 2:36-38)
15. Samuel
16. Balaam (Numbers 22-24)
17. Abraham (Genesis 20:1-7)
18. Moses (Deuteronomy 18:15)
19. Gad (2 Samuel 24:10-14)
20. Ahijah (1 Kings 11:29-40)
21. Jonah
22. Amos
23. Nahum
24. Hosea
25. Joel
26. Obadiah
27. Miriam (Exodus 15:20)
28. Deborah (Judges 4:4)
29. John

30. This man, who traveled to Antioch with Paul, Silas, and Barnabas, was considered a prophet.
31. This prophet spoke of the need to purify temple worship after the return from exile in Babylon. He spoke of the coming of someone like the prophet Elijah.
32. This man of Moresheth was a contemporary of Isaiah. He spoke of the need to walk humbly with God.
33. This prophet, who posed much of his book in the form of questions and answers, concluded that "the just shall live by faith."
34. Active during Josiah's reign, this prophet spoke about judgment and the coming "day of the Lord."
35. This unlucky prophet delivered an unfavorable message to King Ahab.
36. This false prophet wore a yoke, which Jeremiah broke.
37. This traveling companion of Paul was considered a prophet.
38. Active at the time of the rebuilding of the temple in Jerusalem, this prophet is associated with Zechariah.
39. This prophet, who lived in Jerusalem after the Babylonian exile, had visions of a flying scroll and a gold lampstand.
40. This man is spoken of as being his brother's prophet. He is also famous for having constructed a golden calf.
41. This false prophet wore iron horns and told King Ahab he would be victorious in battle.
42. This prophet told King Rehoboam that Judah would be abandoned to the forces of the Egyptian king.
43. This prophet, who lived in the reign of King Asa in Judah, was the son of the prophet Oded.
44. This false prophet was a sorcerer and an attendant of the proconsul, Sergius Paulus.
45. This prophetess is mentioned as an intimidator of Nehemiah.
46. This evil prophetess is referred to in Revelation by the name of an Old Testament queen.

30. Judas Barsabbas (Acts 15:22, 32)
31. Malachi
32. Micah
33. Habakkuk
34. Zephaniah
35. Micaiah ben-Imlah (1 Kings 22:8-28)
36. Hananiah (Jeremiah 28)
37. Silas (Acts 15:32)
38. Haggai
39. Zechariah
40. Aaron (Exodus 7:1)
41. Zedekiah (1 Kings 22:1-12)
42. Shemaiah (2 Chronicles 12:5-8)
43. Azariah (2 Chronicles 13:1-8)
44. Bar-Jesus (Acts 13:6-11)
45. Noadiah (Nehemiah 6:14)
46. Jezebel (Revelation 2:20)

✦Notable Women, and Some Less Notable (II)

1. Who was the mother of the Midianites?
2. What Gospel mentions Susanna, who had been healed by Jesus?
3. Who is the only Egyptian queen mentioned in the Bible?
4. What Egyptian woman found the infant Moses in the river?
5. What daughter of David was raped by her half brother?
6. What epistle mentions Tryphena, a faithful church worker?
7. Who was the wife of Haman of Persia?
8. Who were the first two women to hear that their husband had killed a man?
9. What servant woman of Leah's became the mother of two of the twelve tribes of Israel?
10. What were the names of Adam's daughters?
11. Whose daughters became the mothers of the Moabites and the Ammonites?
12. What priest of Midian had seven daughters, one of which became the wife of Moses?
13. What girl was offered as a sacrifice by her father, one of Israel's judges?
14. What daughter of a troublemaker married a Jewish priest, a marriage that caused him to lose his post?
15. What was the name of Melchizedek's mother?
16. What little girl was referred to as "Talitha" by Jesus?
17. What two Hebrew servant women risked their lives by disobeying the command of the pharaoh?
18. What harlot fled from a burning city, taking her family with her?
19. Whose ten concubines were forced to engage in public lewdness with the king's sons?
20. Who had an Israelite servant girl who told him about a cure for leprosy?
21. Who urged her husband to curse God and die?
22. What apostle had a sister whose son informed soldiers of a murderous plot?
23. Who was forbidden to mourn the death of his beautiful wife?

Notable Women, and Some Less Notable (II)
(Answers)

1. Keturah, wife of Abraham (Genesis 25:1, 4)
2. Luke (8:3)
3. Tahpenes (1 Kings 11:19)
4. Pharaoh's daughter (Exodus 2:5)
5. Tamar (2 Samuel 13)
6. Romans (16:12)
7. Zeresh (Esther 5:10)
8. Zilah and Adah, wives of Lamech (Genesis 4:19-23)
9. Zilpah, mother of Asher and Gad (Genesis 30:11-13)
10. They are not named.
11. Lot's (Genesis 19:30-38)
12. Jethro, or Reuel (Exodus 2:16-20)
13. Jephthah's daughter (Judges 11)
14. The daughter of Sanballat, and wife of Joiada (Nehemiah 13:28)
15. He didn't have a mother (Hebrews 7:3)
16. Jairus's daughter (Matthew 9:18-25)
17. Puah and Shiprah (Exodus 1:15)
18. Rahab (Joshua 6:25)
19. David's (2 Samuel 15:16; 16:22; 20:3)
20. Naaman (2 Kings 5:2)
21. Job's wife (Job 2:9)
22. Paul (Acts 23:16)
23. Ezekiel (24:16-18)

24. What invading general had a loving mother who never saw her son return from battle?
25. What woman in the time of the judges had dedicated 1,100 shekels of silver to the making of idols?
26. Whose mother took refuge in Moab while her son was fleeing the wrath of Israel's king?
27. What woman put on an act to convince David to recall Absalom from exile?
28. What was the occupation of the two women who disputed over a child and asked Solomon for a decision?
29. What city suffered such a terrible famine that two women agreed to eat their sons for dinner?
30. What woman is mentioned in Proverbs as having taught wise sayings to her son?
31. What book portrays Wisdom as a woman?
32. What grief-stricken woman turned away from her diseased husband because his breath was so offensive?
33. Where did the faithful mother of Rufus live?
34. What violent son of Gideon was killed by a woman who dropped a millstone on his skull?
35. Who tricked his enemies by leaving a harlot's house earlier than expected?
36. Who is the only woman in the Bible described as a "wench"?
37. Who helped David by hiding two of his messengers in her cistern?
38. What woman saved her city by negotiating peacefully with Joab?
39. What prophet pictures women weeping for the god Tammuz?
40. Who is the first female barber mentioned in the Bible?
41. Where did Paul exorcise a spirit from a girl who later became a believer?
42. Which epistle mentions "silly women" who are always learning but never aware of the truth?
43. Which epistle is addressed to a woman?
44. How many times does Eve's name appear in Genesis?
45. How many times does Eve's name appear in the New Testament?
46. Which Gospel records Jesus saying "Remember Lot's wife"?

24. Sisera's mother (Judges 5:28)
25. Micah's mother (Judges 17:2-4)
26. David's (1 Samuel 22:3-4)
27. The wise woman of Tekoa (2 Samuel 14)
28. Harlots (1 Kings 3:16-28)
29. Samaria (2 Kings 6:20, 26-30)
30. King Lemuel's mother (Proverbs 31:1)
31. Proverbs (chapter 8)
32. Job's wife (Job 19:17)
33. Rome (Romans 16:13)
34. Abimelech (Judges 9:53)
35. Samson (Judges 16:1-3)
36. The woman of En-rogel who acted as a liaison between David and the high priest (2 Samuel 17:17)
37. The Bahurim woman (2 Samuel 17:19)
38. The wise woman of Abel (2 Samuel 20:16-22)
39. Ezekiel (8:14)
40. Delilah (Judges 16:19)
41. Philippi (Acts 16:16)
42. 2 Timothy (3:6-7)
43. 2 John
44. Twice (Genesis 3:20; 4:1)
45. Twice (2 Corinthians 11:3; 1 Timothy 2:13)
46. Luke (17:32)

47. What shepherd girl became the much-loved wife of Jacob?
48. What daughter of Jacob caused major problems by venturing into strange territory?
49. What quick-witted widow secured children through her deceived father-in-law?
50. What Egyptian wife caused Joseph to be thrown into prison?
51. What Midianite woman married Moses?
52. What Moabite was an ancestor of Jesus?
53. Who is the first female singer mentioned in the Bible?
54. What woman was married to a fool with a name that meant "fool"?
55. What singer was shut out of the Israelite camp for seven days when she was stricken with leprosy?
56. What five women demanded that Moses give them their deceased father's estate, though women had no property rights at the time?
57. What woman of Jericho was spared when Joshua's men took the city?
58. What unfortunate woman was gang-raped, then cut into twelve pieces and sent to the tribes of Israel?
59. Who brought down Samson for the price of 1,100 pieces of silver from each of the Philistine chieftains?
60. At whose house did Peter confront maids who asked him if he was one of Jesus' disciples?
61. What famous Moabite woman was married to Chilion of Israel?
62. Who was the Kate Smith of the Hebrews?
63. What woman was suspected of drunkenness as she prayed in the sanctuary at Shiloh?
64. Who was David's first wife?
65. What young girl was brought in to warm the cold bones of old King David?
66. What name was borne by one of David's wives and one of his mothers-in-law?
67. Who was stricken with leprosy for speaking out against her brother?
68. What famous woman judge was married to the obscure man named Lapidoth?
69. What was Moses' mother's name?

47. Rachel (Genesis 29:6)
48. Dinah (Genesis 34)
49. Tamar (Genesis 38)
50. The wife of Potiphar (Genesis 39:7-20)
51. Zipporah (Exodus 2:21)
52. Ruth (4:17)
53. Miriam (Exodus 15:21)
54. Abigail (1 Samuel 25:23-25)
55. Miriam (Numbers 12)
56. The five daughters of Zelophehad (Numbers 26–27)
57. Rahab (Joshua 6:17)
58. The Levite's concubine (Judges 19–20)
59. Delilah (Judges 16:5)
60. The high priest's (Matthew 26:69-71; Mark 14:66-69)
61. Ruth (1:2-5)
62. Miriam, who sang a patriotic song after the crossing of the Red Sea (Exodus 15:21)
63. Hannah (1 Samuel 1:13-14)
64. Michal (1 Samuel 18:27)
65. Abishag (1 Kings 1:3, 15)
66. Ahinoam (1 Samuel 14:50; 25:43)
67. Miriam (Numbers 12)
68. Deborah (Judges 4:4)
69. Jochebed (Exodus 6:20)

70. What woman gave up her son to the household of an Egyptian but came to raise him in her own home anyway?
71. What Midianite woman was the daughter of a priest and the wife of a former Egyptian prince?
72. What woman of dubious character hid Israelite spies under piles of flax?
73. What woman from an idol-worshiping nation became an ancestor of Christ?
74. What barren woman begged the Lord for a son, and later gave up her only son to live in the house of the priest Eli?
75. Who took great pains to make peace between David and her foolish and obnoxious husband?
76. What unnamed woman broke the king's law by order of the king himself?
77. What wife of David took enormous pains to secure the throne for her son?
78. What son of David was always referred to as the "son of Haggith"?
79. What wife of David is mentioned in Matthew's genealogy of Jesus?
80. Who came to Jesus at the wedding of Cana and said, "They have no wine"?
81. What queen of Israel ordered the extermination of the prophets of the Lord?
82. Who was killed after being thrown from a window by two eunuchs?
83. What woman, associated with the prophet Elijah, was mentioned by Jesus?
84. What wealthy woman had a son that died of a sunstroke?
85. What daughter of Jezebel was killed at Jerusalem's Horse Gate?
86. What wise woman was sought out by Josiah when the Book of the Law was discovered in the temple?
87. What book of the Bible mentions a virtuous woman who is more valuable than rubies?
88. Who was the first woman to ask the Lord for help?
89. Who was Jesus speaking of when he said, "Behold your mother"?
90. What servant of David was desired as a prize by his son Adonijah?

70. Jochebed, Moses' mother (Exodus 2:8-10)
71. Zipporah, Moses' wife (Exodus 2:21)
72. Rahab (Joshua 2:6)
73. Ruth (4:17)
74. Hannah (1 Samuel 1:20-25)
75. Abigail (1 Samuel 25:23-35)
76. The witch of Endor (1 Samuel 28:7-25)
77. Bathsheba, mother of Solomon (1 Kings 1)
78. Adonijah (1 Kings 1:11)
79. Bathsheba (Matthew 1:6)
80. Mary (John 2:3)
81. Jezebel (1 Kings 18:4)
82. Jezebel (2 Kings 9:33)
83. The widow of Zarephath (Luke 4:25-26)
84. The woman of Shunam (2 Kings 4:19)
85. Athaliah (2 Chronicles 23:14)
86. Huldah the prophetess (2 Kings 22:14)
87. Proverbs (31:10-31)
88. Rebekah (Genesis 25:22)
89. Mary (John 19:27)
90. Abishag, the Shunnamite (1 Kings 2:17)

✦The Inventors

1. Who was the first person to practice wine-making?
2. What righteous man started the practice of herding sheep?
3. What mighty man was the first hunter?
4. Who invented farming?
5. Who invented the art of working with metal?
6. Who was the first man to build a city?
7. Who invented music-making?
8. Who invented tents?

✦Down on the Farm

1. What was the farmer Elisha doing when Elijah threw his mantle upon him?
2. What suffering man was a farmer?
3. Who planted the first garden?
4. What judge was a wheat farmer?
5. What king of Judah loved farming?
6. Who was the first man to plant a vineyard?
7. What barley farmer married a Moabite woman and became an ancestor of David?
8. Who was the first farmer?
9. For what cripple did David order Ziba to farm the land?
10. Who had a vineyard that Ahab coveted?
11. What patriarch farmed in Gerar and received a hundredfold harvest?
12. What lieutenant of David had his barley fields destroyed by Absalom?
13. What king, famous for his building projects, also planted vineyards, gardens, and orchards?

✦Late-Night Callers

1. Who came to Peter late at night and released him from prison?
2. Who had a late night visit from an angel, who assured him that he would be safe aboard a storm-tossed ship?

The Inventors (Answers)

1. Noah (Genesis 9:20-21)
2. Abel (Genesis 4:2)
3. Nimrod (Genesis 10:8-9)
4. Cain (Genesis 4:2)
5. Tubal-Cain (Genesis 4:22)
6. Cain (Genesis 4:17)
7. Jubal, inventor of the harp and organ (Genesis 4:21)
8. Jabal (Genesis 4:20)

Down on the Farm (Answers)

1. Plowing (1 Kings 19:19)
2. Job (1:14)
3. God (Genesis 2:8)
4. Gideon (Judges 6:11)
5. Uzziah (2 Chronicles 26:9-10)
6. Noah (Genesis 9:20)
7. Boaz (Ruth 1:22–2:3)
8. Cain (Genesis 4:2)
9. Mephibosheth, Saul's grandson (2 Samuel 9:9-10)
10. Naboth (1 Kings 21:1-2)
11. Isaac (Genesis 26:12)
12. Joab (2 Samuel 14:30)
13. Solomon (Ecclesiastes 2:4-5)

Late-Night Callers (Answers)

1. An angel (Acts 12:6-17)
2. Paul (Acts 27:23-24)

3. Who led some officers of the chief priests to pay a late night call on Jesus?
4. What Pharisee came to Jesus late at night?
5. Who met a man with whom he engaged in an all-night wrestling match?
6. Who came through Egypt on a late-night visit to almost every household?
7. Where did shepherds receive angels as late visitors?
8. Who took Saul's spear after sneaking into his camp late one night?
9. Who visited a medium at night?
10. Who attacked a Midianite camp late at night?
11. Who paid the young Samuel a late-night call?
12. Who frightened his followers, who thought he was a ghost when he passed by them late at night?

◆They Heard Voices

1. What New Testament character was the "voice crying in the wilderness"?
2. What blind father recognized Jacob's voice but was deceived by his glove-covered hands?
3. When Moses was in the tabernacle, where did God's voice come from?
4. Who heard a voice that said, "Write down what you see"?
5. Where did God speak to Moses in a voice like thunder?
6. What barren woman moved her lips in prayer but made no sound?
7. According to Deuteronomy, where did God's voice come from?
8. Who told Saul that obeying God's voice was more important than sacrificing animals?
9. Which Gospel mentions the voice of Rachel weeping for her children?
10. Who heard the voice of an angel ordering that a large tree be chopped down?
11. What book says that the divine voice sounds like a waterfall?
12. Who said, "Is that your voice, David my son"?

3. Judas (John 18:3, 12)
4. Nicodemus (John 3:1-2)
5. Jacob (Genesis 32:22-31)
6. The angel of death (Exodus 12:29-31)
7. Near Bethlehem (Luke 2:8-16)
8. David and Abishai (1 Samuel 26:7-12)
9. Saul (1 Samuel 28:8)
10. Gideon and his men (Judges 7:19)
11. The Lord (1 Samuel 4:1-14)
12. Jesus, when he walked on the lake (Mark 6:48)

They Heard Voices (Answers)

1. John the Baptist (Mark 1:3)
2. Isaac (Genesis 27:22)
3. Above the ark of the covenant (Numbers 7:89)
4. John (Revelation 1:10)
5. Mount Sinai (Exodus 19:19)
6. Hannah (1 Samuel 1:13)
7. The fire (Deuteronomy 5:24)
8. Samuel (1 Samuel 15:22)
9. Matthew (2:18)
10. Daniel (4:14)
11. Revelation (1:15)
12. Saul (1 Samuel 26:17)

13. To which church did Jesus say, "If any man hear my voice, and open the door, I will come in to him"?
14. What apostle addressed the Pentecost crowd in a loud voice?
15. Who cried out at the top of her voice when she saw Samuel raised from the dead?
16. At what event did a voice from heaven say, "This is my beloved Son, in whom I am well pleased"?
17. What boy was sleeping near the ark of the covenant when he heard God's voice calling to him?
18. Where was Jesus when the divine voice said, "This is my beloved Son . . . hear ye him"?
19. What king heard the voice of God in the temple—although there was no temple at the time?
20. Who heard the voice of those who had been killed for proclaiming God's word?
21. Who heard God's voice after running away from Queen Jezebel?
22. Who screamed in a loud voice, asking Jesus not to punish him?
23. What king was told by Isaiah that the king of Assyria had raised his voice up against God?
24. What was the problem of the ten men who called to Jesus in loud voices, begging him for mercy?
25. Who heard the "still, small voice" of God?
26. What criminal did the people of Jerusalem cry out for in a loud voice?
27. Who heard God speaking out of a whirlwind?
28. What bird did John hear crying in a loud voice, "Woe, woe to the inhabiters of the earth"?
29. According to Psalm 19, what has a voice that goes out to all the world?
30. Who said that the bridegroom's friend is happy when he hears the bridegroom's voice?
31. According to Psalms, what trees are broken by the power of God's voice?
32. Who heard a voice telling of the fall of Babylon?
33. Which Gospel mentions the dead awakening to the voice of the Son of God?
34. What, according to Proverbs, lifts its voice up in the streets?

13. Laodicea (Revelation 3:20)
14. Peter (Acts 2:14)
15. The witch of Endor (1 Samuel 28:12)
16. Jesus' baptism (Matthew 3:17)
17. Samuel (1 Samuel 3:3-14)
18. On the Mount of Transfiguration (Matthew 17:5)
19. David (2 Samuel 22:7)
20. John (Revelation 6:10)
21. Elijah (1 Kings 19:13)
22. The Gerasene demoniac (Mark 5:7)
23. Hezekiah (2 Kings 19:22)
24. Leprosy (Luke 17:13)
25. Elijah (1 Kings 19:12)
26. Barabbas (Luke 23:18)
27. Job (38:1)
28. An eagle (Revelation 8:13)
29. The heavens (Psalm 19:4)
30. John the Baptist (John 3:29)
31. The cedars of Lebanon (Psalm 29:5)
32. John (Revelation 18:2)
33. John (5:25)
34. Wisdom (Proverbs 1:20)

35. What city in Revelation was seen as a place that would never again hear the voices of brides and grooms?
36. According to Jesus, whose voice do the sheep know?
37. What book mentions the sweet voices of lovers in the garden?
38. In Revelation, where did the voice proclaiming the new heaven and earth come from?
39. Who heard God's voice in the temple in the year that King Uzziah died?
40. Who came forth when Jesus called to him in a loud voice?
41. What prophet predicted that Rachel's voice would be heard, wailing for her dead children?
42. Which Gospel mentions the voice of God speaking during Jesus' farewell address to his disciples?
43. What prophet mentions Jerusalem with the voice of a ghost?
44. Who heard the voice of Jesus many months after Jesus' ascension to heaven?
45. What epistle mentions an archangel's voice in connection with the resurrection of believers?
46. What prophet's voice did the returned Jewish exiles obey?
47. What prophet mentions a voice crying in the wilderness?
48. Who heard the divine voice telling him to eat unclean animals?
49. What king heard God's voice just as he was boasting about how great Babylon was?
50. Who heard the voice of God as he watched four mysterious creatures flying under a crystal dome?
51. Who recognized Peter's voice after he was miraculously delivered from prison?
52. According to Isaiah, what noble person will not lift up his voice in the streets?
53. According to Paul, what language did the divine voice use on the Damascus road?
54. What king called to Daniel in an anguished voice?
55. Which epistle mentions the voice of Balaam's donkey?

35. Babylon (Revelation 18:23)
36. The shepherd's (John 10:4)
37. Song of Solomon (2:14; 8:13)
38. The throne (Revelation 21:3)
39. Isaiah (6:8)
40. Lazarus (John 11:43)
41. Jeremiah (31:15)
42. John (12:28-30)
43. Isaiah (29:4)
44. Paul (Acts 9:4)
45. 1 Thessalonians (4:16)
46. Haggai's (1:12)
47. Isaiah (40:3)
48. Peter (Acts 10:13-15)
49. Nebuchadnezzar (Daniel 4:31)
50. Ezekiel (1:24)
51. Rhoda (Acts 12:14)
52. The Lord's servant (Isaiah 42:2)
53. Hebrew (or, in some translations, Aramaic) (Acts 26:14)
54. Darius (Daniel 6:20)
55. 2 Peter (2:16)

✦Teacher, Teacher

1. What famous rabbi was Paul's teacher?
2. Who commissioned Ezra to teach the law to Israel?
3. According to Jesus, who would teach his followers all they needed to know?
4. What two men were to instruct the people involved in the construction of the tabernacle?
5. What king of Judah sent his princes throughout the land to teach the law to the people?
6. What learned Greek taught in the synagogue at Ephesus but was himself instructed by Aquila and Priscilla?
7. What king sent an exiled priest back to Samaria to teach the Gentiles there how to follow God?
8. What apostle taught and disputed in the lecture hall of a man named Tyrannus?
9. Who was supposed to teach the Israelites how to deal with lepers?
10. What New Testament word means "teacher"?

✦Sleepers and Nonsleepers

1. Who had surgery performed on him while he slept?
2. Who was killed as he slept in the tent of Jael?
3. Who slept in the bottom of a ship as it rolled in a storm?
4. Who suggested to Jezebel's priests that Baal was sleeping on duty?
5. Who slept at Bethel and dreamed about angels?
6. Who slept at David's door while he was home on furlough?
7. Who could not sleep on the night after Haman built a gallows for hanging Mordecai?
8. Who had troublesome dreams that kept him from sleeping?
9. Who was visited by an angel of the Lord while sleeping?
10. Who slept while Jesus prayed in Gethsemane?
11. Who sneaked into Saul's camp while he was asleep?
12. Who spoke to Abram while he was in a deep sleep?
13. Who did not sleep while Daniel was in the lions' den?
14. Who slept through a haircut?

Teacher, Teacher (Answers)

1. Gamaliel (Acts 22:3)
2. King Artaxerxes (Ezra 7:25)
3. The Comforter (John 14:26)
4. Bezaleel and Aholiab (Exodus 35:30-35)
5. Jehoshaphat (2 Chronicles 17:7-9)
6. Apollos (Acts 18:24-26)
7. The king of Assyria (2 Kings 17:28)
8. Paul (Acts 19:9)
9. The priests (Deuteronomy 24:8)
10. Rabbi (John 1:38)

Sleepers and Nonsleepers (Answers)

1. Adam (Genesis 2:21)
2. Sisera (Judges 4:21)
3. Jonah (1:5)
4. Elijah (1 Kings 18:27)
5. Jacob (Genesis 28:11-15)
6. Uriah (2 Samuel 11:9)
7. King Ahasuerus (Esther 6:1)
8. Nebuchadnezzar (Daniel 2:1)
9. Joseph (Matthew 2:13)
10. The disciples (Luke 22:45)
11. David and Abishai (1 Samuel 26:7)
12. God (Genesis 15:12-16)
13. King Darius (Daniel 6:18)
14. Samson (Judges 16:19)

15. Who slept during a storm on the Sea of Galilee?
16. Who fell asleep during Paul's sermon and was later raised from the dead by Paul?
17. Who was sleeping between two soldiers when an angel came to release him?
18. Who was awakened from a deep sleep by an earthquake that toppled a prison?
19. According to Jesus, this person was not dead, but only sleeping. Who was it?
20. Who told Laban he had gone twenty years without a decent sleep?
21. According to Proverbs, what does it take for the wicked to sleep well?
22. Which epistle tells sleepers to rise from the dead?
23. Which epistle uses sleep as a metaphor for physical death?
24. What boy was called out of his sleep by the voice of God?
25. Which epistle urges believers to be alert, not asleep?
26. Who was in a deep sleep as the angel Gabriel explained a vision?

◆Godly Government Workers in Ungodly Places

1. What Hebrew governed Egypt?
2. What upright young man was made ruler over the whole province of Babylon?
3. What island was Sergius Paulus, who became a Christian, the deputy of?
4. What Persian king did Nehemiah serve under?
5. What church in Greece had believers that were workers in "Caesar's household"?
6. From what country was the eunuch that was baptized by Philip?
7. What Jewish man served as an honored official under Ahasuerus of Persia?
8. What Roman centurion of Caesarea was a godly man?
9. What three Hebrew men were appointed Babylonian administrators by Nebuchadnezzar?

15. Jesus (Luke 8:23-24)
16. Eutychus (Acts 20:9-12)
17. Peter (Acts 12:6-7)
18. The Philippian jailor (Acts 16:27)
19. Jairus's daughter (Luke 8:52)
20. Jacob (Genesis 31:38, 40)
21. Causing trouble (Proverbs 4:16)
22. Ephesians (5:14)
23. 1 Corinthians 15
24. Samuel (1 Samuel 3:2-10)
25. 1 Thessalonians (5:4-8)
26. Daniel (8:15-18)

Godly Government Workers in Ungodly Places
(Answers)

1. Joseph (Genesis 42:6)
2. Daniel (2:48)
3. Cyprus (Acts 13:4-7)
4. Artaxerxes (Nehemiah 1:11)
5. Philippi (Philippians 4:22)
6. Ethiopia (Acts 8:27)
7. Mordecai (Esther 10:3)
8. Cornelius (Acts 10:1-2)
9. Shadrach, Meshach, and Abednego (Daniel 2:49)

10. What was the occupation of the Roman who had his beloved servant healed by Jesus?
11. What Jewish girl became queen of Persia?

✦Notable Women, and Some Less Notable (III)

1. What New Testament woman was married to a priest named Zacharias?
2. Who begged her sister for some mandrakes, hoping they would help her bear children?
3. To what woman did Jesus declare, "I am the resurrection and the life"?
4. Who sat at Jesus' feet while her sister kept house?
5. What two women witnessed Jesus' tears over their dead brother?
6. What disciple's mother-in-law was healed of a fever by Jesus?
7. What wicked woman, the wife of a wicked king, brought about the death of John the Baptist?
8. How long did cousins Mary and Elisabeth spend together during their pregnancies?
9. Who offered to bear the guilt if her scheme to deceive her aged husband was found out?
10. Who said to her husband, "Give me children, or else I die"?
11. Which of Jacob's wives was the first to bear children?
12. What woman was called a prophetess by Luke?
13. Who died in giving birth to Benjamin?
14. What clever woman hoodwinked her father-in-law out of a signet ring and bracelets?
15. Who falsely accused her Hebrew servant of trying to seduce her?
16. What woman was the mother of two of Jesus' disciples?
17. Who asked Jesus for the special water that would quench her thirst forever?
18. Who called Jesus "Rabboni"?
19. To what earthy woman did Jesus say, "God is a spirit"?

10. A centurion (Luke 7:2-10)
11. Esther (2:17)

Notable Women, and Some Less Notable (III)
(Answers)

1. Elisabeth (Luke 1:5)
2. Rachel (Genesis 30:14)
3. Martha (John 11:24-26)
4. Mary (Luke 10:39-42)
5. Mary and Martha (John 11:32-39)
6. Peter's (Mark 1:30-31)
7. Herodias, wife of Herod (Luke 3:19)
8. Three months (Luke 1:56)
9. Rebekah (Genesis 27:13)
10. Rachel (Genesis 30:1)
11. Leah (Genesis 29:31)
12. Anna (Luke 2:36)
13. Rachel (Genesis 35:18)
14. Tamar (Genesis 38:17)
15. Potiphar's wife (Genesis 39:14)
16. Salome (Mark 15:40). While this verse does not specifically say that Salome is the mother of James and John, Matthew 27:56 mentions that two Marys and the mother of James and John were watching the crucifixion, so we may assume from Matthew and Mark that the third woman, Salome, was the mother of James and John.
17. The Samaritan woman (John 4:15)
18. Mary Magdalene (John 20:16)
19. The Samaritan woman (John 4:24)

20. Which of David's wives was described as "very beautiful to look upon"?
21. What wife, seeing her husband on the verge of death, circumcised their son?
22. Who criticized her famous brother for being married to an Ethiopian woman?
23. What Old Testament woman is mentioned in the roll of the faithful in Hebrews 11?
24. What woman gave needed courage to the fainthearted military man Barak?
25. Who pouted when her strongman lover kept fooling her about the source of his strength?
26. Who lay down at her future husband's feet and was accepted by him?
27. Which of David's wives "despised him in her heart"?
28. What wife of a sheepherder admitted that her husband was a complete fool?
29. Who killed a fatted calf and made bread for a despairing king?
30. Who was the mother of John Mark?
31. Who was the royal mother of Nathan, Shobab, and Shimea?
32. Who came to Jerusalem with a caravan of camels and loads of jewels?
33. Who ran to tell people that she had met the Christ by a well?
34. What woman set up a special apartment for the prophet Elisha?
35. What book mentions an industrious woman who plants a vineyard with her own hands?
36. Who was the angel Gabriel speaking to when he said, "Blessed art thou among women"?
37. Where was Mary the last time she is mentioned in the New Testament?
38. Who was the first woman to tell Jesus she believed he was the Messiah?
39. What was the affliction of the woman who touched the hem of Jesus' robe?
40. To whom did Jesus say, "I am not sent but unto the lost sheep of the house of Israel"?

---

0. Bathsheba, or Bath-shua (2 Samuel 11:2)
1. Zipporah (Exodus 4:25)
2. Miriam (Numbers 12:1)
3. Rahab (Hebrews 11:31)
4. Deborah (Judges 4:8)
5. Delilah (Judges 16)
6. Ruth (3:4-9)
7. Michal (2 Samuel 6:16)
8. Abigail (1 Samuel 25:25)
9. The witch of Endor (1 Samuel 28:24)
0. Mary (Acts 12:12)
1. Bathsheba (1 Chronicles 3:5)
2. The queen of Sheba (1 Kings 10:2)
3. The Samaritan woman (John 4:29)
4. The woman of Shunam (2 Kings 4:9)
5. Proverbs (31:16)
6. Mary (Luke 1:28)
7. With the apostles in the upper room in Jerusalem (Acts 1:13-14)
8. Martha (John 11:24-27)
9. An issue of blood (Mark 5:31)
0. The Syro-Phoenician woman of Canaan (Matthew 15:24)

41. Who asked that her two sons could have places of priority in Jesus' kingdom?
42. What woman had had five husbands and was living with another man?
43. What woman accused Elijah of murdering her son, a son that Elijah then raised from the dead?
44. What woman had been healed of seven demons by Jesus?
45. How many Marys are in the New Testament?
46. Who was the first woman to go against Jesus' words "You cannot serve God and mammon"?
47. What woman had Tabitha as a pet name?
48. What woman had the same name as an old kingdom of Asia?
49. What daughter of Job had a twelve-letter name?
50. What woman was capable enough to instruct the brilliant Apollos in theology?
51. Who was probably the carrier of Paul's epistle to the Romans?
52. What pastor was the son of the devout Eunice?
53. Who was with David when Bathsheba and Nathan pleaded with him to designate Solomon as his successor?
54. Who was given by her Egyptian father as a reward to a Hebrew servant?
55. What evil woman lived in the Valley of Sorek?
56. Who was Timothy's devout grandmother?
57. What woman, wife of the wicked king Amon, gave birth to the future godly king Josiah?
58. What courageous woman risked her life to keep her royal nephew alive?
59. What Jewish Christian woman had lived at Rome, Corinth, and Ephesus?
60. Who called herself Marah, a name meaning "bitter"?
61. Who asked her royal son to surrender his father's concubine to another son?
62. What wealthy woman made her living selling purple dye?
63. What woman had such an influential life that Israel had forty years of peace?
64. Who was better to her widowed mother-in-law than any seven sons could be?
65. Who bore three sons and two daughters after giving up her first son to serve the Lord at Shiloh?

41. The mother of John and James (Matthew 20:21)
42. The Samaritan woman (John 4:18)
43. The widow of Zarephath (1 Kings 17:18)
44. Mary Magdalene (Mark 16:9)
45. Six—Jesus' mother, Mary of Bethany, Mary Magdalene, Mary mother of James and Joses, Mary mother of John Mark, and Mary of Rome
46. Sapphira, wife of Ananias (Acts 5)
47. Dorcas (Acts 9:36, 39)
48. Lydia (Acts 16:14)
49. Keren-happuch (Job 42:14)
50. Priscilla (Acts 18:26)
51. Phoebe (Romans 16:1-2)
52. Timothy (2 Timothy 1:5)
53. Abishag (1 Kings 1:15)
54. Asenath, wife of Joseph (Genesis 41:45)
55. Delilah (Judges 16:4)
56. Lois (2 Timothy 1:5)
57. Jedidah (2 Kings 22:1)
58. Jehosheba, Joash's aunt (2 Kings 11:2-3)
59. Priscilla (Acts 18:2, 18, 24-26)
60. Naomi (Ruth 1:19-21)
61. Bathsheba (1 Kings 2:20)
62. Lydia (Acts 16:14)
63. Deborah (Judges 5:31)
64. Ruth (4:15)
65. Hannah (1 Samuel 2:21)

66. What wife of David had no children because she had criticized her husband's jubilant dancing?
67. Who married David after her stupid husband died out of fear?
68. Who was the last woman to have dinner with King Saul?
69. Who was the first woman to be ashamed of her clothing?
70. Who was given a miraculous supply of food by the prophet Elijah?
71. What faithful woman did Elisha warn of a coming famine?
72. Who said, "Thy father and I have sought thee sorrowing"?
73. Who referred to Mary as the "mother of my Lord"?
74. What New Testament woman holds the record for widowhood—eighty-four years?
75. Who anointed Jesus' feet with precious ointment?
76. Who had her conversation with Jesus interrupted by his disciples, who criticized him for speaking with a woman?
77. Who was the first woman to see Jesus' empty tomb?
78. What two tribes of Israel were descended from an Egyptian woman?
79. What pagan woman of the Gospels is traditionally identified with the Christian woman Claudia mentioned in 2 Timothy?
80. What Christian woman was noted for helping the poor in the early church?
81. What woman, once possessed by demons, was the first to see the risen Christ?
82. What woman's absence made the Israelites pause in their journey to the promised land?
83. What woman was the first Christian convert in Europe?
84. What woman has been proposed as the author of the Epistle to the Hebrews?
85. What devout woman was described by Paul as "our sister" and "a servant of the church"?
86. What book features a dark Shulamite woman who sings to her loved one?
87. In the ridiculous riddle of the Sadducees, how many husbands did the hypothetical woman have?
88. What was the proposed punishment for the woman taken in adultery, later forgiven by Jesus?
89. Where was Paul when he cast demons out from a girl who was a spiritualist?

66. Michal (2 Samuel 6:23)
67. Abigail (1 Samuel 25:36-42)
68. The witch of Endor (1 Samuel 28:25)
69. Eve—actually, she was ashamed of her lack of clothing (Genesis 3:7)
70. The widow of Zarephath (1 Kings 17:16)
71. The woman of Shunem (2 Kings 8:1)
72. Mary (Luke 2:48)
73. Elisabeth (Luke 1:41-43)
74. Anna (Luke 2:36-37)
75. Mary of Bethany (John 12:3)
76. The Samaritan woman (John 4:27)
77. Mary Magdalene (John 20:1)
78. Manasseh and Ephraim—their father Joseph was married to Asenath of Egypt (Genesis 41:50-52)
79. Pilate's wife (Matthew 27:19)
80. Dorcas (Acts 9:36, 39)
81. Mary Magdalene (John 20:14)
82. Miriam's (Numbers 12:15)
83. Lydia (Acts 16:14)
84. Priscilla
85. Phoebe (Romans 16:1-2)
86. The Song of Solomon
87. Seven (Mark 12:20-25)
88. Stoning (John 8:3-11)
89. Philippi (Acts 16:16)

90. What was the hometown of Mary and Martha and Lazarus?
91. What beautiful woman of Israel was married to a Hittite warrior?
92. What distraught woman failed at first to recognize the resurrected Jesus?
93. What doting mother made her absentee son a new coat each year?
94. What book speaks of the "sons of God" taking the "daughters of men" as wives?
95. What woman is significant for keeping her own name when she married instead of taking her husband's name?
96. Who had ten concubines that were sexually assaulted by his wayward son?
97. What book has a chorus of girls of Jerusalem as characters?

90. Bethany (John 11:1)
91. Bathsheba, wife of Uriah (2 Samuel 11:3)
92. Mary Magdalene (John 20:14-15)
93. Hannah (1 Samuel 2:19)
94. Genesis (6:2)
95. The daughter of Barzillai (Ezra 2:61)
96. David (2 Samuel 16:21-22)
97. The Song of Solomon

PART 2

Crimes
and
Punishments

✦All Kinds of Villains

1. Who plotted to have the entire Hebrew nation completely exterminated?
2. Who committed the first murder?
3. Who acknowledged the innocence of Jesus but allowed him to be crucified anyway?
4. Who made numerous attempts to swindle Jacob, who ultimately prospered?
5. What king was constantly making oaths of love and loyalty to David while frequently trying to kill him?
6. What evil king of Israel was led into even more wickedness by his beautiful and scheming wife?
7. Who ordered the killing of infant boys in Bethlehem?
8. What treacherous son led a revolt against his father, the king of Israel?
9. What ruler, who had already had John the Baptist beheaded, was Jesus made to appear before?
10. What two traitorous army captains murdered their king as a favor to David and were then executed by David for treachery?

✦Thieving Types

1. Who stole idols from her father?
2. What robber was released from prison at the time of the Passover?
3. According to Malachi, what were the people of Judah stealing from God?
4. Who was stoned for stealing booty during the battle for Ai?
5. Which epistles say that the day of the Lord will come like a thief?
6. What disciple stole from the treasury?

All Kinds of Villains (Answers)

1. Haman, minister of Persia (Esther)
2. Cain, who murdered his brother (Genesis 4:8)
3. Pontius Pilate (John 18—19)
4. Laban, his father-in-law (Genesis 29—31)
5. Saul (1 Samuel 19—17)
6. Ahab, husband of Jezebel (1 Kings 16)
7. Herod, known to history as Herod the Great (Matthew 2:16)
8. Absalom, son of David (2 Samuel 15)
9. Herod Antipas (Matthew 14:10)
10. Recab and Baanah, captains of Ishbosheth (2 Samuel 4)

Thieving Types (Answers)

1. Rachel (Genesis 31:19)
2. Barabbas (John 18:40)
3. The tithes they owed (Malachi 3:8)
4. Achan (Joshua 7:10-26)
5. 1 Thessalonians (5:2) and 2 Peter (3:10)
6. Judas Iscariot (John 12:4-6)

7. In the time of the judges, what man stole eleven hundred pieces of silver from his own mother?
8. What did Joseph accuse his brothers of stealing?
9. What prophet condemns people who pile up stolen goods?

✦Playing with Fire

1. What group of converts burned their books of magic?
2. Who burned Joab's barley field just to get his attention?
3. Who burned the Philistines' grain by tying torches to the tails of foxes?
4. What king of Babylon burned Jerusalem?
5. What Canaanite city was burned down by the men of Dan?
6. What Israelite had his goods burned after he had been stoned to death?
7. What nation burned David's city of Ziklag?
8. What king committed suicide by burning down his palace with himself inside?
9. What judge killed about a thousand people when he burned down the tower of Shechem?
10. What Israelite city was burned up by Pharaoh?
11. What tribe of Israel sacked Jerusalem and burned it?
12. In the days of the judges, what tribe had its cities burned by the other tribes?

✦People in Exile

1. What apostle was exiled to Patmos?
2. How many years were the Israelites in Egypt?
3. What prophet was exiled in Egypt with other people from Judah?
4. What was the first instance of exile in the Bible?
5. Who was brought down to Egypt and sold to a man named Potiphar?
6. Who chose to go into exile rather than constantly quarrel with his brother?
7. Who was exiled from the rest of the world?
8. Who did Abraham banish to the desert?

7. Micah (Judges 17:1-4)
8. His silver cup (Genesis 44:1-17)
9. Habakkuk (2:6)

Playing with Fire (Answers)

1. The Ephesians (Acts 19:19)
2. Absalom (2 Samuel 14:28-33)
3. Samson (Judges 15:4-5)
4. Nebuchadnezzar (2 Kings 25:9)
5. Laish (Judges 18:26-27)
6. Achan (Joshua 7:24-25)
7. The Amalekites (1 Samuel 30:1)
8. Zimri (1 Kings 16:18)
9. Abimelech (Judges 9:49)
10. Gezer (1 Kings 9:16)
11. Judah (Judges 1:8)
12. Benjamin (Judges 20:48)

People in Exile (Answers)

1. John (Revelation 1:9)
2. 430 years (Exodus 12:40)
3. Jeremiah (43:5-7)
4. God drove Adam and Eve out of the garden (Genesis 3:24)
5. Joseph (Genesis 39:1)
6. Jacob (Genesis 27:41-45)
7. Noah and his family, since everyone else died (Genesis 7:23)
8. Hagar and Ishmael (Genesis 21:14)

9. Who stayed in Egypt until Herod died?
10. Who carried the people of Jerusalem off to Babylon?
11. What future king of Israel fled from Solomon and hid in Egypt?
12. What nation carried Israel into exile?
13. Who was in exile three years after killing his brother Amnon?
14. What land did Moses flee to when he left Egypt?
15. Who was exiled to the land of Nod?
16. What judge fled from his kin and lived in the land of Tob?
17. Christians were scattered throughout Judea and Samaria because of a persecution that began after whose death?
18. What exiled king of Judah became a friend of the king of Babylon?
19. Who predicted the Babylonian exile to Hezekiah?
20. Who was king in Israel when the Assyrians deported the people?
21. What king of Judah was temporarily exiled in Assyria, where he repented of his evil ways?
22. Who was king when Jerusalem fell to the Babylonians?
23. What prophet went into exile in Babylon?
24. Who was appointed governor of Judah after the people went into exile?
25. When the Assyrians deported the people of Israel, how many of the twelve original tribes were left?
26. What blind king died in exile in Babylon?
27. What king issued an edict ending the exile of the Jews?
28. What Assyrian king carried the people of Israel into exile?
29. What interpreter of dreams was in exile in Babylon?
30. What prophet warned the wicked priest Amaziah that Israel would go into exile?
31. Which epistles are addressed to God's people in exile?
32. Which psalm is a lament of the exiles in Babylon?

✦A Collection of Traitors

1. What infamous Philistine woman tricked Samson into revealing the secret of his strength?
2. What son of David led a major revolt against his father?

9. Joseph, Mary, and Jesus (Matthew 2:13-15)
10. Nebuchadnezzar (2 Kings 24:14-15)
11. Jeroboam (1 Kings 11:40)
12. Assyria (2 Kings 17:6)
13. Absalom (2 Samuel 13:37-38)
14. Midian (Exodus 2:15)
15. Cain (Genesis 4:13-16)
16. Jephthah (Judges 11:3)
17. Stephen's (Acts 8:1)
18. Jehoiachin (2 Kings 25:27-30)
19. Isaiah (2 Kings 20:12-19)
20. Pekah (2 Kings 15:29)
21. Manasseh (2 Chronicles 33:11-13)
22. Zedekiah (2 Chronicles 36:11-20)
23. Ezekiel (1:1-2)
24. Gedaliah (2 Kings 25:22)
25. One—Judah (2 Kings 17:18)
26. Zedekiah (Jeremiah 52:11)
27. Cyrus of Persia (2 Chronicles 36:22-23)
28. Tiglath-Pileser (2 Kings 15:29)
29. Daniel (1:1-6)
30. Amos (7:17)
31. James and 1 Peter
32. Psalm 137

A Collection of Traitors (Answers)

1. Delilah (Judges 16)
2. Absalom (2 Samuel 15)

3. When Pekah the usurper reigned in Israel, who murdered him and took over the throne?

4. What fiery chariot driver slew the king of Israel and the king of Judah and later had Jezebel murdered, after which he reigned as king in Israel?

5. Hazael of Syria usurped the throne after he murdered the king, Ben-hadad. What unusual method did he use for the murder?

6. What traitor murdered Elah, king of Israel, and then later, after a seven-day reign, committed suicide?

7. Who murdered Shallum and took his place on the throne of Israel?

8. When Judas appeared in Gethsemane to betray Jesus, he was accompanied by a crowd. What were the people of the crowd carrying?

◆A Gallery of Prisoners

1. Who was put in prison as a political enemy of the Philistines?

2. What king of Israel was imprisoned for defying Assyrian authority?

3. What kinsman of Jesus was imprisoned for criticizing King Herod's marriage to Herodias?

4. What famous dreamer was imprisoned after being accused of trying to seduce Potiphar's wife?

5. Whose brothers were imprisoned after being falsely accused of being spies in Egypt?

6. Who was imprisoned for prophesying the destruction of the kingdom of Judah?

7. What king of Judah was blinded and imprisoned because he defied Babylonian authority?

8. Who prophesied doom for King Asa and was put in prison?

9. What king of Judah was sent into exile in Babylon and put in prison, but was later released and treated as a friend of the king of Babylon?

10. Who prophesied doom and defeat for King Ahab and was put in prison for his harsh words?

3. Hoshea (2 Kings 15:30)
4. Jehu (2 Kings 9)
5. He took a thick cloth, dipped it in water, and smothered the king (2 Kings 8:15)
6. Zimri (1 Kings 16:8-10)
7. Menahem (2 Kings 15:14)
8. Swords and clubs (Mark 14:43)

A Gallery of Prisoners (Answers)

1. Samson (Judges 16:24)
2. Hoshea (2 Kings 17:4)
3. John the Baptist (Matthew 14:3-5)
4. Joseph (Genesis 39:7-19)
5. Joseph's (Genesis 42)
6. Jeremiah (37–38)
7. Zedekiah (2 Kings 25:6-7)
8. Hanani (2 Chronicles 16:10)
9. Jehoiachin (2 Kings 24:12; 25:27-30)
10. Micaiah (1 Kings 22:26-27)

11. What two apostles were put into prison in Jerusalem for preaching the gospel?
12. Who remained in the prison at Philippi even after an earthquake opened the prison doors?

✦Courts, Councils, and Trials

1. When Jesus was brought before the Council, how many false witnesses were brought in to accuse him?
2. Who suggested to Moses that he appoint judges so that he would not have to judge all cases himself?
3. According to the Law, how many witnesses are necessary before a man could be tried and put to death?
4. What cynical king asked Jesus questions and then allowed him to be mocked?
5. According to Jesus, when his followers were dragged into court, they would not need to worry about their defense, for someone else would speak through them. Who?
6. What stinging accusation of the Jews finally convinced Pilate to allow Jesus to be executed?
7. What person's presence at the trial of Peter and John kept the rulers and priests from punishing the two apostles?
8. When Stephen was brought to trial, what was the charge laid against him?
9. In what city were Paul and Silas tried, flogged, and jailed after they cast a demon out of a fortune-teller?
10. When Paul was mobbed in the temple, who rescued him?
11. What Roman official gave Paul a centurion as a guard and told the centurion to allow Paul freedom to see whomever he wished?
12. What three rulers, hearing Paul defend himelf in Caesarea, agreed that he deserved no punishment?

✦Lies and More Lies

1. Who was the first person to lie to God about a murder?
2. Who was probably the most deceptive future father-in-law in the Bible?

11. Peter and John (Acts 4:3)
12. Paul and Silas (Acts 16:16-24)

Courts, Councils, and Trials (Answers)

1. Two (Matthew 26:57-66)
2. His father-in-law, Jethro (Exodus 18)
3. At least two (Deuteronomy 17:6)
4. Herod (Luke 23:1-11)
5. The Spirit (Matthew 10:16-20)
6. They claimed that Pilate was no friend of Caesar (John 19:12)
7. The lame man Peter and John had healed (Acts 4:14)
8. That he had taught that Jesus had aimed to change the customs taught by Moses (Acts 6:11-14)
9. Philippi (Acts 16:16-22)
10. The chief Roman captain (Acts 22:30; 23:1-10)
11. Felix (Acts 24:23)
12. Festus, Agrippa, and Bernice (Acts 25:23–26:32)

Lies and More Lies (Answers)

1. Cain (Genesis 4:8-9)
2. Laban, father-in-law of Jacob (Genesis 29)

3. What doting mother lied to procure a blessing for her favorite son?
4. Who was the only animal that lied?
5. What frustrated Egyptian wife claimed her Hebrew servant tried to seduce her?
6. What lying prophet put Jeremiah in the stocks and was later told that he and his whole household would die in exile?
7. Who was turned into a leper for lying to the prophet Elisha?
8. What owner of a vineyard was executed by Ahab because lying witnesses claimed he had blasphemed against God and the king?
9. What king of Israel claimed to be a devout worshiper of Baal in order to gather together Baal-worshipers and butcher them?
10. Who died after lying to Peter about the value of the possessions they had sold?
11. What godly prophet lied to Ahab about the outcome of a battle?
12. Who is the father of lies?
13. What two men—father and son—claimed at different times that their wives were actually their sisters?

◆Violent People and Things

1. What oversized warrior had bronze armor weighing over 125 pounds?
2. What Roman official in Jerusalem bowed to the wishes of an uncontrollable mob?
3. In what city in Greece did a group of Jews whip up a company of thugs in an anti-Paul riot?
4. Who carried five smooth stones as his weapons?
5. What did Ehud use to kill fat King Eglon of Moab?
6. Who killed six hundred Philistines with an ox goad?
7. What did Jael use to murder Sisera?
8. What rebel was killed by three darts, shot into his heart by Joab?
9. What prophet was commanded to make a model of Jerusalem and set battering rams against it?

3. Rebecca, mother of Jacob and Esau (Genesis 27)
4. The serpent (Genesis 3:1-5)
5. The wife of Potiphar, Joseph's master (Genesis 39)
6. Pashur (Jeremiah 20:1-3, 6)
7. His servant, Gehazi (2 Kings 5:20-27)
8. Naboth (1 Kings 21)
9. Jehu (2 Kings 10)
10. Ananias and Sapphira (Acts 5:1-9)
11. Micaiah (1 Kings 22)
12. The devil (John 8:44)
13. Abraham (Genesis 12:11-13) and Isaac (26:6-7)

Violent People and Things (Answers)

1. Goliath (1 Samuel 17:4-6)
2. Pilate (Matthew 27:23-24)
3. Thessalonica (Acts 17:5)
4. David (1 Samuel 17:40)
5. A two-edged dagger (Judges 3:16-21)
6. Shamgar (Judges 3:31)
7. A tent peg through his temple (Judges 4:17-21)
8. Absalom (2 Samuel 18:14)
9. Ezekiel (19:34)

10. Who threw a javelin at David?
11. In what city was Jesus almost killed by an angry mob?
12. What city had a riot on behalf of the goddess Artemis?
13. What king fortified Jerusalem with catapults for throwing stones?
14. What apostle was almost done in by forty men waiting to ambush him at Jerusalem?
15. Who drew the army of Ai out of the city while another group ambushed the city and destroyed it?
16. What paranoid king ordered the execution of the infants in Bethlehem?
17. Who killed Abner?
18. What evil king of Judah was killed by his servants?
19. What Christian witness was killed by the people of Pergamos?
20. Who killed Ben-Hadad with a wet cloth?
21. What two women brought about the execution of John the Baptist?
22. What king of Israel had the whole dynasty of Ahab murdered?
23. What former member of the Egyptian court killed an Egyptian official?
24. Who did Rechab and Baanah murder to get in good with David?
25. What king of Assyria was murdered at worship by his two sons?
26. What good king of Judah was murdered by his court officials?
27. What saintly deacon was murdered by the Jewish elders for his testimony?
28. Who had one of his army men killed in order to cover up an adulterous affair?
29. Who killed Hamor and Shechem for offending their sister Dinah?
30. What Old Testament figure boasted to his two wives that he had killed a young man?
31. What son of Abraham was supposed to have been against everyone, and everyone against him?
32. Who caused a riot when people thought he had taken a Gentile into the temple?

---

10. Saul (1 Samuel 18:11)
11. Nazareth (Luke 4:29)
12. Ephesus (Acts 19:28-29)
13. Uzziah (2 Chronicles 26:14-15)
14. Paul (Acts 23:21-23)
15. Joshua (8:12-22)
16. Herod (Matthew 2:16)
17. Joab (2 Samuel 3:27)
18. Amon (2 Kings 21:23)
19. Antipas (Revelation 2:13)
20. Hazael (2 Kings 8:7, 15)
21. Herodias and her daughter (Mark 6:25, 27)
22. Jehu (2 Kings 9)
23. Moses (Exodus 2:12)
24. Ishbosheth (2 Samuel 4:6)
25. Sennacherib (2 Kings 19:37)
26. Joash (2 Kings 12:20-21)
27. Stephen (Acts 7:58-59)
28. David (2 Samuel 12:9)
29. Levi and Simeon (Genesis 34:26)
30. Lamech (Genesis 34:26)
31. Ishmael (Genesis 16:12)
32. Paul (Acts 21:30-35)

33. What tribe was ambushed at Gibeah by the other tribes of Israel?
34. In the time of the judges, what did the Levite do when his concubine had been savagely abused by the men of Gibeah?
35. Who killed Amasa after holding his beard and kissing him?
36. What rebel killed Gedaliah, the governor of Judah after the fall of Judah to the Babylonians?
37. Where did Cain kill Abel?
38. What king was critically wounded by Philistine arrows?
39. Who slew a thousand men with the jawbone of an ass?
40. Who carried a staff that was as big as a weaver's beam?
41. Who pelted King David with stones while telling him what a violent king he was?

◆The Impersonators

1. What king disguised himself in order to consult with a sorceress?
2. Who fooled Jacob by posing as her sister?
3. Who pretended to be a madman in order to escape from King Achish?
4. Who disguised himself while going to battle against the forces of Pharaoh Neco of Egypt?
5. Who posed as her husband's sister while in Egypt?
6. What king's wife disguised herself in order to consult the prophet Ahijah?
7. What smooth-skinned man disguised himself so well that he passed himself off as his hairy brother?
8. Who persuaded the clever woman of Tekoa to pretend to be a widow in order to play on David's sympathy?
9. Who posed as Isaac's sister?
10. Who fooled Joshua by pretending to be ambassadors from a distant country?
11. What evil king of Israel disguised himself while going against the armies of Syria?
12. Who sent spies to act as followers of Jesus and to try to trap him?

33. Benjamin (Judges 20:29-33)
34. He cut her into twelve pieces and sent a piece to each tribe of Israel (Judges 19)
35. Joab (2 Samuel 20:9-10)
36. Ishmael (2 Kings 25:25)
37. Out in the fields (Genesis 4:8)
38. Saul (1 Samuel 31:3)
39. Samson (Judges 15:15)
40. Goliath (1 Samuel 17:7)
41. Shimei (2 Samuel 16:5-8)

The Impersonators (Answers)

1. Saul (1 Samuel 28:8)
2. Leah (Genesis 29:21-25)
3. David (1 Samuel 21:12–22:1)
4. King Josiah (2 Chronicles 35:20-24)
5. Sarai, wife of Abram (Genesis 12:10-20)
6. Jeroboam's (1 Kings 14:1-6)
7. Jacob (Genesis 27:1-29)
8. Joab (2 Samuel 14:1-24)
9. His wife Rebekah (Genesis 26:6-11)
10. The Gibeonites (Joshua 9:4-16)
11. Ahab (1 Kings 22:30-40)
12. The chief priests and scribes (Luke 20:19-20)

13. What king was confronted by a prophet posing as a wounded soldier?
14. According to Paul, who masquerades as an angel of light?

◆Naughty Ladies

1. What judge of Israel was a prostitute's son?
2. What two New Testament epistles speak of the righteousness of the prostitute Rahab?
3. What king served as judge when two prostitutes fought over a child?
4. Who had a vision of a prostitute with a city's name engraved on her head?
5. What character in a parable wasted his money on prostitutes?
6. According to Jesus, what prophet had prostitutes and tax collectors as followers?
7. What prophet did the Lord tell about two prostitutes named Oholah and Oholibah?
8. Where did the prostitute Rahab live?
9. Who ordered his daughter-in-law Tamar burned because she had acted like a prostitute?
10. Who married a faithless woman named Gomer?
11. Who went on a killing spree when their sister Dinah was treated like a prostitute?
12. Who tricked the people of Gaza by leaving a prostitute's house earlier than they expected?
13. What epistle warns Christians against patronizing prostitutes?
14. What prophet warned the priest Amaziah that his wife would become a prostitute?
15. According to tradition, what follower of Jesus had been a prostitute, though the Bible does not refer to her as one?

◆Sexual Sinning

1. Who had two daughters who got him drunk and committed incest?

13. Ahab (1 Kings 20:35-43)
14. Satan (2 Corinthians 11:14)

Naughty Ladies (Answers)

1. Jephthah (Judges 11:1)
2. James (2:25) and Hebrews (11:31)
3. Solomon (1 Kings 3:16)
4. John (Revelation 17:5)
5. The prodigal son (Luke 15:30)
6. John the Baptist (Matthew 21:32)
7. Ezekiel (23:1-21)
8. Jericho (Joshua 2:1-6)
9. Judah (Genesis 38:24)
10. Hosea (chapters 1-3)
11. Levi and Simeon (Genesis 34:25-31)
12. Samson (Judges 16:1-3)
13. 1 Corinthians (6:15-16)
14. Amos (7:17)
15. Mary Magdalene

Sexual Sinning (Answers)

1. Lot (Genesis 19:30-38)

2. What church in Greece had a scandalous member who was cohabiting with his stepmother?
3. How many times had the immoral Samaritan woman, who was living with her present lover, been married?
4. What son of David forced his half-sister to have sexual relations with him?
5. What book of the Old Testament mentions a gang rape of a concubine belonging to a Levite?
6. What daughter-in-law of Judah enticed him to have relations with her?
7. What Israelite sinned in the wilderness by taking a Midianite woman as his harlot companion?
8. What daughter of Jacob was raped by Shechem?
9. What city has given its name to homosexual behavior?
10. Who was killed by God because he spilled out his seed on the ground rather than father a child by his brother's wife?
11. What sin were the men of Gibeah hoping to commit when they stormed the house of a man who had taken in a traveler?
12. What priest had two sons who slept with the women who worked at the entrance of the tabernacle?
13. What beautiful woman committed adultery with David?
14. What son of Jacob had sexual relations with one of his father's concubines?
15. Who had sex with his father's concubines on the palace roof while everyone was watching?
16. What prophet's wife was a harlot before marriage and an adulteress afterward?
17. What church was home to a sexually immoral woman named Jezebel?
18. What king did John the Baptist call an adulterer?
19. What sexual sin did Paul see as the result of not worshiping the true God?
20. According to the Law, what is the punishment for committing adultery?

◆Taxes, Extortion, and Bribes

1. What noble prophet's sons were notorious for taking bribes?

2. Corinth (1 Corinthians 5:1)
3. Five (John 4)
4. Amnon (2 Samuel 13:14)
5. Judges (19:22-28)
6. Tamar (Genesis 38:14-18)
7. Zimri (Numbers 25:6-14)
8. Dinah (Genesis 34:1-2)
9. Sodom
10. Onan (Genesis 38:9)
11. Homosexual rape (Judges 19:22)
12. Eli (1 Samuel 2:22)
13. Bathsheba (2 Samuel 11)
14. Reuben (Genesis 35:22)
15. Absalom (2 Samuel 16:22)
16. Gomer, wife of Hosea (1–2)
17. Thyatira (Revelation 2:20)
18. Herod (Mark 6:17)
19. Homosexuality (Romans 1:26-27)
20. Death (Leviticus 20:10)

Taxes, Extortion, and Bribes (Answers)

1. Samuel's (1 Samuel 8:1-3)

2. What tax collector climbed a tree to see Jesus?
3. Who kept Paul in prison, hoping Paul would try to bribe him for release?
4. Who advised that the Egyptians be taxed 20 percent of their produce in order to prepare for famine?
5. Who taxed the Israelites in order to pay off Pul, the king of Assyria?
6. Who did Jesus send fishing in order to get money for taxes?
7. Who warned the people of Israel that having a king would mean having taxation?
8. What figure did Jesus use as a contrast to the humble tax collector?
9. What did the hungry Esau give up to Jacob in exchange for food?
10. What was Judas given to betray Jesus?
11. By what other name was the tax collector Matthew known?
12. What did John the Baptist tell the tax collectors who came to him for baptism?
13. Who offered Delilah silver if she could find out the secret of Samson's strength?
14. Who bribed the guards at Jesus' tomb to say that the disciples had stolen the body?
15. According to the Law, how much tax did all adult Israelites have to pay when the census was taken?
16. What ruler imposed tribute in Jesus' day?
17. Who taxed his subjects in order to pay tribute to Pharaoh Necho of Egypt?
18. What king is remembered as placing a "heavy yoke" of taxation on Israel?
19. What king of Israel paid tribute money to King Shalmaneser of Assyria?
20. Who laid a tax on the whole Persian Empire?
21. To what king of Judah did the Philistines bring tribute?
22. What Persian king exempted the priests and Levites from paying taxes?
23. What empire's taxation led to Jesus being born in Bethlehem?

2. Zacchaeus (Luke 19:1-10)
3. Felix (Acts 24:26)
4. Joseph (Genesis 41:34)
5. King Menahem (2 Kings 15:19-20)
6. Peter (Matthew 17:24-27)
7. Samuel (1 Samuel 8)
8. A Pharisee (Luke 18:9-14)
9. His birthright (Genesis 25:29-34)
10. Thirty pieces of silver (Matthew 26:14-16)
11. Levi (Luke 5:29-32)
12. To collect no more than was legal (Luke 3:12-13)
13. The lords of the Philistines (Judges 16:5)
14. The chief priests (Matthew 28:11-15)
15. A half shekel each (Exodus 30:12-16)
16. Caesar (Matthew 22:17-22)
17. Jehoiakim (2 Kings 23:33-35)
18. Solomon (1 Kings 12:1-14)
19. Hoshea (2 Kings 17:3-4)
20. King Ahasuerus (Esther 10:1)
21. Jehoshaphat (2 Chronicles 17:11)
22. Artaxerxes (Ezra 7:24)
23. Rome (Luke 2:1-7)

24. Whose wife was threatened with having her family's house burned down unless she would find the answer to Samson's riddle?
25. Who made for Jesus a feast that was attended by many tax collectors?

24. Samson's (Judges 14:15)
25. Levi (or Matthew) (Luke 5:29-32)

PART 3
Military Matters

✦They Spied

1. Who sent spies to watch Jesus?
2. How many spies did Moses send into Canaan?
3. Who sent spies to see if Saul had followed him?
4. What tribe sent out five spies to check out its land?
5. What counselor of Absalom was actually a spy for David?
6. Who sent two spies to Jericho?
7. What epistle warns against people sent in to "spy out our liberty"?
8. What rebel sent his spies throughout Israel, telling them to wait till they heard the sound of the trumpet?
9. What Canaanite city did spies find the entrance of?

✦Military Men

1. Who was sleeping between two soldiers when he was miraculously delivered?
2. What captain of the palace guard did Joseph serve under?
3. What loyal Israelite soldier gave Joshua a positive report about the land of Canaan?
4. What Hittite soldier was put on the front lines of battle so David could take his wife?
5. Which Gospel is the only one to mention the Roman soldiers piercing Jesus' body with a spear?
6. What Gittite soldier supported David during the rebellion of Absalom?
7. What leper was commander of the Syrian troops?
8. What soldier led a revolt against King Elah, made himself king, and then committed suicide after a seven-day reign?
9. What Roman soldier treated Paul kindly on his voyage to Rome?
10. What foreign king had Nebuzaradan as commander of his troops?

They Spied (Answers)

1. The chief priests and scribes (Luke 20:20)
2. Twelve—one from each tribe (Numbers 13:1-16)
3. David (1 Samuel 26:3-4)
4. Dan (Judges 18:2-28)
5. Hushai (2 Samuel 15:32-37)
6. Joshua (2:1)
7. Galatians (2:4)
8. Absalom (2 Samuel 15:10)
9. Bethel (Judges 1:23-25)

Military Men (Answers)

1. Peter (Acts 12:6)
2. Potiphar (Genesis 39:1)
3. Caleb (Joshua 14:6-13)
4. Uriah (2 Samuel 11:3)
5. John (19:34)
6. Ittai (2 Samuel 15:19)
7. Naaman (2 Kings 5:1)
8. Zimri (1 Kings 16:9-20)
9. Julius (Acts 27:1-3)
10. Nebuchadnezzar (2 Kings 25:8)

11. Who was commander of the rebel army when Absalom rebelled against David?
12. What Roman soldier was led to Christ by Peter?
13. Which Gospel does not mention the Roman soldier on Calvary who said, "Truly this was a son of God"?
14. Where was Jesus when a Roman officer asked him to heal a beloved servant?
15. Who had a nephew that informed the Roman soldiers of a plot to kill a prisoner?
16. What was the name of the military commander who sent Paul from Jerusalem to Caesarea?
17. What soldier was in charge of David's bodyguard?
18. Where was Paul when a Roman soldier stopped him from being murdered by an angry mob?
19. What cousin of Saul was commander of the king's troops?
20. What Canaanite commander was murdered by Jael?
21. Who was commander of the Israelites under Moses?
22. Who was the commander of Abimelech's army?
23. Who met the commander of the Lord's army?
24. What judge from Gilead was called to be a commander against the Ammonites?
25. What irate soldier falsely accused Jeremiah of deserting to the Babylonians and arrested him?
26. What Philistine soldier was slain by a boy carrying a bag of stones?
27. Who was commander of Solomon's army?
28. Who was commander of David's army?
29. What commander led a successful revolt against the ill-fated King Zimri?
30. What army commander was anointed by a prophet and told that he was to stamp out Ahab's dynasty?
31. What Assyrian field commander tried to intimidate King Hezekiah by speaking propaganda to the people of Jerusalem?
32. Who was commander of the troops during the rebuilding of the walls of Jerusalem?
33. What Babylonian soldier was ordered to execute Daniel and his friends?
34. What soldier, David's oldest brother, picked on David for coming to the battle lines?

11. Amasa (2 Samuel 17:25)
12. Cornelius (Acts 10:1)
13. John
14. Capernaum (Luke 7:1-5)
15. Paul (Acts 23:16-22)
16. Claudius Lysias (Acts 23:26)
17. Benaiah (2 Samuel 8:18)
18. Outside the temple (Acts 21:30-33)
19. Abner (1 Samuel 14:50)
20. Sisera (Judges 4:2)
21. Joshua (Exodus 17:10)
22. Phichol (Genesis 21:22)
23. Joshua (5:14)
24. Jephthah (Judges 11:6)
25. Irijah (Jeremiah 37:13)
26. Goliath (1 Samuel 17:48-54)
27. Benaiah (1 Kings 4:4)
28. Joab (2 Samuel 8:16)
29. Omri (1 Kings 16:16)
30. Jehu (2 Kings 9:1-11)
31. Rabshakeh (2 Kings 18:17-37)
32. Hananiah (Nehemiah 7:2)
33. Arioch (Daniel 2:14)
34. Eliab (1 Samuel 17:28)

35. What brother of Joab was famous for having killed 300 enemy soldiers in battle?
36. Who told Roman soldiers to be content with their pay and to avoid taking money by force?

◆Battles Won Supernaturally

1. What prophet's word caused the Syrian soldiers to be struck blind?
2. What nation's army was destroyed in the Red Sea?
3. What nation was Israel fighting when Moses' arms, held aloft, caused Israel to win?
4. What weather phenomenon did the Lord use to defeat the Amorites when Joshua and his men were fighting them?
5. What army was defeated when an angel of the Lord struck down 185,000 soldiers?
6. When Samuel was offering a sacrifice, what did the Lord do to rattle the Philistines?
7. What occurred when Jonathan and his armor-bearer attacked the Philistines?
8. What made the Syrians flee, thinking the Israelites had joined forces with the Egyptians and Hittites?
9. Who were the Judeans fighting when God helped them slaughter a half million soldiers?
10. What king led the people in singing and praising God, leading God to destroy the armies of the Ammonites, Moabites, and Edomites?

35. Abishai (1 Chronicles 11:20)
36. John the Baptist (Luke 3:14)

Battles Won Supernaturally (Answers)

1. Elisha's (2 Kings 6:18-23)
2. Egypt's (Exodus 14:13-31)
3. Amalek (Exodus 17:11)
4. Large hailstones (Joshua 10:6-13)
5. Assyria's (2 Kings 19:35)
6. Thundered from heaven (1 Samuel 7:10)
7. An earthquake (1 Samuel 14:11-15)
8. The Lord made a sound like a thundering army (2 Kings 7:6-7)
9. Israel (2 Chronicles 13:15-16)
10. Jehoshaphat (2 Chronicles 20:22)

PART 4
Religious Matters

✦A Book of Covenants

1. The covenant after the Flood was made not only between God and man, but also between God and the animals and the earth. What did God give as the sign of this covenant?
2. In God's covenant with Abraham, what ceremonial rite was made mandatory for all Abraham's male descendants?
3. In the covenant between God and Israel at Sinai, the agreement was broken almost immediately afterward by the Israelites. What did they do that was an infringement of the covenant?
4. According to Jeremiah's vision, where would the new covenant between God and man be written?
5. In the New Testament, a new covenant is instituted by Jesus. What does he use to symbolize this new covenant?

✦The Anointed Ones

1. Who anointed a stone and dedicated it to God?
2. What holy man was anointed by an immoral woman?
3. What substance was usually used for anointing in Israel?
4. Who, according to James, should anoint the sick believer with oil?
5. Who did Moses anoint with the blood of a ram?
6. What New Testament word means "anointed"?
7. What revered judge anointed Saul?
8. What priest anointed Solomon king?
9. Who was anointed by the Holy Spirit?
10. What Persian king was considered to be God's anointed one?
11. What Old Testament word means "anointed"?
12. What apostle told the early Christians that all believers were anointed by the Holy Spirit?
13. Who anointed the tabernacle with oil?

A Book of Covenants (Answers)

1. A rainbow (Genesis 9:13)
2. Circumcision (Genesis 17:9-14)
3. They built and worshiped a graven image, the golden calf (Exodus 32)
4. On men's hearts (Jeremiah 31:33)
5. Wine, which symbolizes the blood of sacrifice (Mark 14:24)

The Anointed Ones (Answers)

1. Jacob (Genesis 28:18)
2. Jesus (Luke 7:38)
3. Olive oil
4. The church elders (James 5:14)
5. Aaron and his sons (Leviticus 8:23)
6. Christ
7. Samuel (1 Samuel 9:16)
8. Zadok (1 Kings 1:39)
9. Jesus (Matthew 3:16)
10. Cyrus (Isaiah 45:1)
11. Messiah
12. Paul (2 Corinthians 1:21)
13. Moses (Exodus 40:9)

14. What leader anointed David as king?
15. What person was, prior to his fall, anointed by God?
16. Where did the men of Judah gather to anoint David as their king?

◆Houses of Worship

1. What gruesome object did the Philistines fasten in the temple of Dagon?
2. Which goddess had a notorious temple at Ephesus?
3. Why did John not see a temple in the New Jerusalem?
4. Whose temple did Abimelech burn while the people of Shechem were hiding inside?
5. Who received a vision of the Jerusalem temple while he was in exile in Babylon?
6. According to Paul, who is called to be the temple of God?
7. What Assyrian emperor was assassinated by his sons while he was worshiping in his pagan temple?
8. Who was told in a vision to measure the temple in Jerusalem?
9. Who carried away furnishings from the Jerusalem temple and put them in the temple at Babylon?
10. What was Jesus talking about when he spoke of destroying the temple and raising it up in three days?
11. What holy object was taken by the Philistines into the temple of Dagon, causing Dagon's image to fall down?
12. Who built the first temple in Jerusalem?
13. Who built a temple for Baal in Samaria?
14. After Saul's death, where did the Philistines carry his armor?
15. Who asked Elisha's forgiveness for worshiping in the temple of the god Rimmon?
16. What king issued an order allowing the Jews to rebuild the temple in Jerusalem?
17. Who was taken to the highest point of the Jerusalem temple?
18. What king tricked the followers of Baal by gathering them in Baal's temple and then slaughtering them?

14. Samuel (1 Samuel 16:12)
15. Lucifer (Ezekiel 28:14—some translations have "the king of Tyre," not Lucifer)
16. Hebron (2 Samuel 2:4)

Houses of Worship (Answers)

1. Saul's head (1 Chronicles 10:10)
2. Diana (or Artemis) (Acts 19:27-28)
3. God and the Lamb are the temple (Revelation 21:22)
4. The temple of the god Berith (Judges 9:46-49)
5. Ezekiel (40–42)
6. All believers (1 Corinthians 6:19)
7. Sennacherib (2 Kings 19:37)
8. John (Revelation 11:1-2)
9. Nebuchadnezzar (2 Chronicles 36:7)
10. His body (John 2:19-21)
11. The ark of the covenant (1 Samuel 5:2-4)
12. Solomon (1 Kings 6)
13. Ahab (1 Kings 16:32)
14. The temple of Ashtoreth (1 Samuel 31:10)
15. Naaman the Syrian (2 Kings 5:18)
16. Darius (Ezra 6:1-12)
17. Jesus (Matthew 4:5)
18. Jehu of Israel (2 Kings 10:18-27)

19. Who had an Assyrian-style altar made for the Jerusalem temple?
20. Who did Solomon hire to take charge of building the temple?

✦Horns of the Altar

1. Who built the first altar?
2. What military leader was killed while holding on to the horns of the altar?
3. What book of the Bible mentions a talking altar?
4. Who almost sacrificed his much-loved son on an altar, but was stopped by an angel?
5. What king of Judah tore down Jeroboam's altar at Bethel and pounded the stones into dust?
6. Who built an altar and called it "The Lord is my banner"?
7. What kind of stone was, according to the Law, not supposed to be used in making an altar?
8. What was the altar in the tabernacle made of?
9. Which of the twelve tribes caused civil war when they built a magnificent altar on the banks of the Jordan?
10. What judge built an altar and called it "The Lord is peace"?
11. What king of Israel built a Baal altar to please his pagan wife?
12. What judge's parents saw an angel going up to heaven in the flames on the altar?
13. What judge and prophet built an altar to the Lord at Ramah?
14. What king was told to build an altar in a threshing place?
15. What rebellious son of David sought refuge from Solomon by holding on to the horns of the altar?
16. Who took bones out of tombs and burned them on an altar to defile it?
17. Who had a vision of the Lord standing beside the altar?
18. What king of Israel changed the religious institutions of the country by building an altar at Bethel?
19. What good king's birth was foretold hundreds of years before the fact by a prophet standing before the altar at Bethel?

19. King Ahaz (2 Kings 16:10-17)
20. Hiram of Tyre (1 Kings 7:13-14)

Horns of the Altar (Answers)

1. Noah (Genesis 8:20)
2. Joab (1 Kings 2:28-34)
3. Revelation (16:7)
4. Abraham (Genesis 22:9)
5. Josiah (2 Kings 23:15)
6. Moses (Exodus 17:15)
7. Cut stones (Exodus 20:25)
8. Acacia wood covered with bronze (Exodus 27:1)
9. Reuben, Gad, and part of Manasseh (Joshua 22:1)
10. Gideon (Judges 6:24)
11. Ahab (1 Kings 16:32)
12. Samson's (Judges 13:20)
13. Samuel (1 Samuel 7:17)
14. David (2 Samuel 24:18)
15. Adonijah (1 Kings 1:50)
16. Josiah (2 Kings 23:16)
17. Amos (9:1)
18. Jeroboam (1 Kings 12:32)
19. Josiah's (1 Kings 13:2)

20. What happened to Jeroboam's altar when he ordered his men to seize a prophet in front of it?
21. What leader was told to tear down his father's altar to Baal?
22. What god's priests danced around the altar while they cut themselves with knives and daggers?
23. What prophet triumphed when God consumed the offering on the altar and shamed the prophets of Baal?
24. What priest of Judah placed a money box near the temple's altar?
25. Who built an altar and named it for El, the God of Israel?
26. What evil king of Judah built an altar modeled on the altars of Syria?
27. Who rebuilt the Jerusalem altar when the exiles returned to Israel?
28. Who had his lips touched by a coal from the altar in the temple?
29. What prophet had a vision of an idol near the altar of God?
30. What prophet foresaw the destruction of the altars of Bethel?
31. Who constructed the first altar covered with gold?
32. What prophet spoke of the Jews weeping and wailing in front of the altar because God would not accept their offerings?
33. What patriarch built an altar after he arrived in Canaan for the first time?
34. What priest saw an angel standing beside the incense altar?
35. Where did Paul see an altar inscribed "To an Unknown God"?
36. Who had a vision of the souls of the martyrs underneath the altar?
37. Who told people to make peace with their brothers before they made a sacrifice on the altar?
38. In what book does the Lord tell Moses to tear down all the pagan altars he finds?
39. What priest led a movement in which the people tore down the Baal altars and killed Mattan, the priest of Baal?
40. What wicked king of Judah built altars for the worship of Baal and the stars?

20. It fell apart and the ashes scattered (1 Kings 13:5)
21. Gideon (Judges 6:25)
22. Baal's (1 Kings 18:26-29)
23. Elijah (1 Kings 18)
24. Jehoiada (2 Kings 12:9)
25. Jacob (Genesis 33:20)
26. Ahaz (2 Kings 16:10)
27. The priest Joshua (Ezra 3:2)
28. Isaiah (6:6)
29. Ezekiel (8:5)
30. Amos (3:14)
31. Solomon (1 Kings 6:20)
32. Malachi (2:13)
33. Abraham (Genesis 12:7)
34. Zacharias (Luke 1:11)
35. Athens (Acts 17:23)
36. John (Revelation 6:9)
37. Jesus (Matthew 5:24)
38. Exodus (34:13)
39. Jehoiada (2 Kings 11:18)
40. Manasseh (2 Kings 21:3-5)

✦A Bevy of Priests

1. What priest in the Bible is mentioned as having no mother or father?
2. What Hebrew married the daughter of an Egyptian priest?
3. What was the penalty in Israel for disobeying a priest?
4. What priest was made mute because he did not believe the prophecy given by an angel?
5. What oil was supposed to be used to anoint Israel's priests?
6. What priest made the first piggy bank by placing a chest with a hole in it near the altar of the temple?
7. What righteous king fired all the priests that had been appointed to serve pagan gods?
8. What are the only books of the Bible named after priests?
9. What kind of head covering did the priest wear?
10. What book mentions the priest of Israel more than any other?
11. What priests—two of Aaron's sons—were killed because they offered "strange fire" to the Lord?
12. What priest was the first head of the Levites?
13. What priest was the "king of peace"?
14. What priest of Midian taught Moses how to administer justice among the Hebrews?
15. What priest in the Old Testament was also a king?
16. Who was priest during Joshua's conquest of Canaan?
17. What priest had the boy Jehoash proclaimed king, causing the death of wicked Queen Athaliah?
18. What priest scolded a distressed woman because he thought she had been drinking at the tabernacle?
19. What was engraved on the twelve stones in the high priest's breastplate?
20. What two gluttonous priests were notorious for keeping the sacrificial meat for themselves?
21. What reform priest was killed by the orders of King Joash, a pupil of his father?
22. What priest had a son named Ichabod, a name meaning "the glory has departed"?
23. What five men were called to be the first priests of Israel?
24. What king ordered the execution of Ahimelech and other priests because they had conspired with David?

A Bevy of Priests (Answers)

1. Melchizedek (Hebrews 7:3)
2. Joseph (Genesis 41:45)
3. Death (Deuteronomy 17:12)
4. Zacharias (Luke 1:20)
5. Olive oil (Exodus 30:24)
6. Jehoiada (2 Kings 12:9)
7. Josiah (2 Kings 23:5)
8. Ezra and Ezekiel
9. A turban (Exodus 28:39)
10. Leviticus
11. Nadab and Abihu (Numbers 3:4)
12. Eleazar, Aaron's son (Numbers 3:32)
13. Melchizedek (Hebrews 7:2)
14. Jethro, also called Reuel (Exodus 18:13-27)
15. Melchizedek (Genesis 14:18)
16. Eleazar (Joshua 17:4)
17. Jehoiada (2 Kings 11:9-16)
18. Eli, who scolded Hannah, future mother of Samuel (1 Samuel 1:9)
19. The names of the tribes of Israel (Exodus 28:21)
20. Hophni and Phinehas (1 Samuel 2:17)
21. Zechariah (2 Chronicles 24:21)
22. Phinehas (1 Samuel 4:21)
23. Aaron and his sons Nadab, Abihu, Eleazar, and Ithamar (Exodus 28:1)
24. Saul (1 Samuel 22:18)

25. Who was the only priest to escape when Saul slaughtered the eighty-five priests of Nob?
26. What priest found the Book of the Law in the temple during Josiah's reign?
27. When Adonijah tried to grab the throne of Israel, what priest took his side?
28. What high priest had John and Peter arrested after the two disciples had healed a lame man?
29. What priest was told by Jeremiah that he would be taken to Babylon as a prisoner?
30. What king of Israel sinned by appointing priests that had not been chosen by God?
31. In the time of the judges, what man was brassy enough to set up one of his sons as priest, though he had no authority to do so?
32. What priest led a reform movement in Judah, so that the people tore down their Baal temple and idols?
33. What priest of Baal was killed in Jerusalem when a reform movement threw out all the idols?
34. What were the names of the two stones worn in the high priest's breastplate and used to determine God's will?
35. What king ordered the priest Uriah to make a copy of a pagan altar he had seen in Damascus?
36. What two men were high priests during David's reign?
37. What priest received the boy Samuel as a servant?
38. When Jerusalem fell to the Babylonians, what priest was taken prisoner to Babylon?
39. What king reversed the reform policies of Jehoiada the priest immediately after Jehoiada died?
40. What fat priest of Israel died when he heard the ark had been captured?
41. What priest scolded King Uzziah for daring to offer incense to God?
42. What leader after the exile traced his ancestry back to the high priest Aaron?
43. What kinds of objects were around the hem of the priest's robe?
44. During Nehemiah's ministry, what priest dedicated the newly rebuilt walls of Jerusalem?
45. Who is the first priest mentioned in the Bible?

25. Abiathar (1 Samuel 22:20)
26. Hilkiah (2 Kings 22:8)
27. Abiathar (1 Kings 1:7)
28. Annas (Acts 4:6)
29. Passhur (Jeremiah 20:6)
30. Jeroboam (1 Kings 13:33)
31. Micah (Judges 17:5)
32. Jehoiada (2 Kings 11:17-20)
33. Mattan (2 Kings 11:18)
34. Urim and Thummim (Exodus 28:30)
35. Ahaz (2 Kings 16:11)
36. Abiathar and Zadok (2 Samuel 20:26)
37. Eli (1 Samuel 2:11)
38. Seraiah (2 Kings 25:18)
39. Joash (2 Chronicles 24:17)
40. Eli (1 Samuel 4:18)
41. Azariah (2 Chronicles 26:18)
42. Ezra (7:5)
43. Bells and pomegranates (Exodus 28:33-34)
44. Eliashib (Nehemiah 3:1)
45. Melchizedek (Genesis 14:18)

46. What book of the Bible mentions a "priest forever, after the order of Melchizedek"?
47. What priest served as a witness when Isaiah gave his son the bizarre name Maher-Shalal-Hash-Baz?
48. What evil priest had Jeremiah beaten and placed in chains?
49. What priest was banished by Solomon, fulfilling a prophecy that Eli's descendants would be stripped of the priesthood?
50. What priest received a letter criticizing him for not putting an iron collar on Jeremiah's neck?
51. What priest, a prisoner in Babylon, was also a prophet?
52. What is the only parable of Jesus to have a priest as a character?
53. What prophet locked horns with the wicked priest Amaziah at Bethel?
54. What miracle of Jesus led the priests to conspire to have him executed?
55. What prophet was sent to encourage the rebuilding of the temple under the priest Joshua?
56. Who had a vision of the high priest Joshua standing beside Satan?
57. What was the affliction of the man who was healed by Jesus then sent to the priest?
58. In what priest's home did the enemies of Jesus meet to plot against him?
59. What disciple angrily cut off the ear of the high priest's servant when Jesus was arrested?
60. What New Testament book says that God has made his people to be a kingdom of priests?
61. What crime did the high priest charge Jesus with?
62. What priest was the father of John the Baptist?
63. What priest gave David the ritual bread when David fled from Saul?
64. According to Ezekiel, what was the one kind of woman a priest could not marry?
65. What priest announced that Jesus should die because it was appropriate for one man to die for the people?
66. What priest was told by the prophet Amos that his wife would become a prostitute?
67. According to John's Gospel, what priest was the first to examine the arrested Jesus?

46. Psalms (110:4)
47. Uriah (Isaiah 8:2)
48. Passhur (Jeremiah 20:1)
49. Abiathar (1 Kings 2:27)
50. Zephaniah (Jeremiah 29:26)
51. Ezekiel
52. The good Samaritan (Luke 10:31)
53. Amos (7:10-17)
54. The raising of Lazarus (John 11:47)
55. Haggai
56. Zechariah (3:1)
57. Leprosy (Matthew 8:4)
58. Caiaphas's (Matthew 26:3)
59. Peter (Matthew 26:51)
60. Revelation (1:6)
61. Blasphemy (Matthew 26:65)
62. Zechariah (Luke 1:5)
63. Ahimelech (1 Samuel 21:1-6)
64. A divorcee (Ezekiel 44:22)
65. Caiaphas (John 11:49)
66. Amaziah (Amos 7:17)
67. Annas (John 18:13)

68. What priest anointed Solomon as king?
69. What man asked the high priest for letters of commendation so he could work in the synagogues of Damascus?
70. What two apostles were met by a priest of Zeus, who tried to offer sacrifices to them?
71. What priest had seven sons who were casting out demons in the name of Jesus?
72. What high priest ordered his men to slap Paul, which caused Paul to call him a "whitewashed wall"?
73. According to the Epistle to the Hebrews, who is the present high priest of Israel?
74. According to the Epistle to the Hebrews, what Old Testament priest is Jesus like?
75. What kinsman of Moses was a priest of Midian?
76. What priest was responsible for taking the first census of Israel?
77. What New Testament epistle mentions the priesthood more than any other?
78. What tribe of Israel did all the priests spring from?
79. What New Testament epistle tells Christians that they are all priests?
80. What priest examined Jesus before the Council?

◆Baptisms

1. What magician came to be baptized by Philip?
2. Who referred to the Israelites crossing of the Red Sea as a baptism?
3. What tradeswoman was baptized by Paul and Silas?
4. How many people were baptized on the day of Pentecost?
5. Who baptized Paul?
6. What Roman official did Peter baptize?
7. What kind of baptism did John promise the Christ would administer?
8. What foreign dignitary did Philip baptize?
9. What man of Philippi took Paul and Silas home and was baptized by them?
10. In what city did Crispus, the synagogue ruler, believe Paul's message and submit to baptism?

68. Zadok (1 Kings 1:45)
69. Paul (Acts 9:2)
70. Paul and Barnabas (Acts 14:13)
71. Sceva (Acts 19:14)
72. Ananias (Acts 23:3)
73. Jesus (Hebrews 3:1)
74. Melchizedek (Hebrews 5:6)
75. Jethro, also called Reuel (Exodus 3:1)
76. Eleazar (Numbers 26:1-2)
77. Hebrews
78. Levi (Exodus 4:14)
79. 1 Peter (2:9)
80. Caiaphas (Matthew 26:62)

Baptisms (Answers)

1. Simon the sorceror (Acts 8:12-13)
2. Paul (1 Corinthians 10:1-2)
3. Lydia (Acts 16:14-15)
4. About 3,000 (Acts 2:41)
5. Ananias (Acts 9:18)
6. Cornelius (Acts 10:23-48)
7. A baptism with the Holy Spirit and with fire (John 3:16)
8. The Ethiopian eunuch (Acts 8:38)
9. The jailor (Acts 16:26-33)
10. Corinth (Acts 18:8)

11. Where did Paul baptize twelve men who had received the baptism of John?
12. Which Gospel opens with John the Baptist preaching in the desert?
13. In which Gospel does John try to dissuade Jesus from being baptized?
14. What did John the Baptist tell the tax collectors who came to him for baptism?
15. Which epistle mentions "one Lord, one faith, one baptism"?
16. Which epistles compare baptism to burial?
17. Which epistle says that the flood waters at the time of Noah symbolize baptism?

✦The Company of Apostles

1. Who was the first apostle to be martyred?
2. Who succeeded Judas Iscariot as an apostle?
3. What apostle was a tax collector from Capernaum?
4. According to tradition, which apostle was a missionary to India?
5. What apostle was probably crucified in Rome, head downward?
6. Who was the only one of the twelve apostles not from Galilee?
7. According to tradition, how did Simon the Zealot die?
8. Who was called the beloved disciple?
9. Who, according to tradition, preached in Assyria and Persia and died a martyr in Persia?
10. Who was not one of the original twelve, though he probably labored harder for the gospel than anyone else?
11. Which apostle was traditionally supposed to have been crucified in Egypt?
12. Which apostle, originally a disciple of John the Baptist, was supposed to have been crucified on an X-shaped cross?
13. Which of the apostles were fishermen?
14. Of all the apostles, which is the only one who is supposed to have died a natural death?

11. Ephesus (Acts 19:1-7)
12. Mark
13. Matthew (3:13-15)
14. Not to collect any more than was legal (Luke 3:12-13)
15. Ephesians (4:5)
16. Romans (6:4) and Colossians (2:12)
17. 1 Peter (3:20-21)

The Company of Apostles (Answers)

1. James (Acts 12:1-2)
2. Matthias (Acts 1:23-26)
3. Matthew
4. Thomas
5. Peter
6. Judas Iscariot
7. Crucifixion or being sawn in pieces
8. John
9. Jude
10. Paul
11. James the less
12. Andrew
13. Peter, Andrew, James, John
14. John

15. Who is supposed to have provided the background information for the Gospel of Mark?
16. Who, according to tradition, preached in Phrygia?
17. What hard-working companion of Paul was called an apostle?
18. Who, in Romans 16, did Paul refer to as apostles?
19. Who is supposed to have been a missionary to Armenia?
20. Who preached at Pentecost?
21. Who is supposed to have suffered martyrdom in Ethiopia?
22. Who was banished to the island of Patmos?
23. Who is supposed to have been flayed to death?
24. Who is thought to have been pushed from a summit of the temple, then beaten to death?
25. By what other name was Matthew known?
26. Who is supposed to have been executed by being sawn in pieces?
27. Who doubted the resurrected Jesus?
28. What was Peter's original name?
29. Who were the sons of Zebedee?
30. Who was the apostle to the Gentiles?
31. What was Paul's original name?
32. Who brought Peter to Jesus?
33. Who had Jesus as a guest at a meal with many tax collectors?
34. Who, according to Catholic tradition, was the first pope?
35. Who requested special places for themselves in Jesus' kingdom?
36. Who is identified with Nathanael of Cana, mentioned in John 1:45?
37. Who brought Nathanael to Jesus?
38. Who said to Jesus, "My Lord and my God"?
39. Who asked Jesus to show the disciples the Father?
40. Who were the "sons of thunder"?
41. Who was with Jesus at the Transfiguration?
42. Who was the only apostle we know for sure was married?
43. In which Gospel is John not mentioned by name?
44. Who spoke for all the apostles at Caesarea Philippi?
45. Who, in John's Gospel, is the "son of perdition"?
46. Who criticized the woman who anointed Jesus?
47. Who was absent when the risen Jesus appeared to the apostles?

15. Peter
16. Philip
17. Barnabas (Acts 13:1-3; 14:4)
18. Andronicus and Junias
19. Bartholomew
20. Peter (Acts 2)
21. Matthias
22. John
23. Bartholomew
24. James the less
25. Levi
26. Simon the Zealot
27. Thomas (John 21:25)
28. Simon
29. James and John
30. Paul
31. Saul
32. Andrew
33. Matthew (Luke 5:29)
34. Peter
35. James and John (Mark 10:39)
36. Bartholomew
37. Philip (John 1:43-46)
38. Thomas (John 20:28)
39. Philip (John 14:8)
40. James and John (Mark 3:17)
41. Peter, James, and John (Mark 9:2)
42. Peter (Mark 1:30)
43. John
44. Peter (Mark 8:27-33)
45. Judas Iscariot (John 17:12)
46. Judas Iscariot (John 12:3-5)
47. Thomas (John 20:24)

48. Who brought Greeks to Jesus?
49. Who had Silas as a traveling companion on his second journey?
50. Which apostles were present at the raising of Jairus's daughter?
51. Who was a Roman citizen?
52. Who healed the crippled man at the Beautiful Gate?
53. Who healed a paralytic named Aeneas in Lydda?
54. Who was baptized by a man named Ananias?
55. What was Barnabas's original name?
56. Who did the Sanhedrin put in jail for disturbing the peace?
57. Who raised a young man named Eutychus from the dead?
58. Whom did Paul oppose when he met him in Antioch?
59. Who asked Jesus why he intended to show himself to the disciples but not to the world?
60. To whom did Jesus say, "Feed my lambs"?
61. Who preached to the intellectuals of Athens?
62. Who had a vision of a sheet filled with unclean animals?
63. Who did Jesus say he would make into fishers of men?
64. Who told Jesus he had seen a man driving out demons in Jesus' name?
65. Who did Jesus take with him to Gethsemane?
66. Who expressed dismay over how to feed the five thousand?
67. Who had a beef against a Greek silversmith named Demetrius?
68. Who brought to Jesus the boy with loaves and fishes?
69. Who was reluctant to have Jesus wash his feet?
70. Who was bitten by a viper on the island of Malta?
71. What brother of Jesus does Paul call an apostle?
72. What young friend of Paul, a co-author of 1 Thessalonians, was an apostle?
73. What apostle, a traveling companion of Paul, was sometimes called Silvanus?
74. According to tradition, what apostle lived to a ripe old age after miraculously living through being boiled in oil?

48. Philip and Andrew (John 12:20-28)
49. Paul (Acts 15-18)
50. Peter, John, and James (Mark 5:37)
51. Paul (Acts 23:27)
52. Peter and John (Acts 3:1-10)
53. Peter (Acts 9:32-35)
54. Paul (Acts 9:10-18)
55. Joseph (Acts 4:36)
56. Peter and John (Acts 4:1-4)
57. Paul (Acts 20:7-12)
58. Peter (Galatians 2:11-21)
59. Jude (John 14:22)
60. Peter (John 21:15-19)
61. Paul (Acts 17:16-34)
62. Peter (Acts 10:9-16)
63. Peter and Andrew (Mark 1:17)
64. John (Mark 9:38)
65. Peter, James, and John (Mark 14:33)
66. Philip (John 6:7)
67. Paul (Acts 19:23-41)
68. Andrew (John 6:8-9)
69. Peter (John 13:6-9)
70. Paul (Acts 28:1-6)
71. James (Galatians 1:19)
72. Timothy (1 Thessalonians 1:1; 2:7)
73. Silas (1 Thessalonians 1:1; 2:7)
74. John

✦Speaking of Churches

1. What church was neither hot nor cold?
2. What church began in the home of Lydia, the seller of purple?
3. At what church was Paul accused of turning the world upside down?
4. What church had two bickering women named Euodia and Syntyche?
5. In what church did Paul raise up Eutychus, who had fallen to his death out of a window?
6. What church was the scene of a burning of wicked books?
7. At what church were believers first called Christians?
8. Who founded the church at Colossae?
9. What church had a false prophetess named Jezebel as a member?
10. Who visited the church at Babylon?
11. What church suffered because of the "synagogue of Satan"?
12. What member of the Colossian church received a letter from Paul?
13. What church received epistles from two different apostles?
14. At what church did Paul preach his first recorded sermon?
15. What church had a former demon-possessed girl as a member?
16. What was the first church to appoint deacons?
17. Who helped Paul establish the church in Corinth?
18. What church tolerated the heresy of the Nicolaitans?
19. What church had fallen prey to the legalistic Judaizers?
20. What is the most commended church in Revelation?
21. What church received from Paul an epistle that has never been found?
22. What church took up a large love offering for the needy believers in Jerusalem?
23. On what Greek island did Titus supervise the churches?
24. What church saw the martyrdom of faithful Antipas?
25. What was the first church to send forth missionaries?
26. What church was Silas from?
27. What love-filled church sent members to accompany Paul all the way to Athens?
28. What church was noted for hating the Nicolaitan heresy?

Speaking of Churches (Answers)

1. Laodicea (Revelation 3:15-16)
2. Philippi (Acts 16:15, 40)
3. Thessalonica (Acts 17:6)
4. Philippi (Philippians 4:1-3)
5. Troas (Acts 20:7-12)
6. Ephesus (Acts 19:19)
7. Antioch (Acts 11:26)
8. Epaphras (Colossians 1:7)
9. Thyatira (Revelation 2:18-29)
10. Peter (1 Peter 5:13)
11. Smyrna (Revelation 2:8-11)
12. Philemon
13. Ephesus (the Letter to the Ephesians from Paul and Revelation 2:1-7 from John)
14. Antioch of Pisidia (Acts 13:16)
15. Philippi (Acts 16:18)
16. Jerusalem (Acts 6:1-7)
17. Priscilla and Aquila (Acts 18:2)
18. Pergamos (Revelation 2:12-17)
19. Galatia (Galatians 1:6-9)
20. Philadelphia (Revelation 3:7-13)
21. Laodicea (Colossians 4:16)
22. Antioch (Acts 11:30)
23. Crete (Titus 1:5)
24. Pergamum (Revelation 2:13)
25. Jerusalem (Acts 8:5, 14)
26. Antioch (Acts 15:34)
27. Berea (Acts 17:10-15)
28. Ephesus (Revelation 2:6)

29. To what church did Jesus say, "Behold, I stand at the door and knock"?
30. At what church did believers hold their property in common?
31. Who was sent by the Jerusalem church to oversee the church at Antioch?
32. To what church did Paul send Epaphroditus as a minister?
33. What church began at Pentecost?
34. What church had Crispus, a synagogue leader, as a member?
35. Where did Paul have a vision asking him to found churches in Europe?
36. At what church were Paul and Barnabas set apart by the Holy Spirit to do missionary work?
37. Who reported his vision of unclean animals to the church at Jerusalem?
38. At what church did Paul have a "loyal yokefellow"?
39. At what church did some people follow the teachings of Balaam?
40. What church was told by John to buy white clothing to hide its nakedness?
41. At what church did the Egyptian-born Apollos first serve?
42. What church did Timothy grow up in?
43. What apostle was supposed to be the rock on which the church was built?
44. Who founded the church at Antioch of Pisidia?
45. From what Asian church was Paul driven out by unbelieving Jews?
46. What church was overseen by James?
47. In what church were Christians guilty of taking other Christians to court?
48. Who established the church at Ephesus?

◆Curses, Curses
1. What was the only animal to be cursed by God?
2. Who was sent by the king of Moab to put a curse on Israel?
3. What grandson of Noah was cursed for his father's sins?
4. Who cursed a fig tree for not bearing fruit?

29. Laodicea (Revelation 3:20)
30. Jerusalem (Acts 2:44-45)
31. Barnabas (Acts 11:22)
32. Philippi (Philippians 2:25)
33. Jerusalem (Acts 2:47)
34. Corinth (Acts 18:8)
35. Troas (Acts 16:9)
36. Antioch (Acts 13:2)
37. Peter (Acts 11:1-18)
38. Philippi (Philippians 4:3)
39. Pergamum (Revelation 2:14)
40. Laodicea (Revelation 3:18)
41. Ephesus (Acts 18:24-28)
42. Lystra (Acts 16:1)
43. Peter (Matthew 16:18)
44. Paul (Acts 13:14)
45. Iconium (Acts 14:5)
46. Jerusalem (Acts 15:13)
47. Corinth (1 Corinthians 6:1-4)
48. Paul (Acts 18:19; 19:1-10)

Curses, Curses (Answers)

1. The serpent (Genesis 3:14-15)
2. Balaam (Numbers 22:1-6)
3. Canaan (Genesis 4:11)
4. Jesus (Mark 11:21)

5. Who put a curse on Cain and made him a wanderer?
6. What son of Josiah was cursed by God?
7. In what story did Jesus place a curse on the unrighteous?
8. According to Paul, what was put under a curse because of man's sin?
9. What nation did God say would have its towns and fields cursed because of disobedience?
10. What happened to the ground as a result of God's curse?
11. Who received a promise from God that all persons who cursed him would be cursed themselves?
12. According to Galatians, what people remain under a curse?
13. Who said that people who taught a false gospel would be cursed?
14. According to Paul, who was made a curse for our sins?
15. According to the Law, what sort of handicapped people should we not curse?
16. Who was told by his wife to curse God and die?
17. What prophet ended his book with God's threat to come and strike the land with a curse?
18. What epistle says that blessing and cursing should not come out of the same mouth?
19. Who had enemies that bound themselves under a curse because they were so determined to kill him?
20. Who told God that Job would curse him to his face?
21. What book says that kings should not be cursed, for little birds will tell on the cursing person?

◆Healthy Confessions

1. What wicked king of Judah confessed his sins when he was taken into captivity in Assyria?
2. Who confessed to God that he had done wrong in taking a census of Israel?
3. Who confessed his denial of Jesus?
4. What sneaky Israelite confessed that he had stolen goods from fallen Jericho?
5. Who confessed his own sin and Israel's after seeing a vision of God on his throne?
6. What king confessed his adulterous affair after being confronted by the prophet Nathan?

5. God (Genesis 4:11)
6. Jehoiakim (Jeremiah 22:18; 36:30)
7. The story of the sheep and the goats (Matthew 25:31-41)
8. Nature (Romans 8:19-22)
9. Israel (Deuteronomy 28:15-16)
10. It brought forth thorns and weeds (Genesis 3:17-18)
11. Abraham (Genesis 12:3)
12. Those who attempt to remain under the Law (Galatians 3:10)
13. Paul (Galatians 1:8)
14. Christ (Galatians 3:13)
15. The blind and the deaf (Leviticus 19:14)
16. Job (2:9)
17. Malachi (4:6)
18. James (3:10)
19. Paul (Acts 23:12)
20. Satan (Job 1:11; 2:5)
21. Ecclesiastes (10:20)

Healthy Confessions (Answers)

1. Manasseh (2 Chronicles 33:11-13)
2. David (2 Samuel 24:10)
3. Peter (Matthew 26:75)
4. Achan (Joshua 7:20)
5. Isaiah (6:5)
6. David (2 Samuel 12:13)

7. What scribe bowed in front of the temple and confessed the sins of Israel while the people around him wept bitterly?

8. What young man confessed his riotous living to his forgiving father?

9. Who confessed the building of the golden calf to God?

10. Who confessed his sexual immorality with his daughter-in-law, Tamar?

11. Who made a false confession to Aaron and Moses?

12. Who confessed his remorse over betraying his master?

13. Who confessed Israel's sins after he heard the walls of Jerusalem were in ruins?

14. Who was visited by the angel Gabriel while he was confessing his sins?

15. Who confessed that he had been self-righteous?

16. Who confessed his sin to an angel that only his donkey had seen?

17. Who was pardoned by David after confessing his sin and begging for mercy?

18. Who confessed to Samuel that he had disobeyed God by not destroying all the spoils of war?

7. Ezra (10:1)
8. The prodigal son (Luke 15:18)
9. Moses (Exodus 32:31)
10. Judah (Genesis 38:26)
11. Pharaoh (Exodus 10:16)
12. Judas (Matthew 27:4)
13. Nehemiah (1:6)
14. Daniel (9:20)
15. Job (42:6)
16. Balaam (Numbers 22:34)
17. Shimei (2 Samuel 19:20)
18. Saul (1 Samuel 15:24)

PART 5
Encounters with the Divine

◆Supernatural Fire

1. What two sinful cities were destroyed by fire and brimstone from heaven?
2. When the Israelites were wandering in the wilderness, what did they follow by night?
3. According to Daniel, this astonishing person had a throne like a fire of flame. Who was he?
4. What did the seraph touch the trembling Isaiah's tongue with?
5. According to Revelation, where is the place reserved for those whose names are not in the book of life?
6. What did the cherubim use to guard the entrance to Eden?
7. How did God first appear to Moses?
8. What strange phenomenon accompanied the plague of hail in Egypt?
9. What mountain did the Lord descend upon in fire?
10. What two sons of Aaron were devoured by fire for making an improper offering to the Lord?
11. How did God deal with the Israelites who were complaining about their misfortunes in the wilderness?
12. What judge of Israel was visited by an angel whose staff caused meat and bread to be consumed by fire?
13. How did Elijah respond to an army captain's summons to present himself to King Ahaziah?
14. What two men saw a chariot of fire drawn by horses of fire?
15. Where, in answer to Elijah's prayer, did fire from the Lord consume both the sacrifice and the altar?

Supernatural Fire (Answers)

1. Sodom and Gomorrah (Genesis 19:24)
2. A pillar of fire (Exodus 13:21)
3. The Ancient of Days (Daniel 7:9)
4. A live coal from the altar (Isaiah 6:6)
5. A lake of fire and brimstone (Revelation 20)
6. A flaming sword (Genesis 3:24)
7. In a burning bush that was not consumed (Exodus 3:2)
8. Fire that ran along the ground (Exodus 9:23)
9. Sinai (Exodus 19:18)
10. Nadab and Abihu (Leviticus 10:1-2)
11. His fire devoured them (Numbers 11:1-3)
12. Gideon (Judges 6:21)
13. He called down fire from heaven on the captain and his men (2 Kings 1:9-12)
14. Elijah and Elisha (2 Kings 2:11)
15. Mount Carmel (1 Kings 18:16-40)

✦Who Asked God the Question?

1. "Why dost thou show me iniquity, and cause me to behold grievance?" (Hint: a prophet.)
2. "Why is my pain perpetual, and my wound incurable?" (Hint: a prophet.)
3. "Shall I go and smite these Philistines?" (Hint: a king.)
4. "Am I my brother's keeper?" (Hint: you don't need one.)
5. "Lord, wilt thou slay also a righteous nation?" (Hint: a king.)
6. "Shall not the judge of all the earth do right?" (Hint: a patriarch.)
7. "Who am I, that I should go unto Pharaoh?"
8. "Ah, Lord God, wilt thou make a full end of the remnant of Israel?" (Hint: a prophet.)
9. "Behold, I am vile; what shall I answer thee?" (Hint: a righteous man.)
10. "Lord God, whereby shall I know that I inherit it?" (Hint: a patriarch.)
11. "Why is it that thou hast sent me?" (Hint: a leader and miracle worker.)
12. "Hast thou also brought evil upon the widow with whom I sojourn, by slaying her son?" (Hint: a prophet.)
13. "What wilt thou give me, seeing I go childless?" (Hint: a patriarch.)
14. "Shall one man sin and wilt thou be wroth with all the congregation?" (Hint: a leader and his brother.)
15. "Who is able to judge this thy so great a people?" (Hint: a king.)
16. "When I come unto the children of Israel and shall say unto them, The God of your fathers hath sent me unto you; and they shall say to me, What is his name? what shall I say to them?" (Hint: a leader.)
17. "Shall I pursue after this troop? Shall I overtake them?" (Hint: a king.)
18. "Why is this come to pass, that there should today be one tribe lacking in Israel?" (Hint: a nation.)
19. "What shall I do unto this people? They are almost ready to stone me." (Hint: a leader.)

Who Asked God the Question? (Answers)

1. Habakkuk (1:1-3)
2. Jeremiah (15:18)
3. David (1 Samuel 23:1-2)
4. Cain (Genesis 4:9)
5. Abimelech (Genesis 20:4)
6. Abraham (Genesis 18:25)
7. Moses (Exodus 3:10-11)
8. Ezekiel (11:13)
9. Job (40:3-4)
10. Abram (Genesis 15:7-8)
11. Moses (Exodus 5:22)
12. Elijah (1 Kings 17:20)
13. Abraham (Genesis 15:2)
14. Moses and Aaron (Numbers 16:22)
15. Solomon (1 Kings 3:5-9)
16. Moses (Exodus 3:13)
17. David (1 Samuel 30:3-8)
18. The Israelites (Judges 21:2-3)
19. Moses (Exodus 17:3-4)

20. "Wherefore hast thou at all brought this people over Jordan, to deliver us into the hand of the Amorites, to destroy us?" (Hint: a leader.)

✦Whom Did God Ask?

1. "How long will this people provoke me?" (Hint: a leader.)
2. "Whom shall I send, and who will go for us?" (Hint: a prophet.)
3. "Have I any pleasure at all that the wicked should die?" (Hint: a prophet.)
4. "Doest thou well to be angry?" (Hint: a reluctant prophet.)
5. "Who told thee that thou wast naked?"
6. "Why is thy countenance fallen? If thou doest well, shalt thou not be accepted?" (Hint: a farmer.)
7. "How long wilt thou mourn for Saul, seeing I have rejected him from reigning over Israel?" (Hint: a judge and prophet.)
8. "I am the Lord, the God of all flesh; is there anything too hard for me?" (Hint: a prophet.)
9. "Son of man, can these bones live?" (Hint: a prophet.)
10. "Who is this that darkeneth counsel by words without knowledge?" (Hint: a righteous man.)
11. "Who hath made man's mouth?" (Hint: a leader.)
12. "What is this that thou hast done?" (Hint: a woman.)
13. "Shall the clay say to him that fashioneth it, What makest thou?" (Hint: a foreign king.)
14. "Shall seven years of famine come unto thee in thy land? Or wilt thou flee three months before thine enemies?" (Hint: a king.)
15. "Shall I not spare Nineveh, that great city?" (Hint: a prophet.)
16. "Hast thou an arm like God? Or canst thou thunder with a voice like him?" (Hint: a righteous man.)
17. "Why is this people of Jerusalem slidden back by a perpetual backsliding?" (Hint: a prophet.)
18. "Have I not commanded thee? Be strong and of good courage; be not afraid." (Hint: a conqueror.)

20. Joshua (7:7)

Whom Did God Ask? (Answers)

1. Moses (Numbers 14:11)
2. Isaiah (6:8)
3. Ezekiel (18:23)
4. Jonah (4:9)
5. Adam (Genesis 3:11)
6. Cain (Genesis 4:6-7)
7. Samuel (1 Samuel 16:1)
8. Jeremiah (32:26-27)
9. Ezekiel (37:3)
10. Job (38:2)
11. Moses (Exodus 4:11)
12. Eve (Genesis 3:13)
13. Cyrus (Isaiah 45:1-9)
14. David (2 Samuel 24:13)
15. Jonah (4:11)
16. Job (40:9)
17. Jeremiah (8:4-12)
18. Joshua (1:1, 9)

19. "Is anything too hard for the Lord?" (Hint: a patriarch.)
20. "Hast thou killed, and also taken possession?" (Hint: a king.)

◆Encounters with Angels

1. The angel of the Lord appeared to the banished Hagar and told her what to name her child. What was the child's name?
2. How many angels rescued Lot and his family from the doomed city of Sodom?
3. What apostle was released from prison by an angel who opened the prison's iron gate?
4. The prophet Balaam could not see the Lord's angel, but his talking donkey could. What was it about the angel that made the donkey turn away?
5. Joshua encountered an angel who was captain of the host of the Lord. What was the angel's purpose in appearing to Joshua?
6. The angel of the Lord instructed Philip to go to Gaza. What person did Philip encounter afterward?
7. What was the name of the angel who appeared to Mary and to Zacharias?
8. This man's mother was visited by the angel of the Lord, who told her she would have a son who would be dedicated as a Nazarite. Who was he?
9. Elijah was nurtured by an angel after his flight from Israel's evil queen. Who was the queen?
10. Jacob is the only person known to have wrestled with an angel. What kindly act did the angel perform after the wrestling match?
11. What Roman official was visited by an angel who told him God had heard his prayers?
12. Who was commissioned by an angel to save Israel from the Midianites?
13. What kind of angelic beings guarded the entrance to Eden?
14. Who had his lips touched by a live coal held by a seraph?
15. What foreign army had 185,000 men killed by the angel of the Lord?

19. Abraham (Genesis 18:13)
20. Ahab (1 Kings 21:19)

Encounters with Angels (Answers)

1. Ishmael (Genesis 16:1-12)
2. Two (Genesis 19:1-22)
3. Peter (Acts 12:1-19)
4. He was holding a drawn sword (Numbers 22:22-35)
5. To give him instructions on conquering Jericho (Joshua 5:13-15)
6. The Ethiopian eunuch (Acts 8:26-39)
7. Gabriel (Luke 1:5-38)
8. Samson (Judges 13:1-20)
9. Jezebel (1 Kings 19:1-8)
10. He blessed Jacob (Genesis 32:24-20)
11. Cornelius (Acts 10:1-8)
12. Gideon (Judges 6:11-23)
13. Cherubim (Genesis 3:24)
14. Isaiah (6:5-7)
15. The Assyrians (2 Kings 19:35)

16. What person did an angel prevent from the act of child sacrifice?
17. What two guides did the angel of the Lord provide for the Israelites in the wilderness?
18. What ungodly ruler in New Testament times was struck down by an angel?
19. Who was carried by angels to Abraham's bosom?
20. What angel helped Daniel understand the future?
21. Who was told by an angel that the angel's name was a secret?
22. According to Revelation, what angel fights against Satan?
23. What kind of angels did Isaiah see in the temple praising God?
24. Who had a dream about an angel and goats?
25. What person saw the angel of the Lord in the form of a flame?
26. What prophet was fed two meals by an angel?
27. According to Jude, who fought with Satan over the body of Moses?
28. Where was Jesus when an angel came and strengthened him?
29. Where was Paul when an angel assured him that he would stand trial before Caesar?
30. How many angels will be at the gates of the New Jerusalem?
31. According to Jesus, what causes the angels to rejoice?
32. Who had a vision of four angels holding the four winds of the earth?
33. Which Gospel says that an angel rolled away the stone from Jesus' tomb?
34. At the end time, what will an angel bind Satan with?
35. How many angels pour out the bowls of wrath on the earth?
36. What prophet saw the Lord's angel riding on a red horse?
37. What is the name of the evil angel of the Abyss in Revelation?

16. Abraham (Genesis 22:11-18)
17. A pillar of fire and a pillar of cloud (Exodus 14:19-20)
18. Herod (Acts 12:23)
19. Lazarus (Luke 16:22)
20. Gabriel (Daniel 8:15-26; 9:21-27)
21. Samson's parents (Judges 13:17-18)
22. Michael (Revelation 12:7)
23. Seraphim (Isaiah 6:1-6)
24. Jacob (Genesis 31:11-12)
25. Moses (Exodus 3:1-22)
26. Elijah (1 Kings 19:5-8)
27. The archangel Michael (Jude 9)
28. Gethsemane (Luke 22:43)
29. On board ship during a storm (Acts 27:23-24)
30. Twelve (Revelation 21:12)
31. A repentant sinner (Luke 15:10)
32. John (Revelation 7:1)
33. Matthew (28:2)
34. A chain (Revelation 20:2)
35. Seven (Revelation 16:1-21)
36. Zechariah (1:8)
37. Abaddon or Apollyon (Revelation 9:11)

✦Visions of God

1. Who had a vision of the Ancient of Days seated upon a throne?
2. Who looked up steadfastly into heaven and saw Jesus on the right hand of God?
3. Who knew a man who had been caught up into the "third heaven"?
4. What seer described himself as "in the Spirit" when he received his visions?
5. What did Isaiah see filling the temple when he beheld God sitting on his throne?
6. Who saw the back of God, since he could not bear to see him face to face?
7. Who, besides Isaiah, saw the Lord sitting upon his throne?
8. What seer of weird visions beheld a throne like a sapphire?
9. Who saw a heavenly ladder with the Lord standing above it?
10. Who, along with Moses, saw God during the wilderness wanderings?

✦Ordained Before Birth by God

1. What strongman was ordained before birth to deliver Israel from the Philistines?
2. What child, who later ministered with the priest Eli, was ordained before birth to serve God?
3. What apostle was foreordained to minister to the Gentiles?
4. What kinsman of Christ was ordained to be his forerunner?
5. What Greek ruler's reign is usually considered to be predicted in the Book of Daniel?
6. What prophet was ordained before birth to be God's messenger?
7. What king of Judah had his birth and reign foretold to King Jeroboam?
8. What psalm, usually assumed to have been written by David, talks about God knowing him before his birth?
9. Who foretold Jesus' birth and ministry to Mary?

Visions of God (Answers)

1. Daniel (7:9)
2. Stephen (Acts 7:55)
3. Paul (2 Corinthians 12:2)
4. John, author of Revelation (Revelation 4:2)
5. The train of God's robe (Isaiah 6:1)
6. Moses (Exodus 33:23)
7. The prophet Micaiah (2 Chronicles 18:18)
8. Ezekiel (1:26)
9. Jacob (Genesis 28:12-13)
10. Aaron, Nadab, Abihu, and seventy of the Israelite elders (Exodus 24:9-10)

Ordained Before Birth by God (Answers)

1. Samson (Judges 13:2-5)
2. Samuel (1 Samuel 1:11-20)
3. Paul (Galatians 1:15)
4. John the Baptist (Luke 1:13-17)
5. Alexander the Great (Daniel 11:2-4)
6. Jeremiah (1:5)
7. Josiah (1 Kings 13:2)
8. Psalm 139
9. The angel Gabriel (Luke 1:26-38)

◆Supernatural Journeys

1. What prophet was able to travel for forty days on the strength from just a cake and some water?
2. Elijah and Elisha walked across the Jordan river on dry ground after Elijah struck the waters with what?
3. Elijah outran a king's chariot, running all the way from Mount Carmel to Jezreel, almost ten miles. Who was the king?
4. How was Elijah taken up into heaven?
5. Israel crossed the Red Sea on dry ground and also crossed a river on dry ground. Which river?
6. What carried Philip from Gaza to Azotus?
7. What two people walked on water in the midst of a storm?
8. Who took Jesus to a pinnacle of the temple in Jerusalem?
9. Ezekiel was lifted up by a spirit, which held him between earth and heaven. What was the spirit holding on to?
10. Who was taken up into heaven in the sight of his followers?
11. What man knew someone who had been caught up to the third heaven?

◆Moses and Miracles

1. What did Moses mount on a pole as a way for healing the ailing Israelites?
2. What bird served as miracle food for the Israelites?
3. What did Moses do to bring forth water from the rock at Kadesh?
4. What animal came forth out of the Nile in droves?
5. What miraculous thing happened to Moses' hand?
6. What was the unique feature of the hailstorm that God sent upon the Egyptians?
7. What did Moses' staff turn into?
8. What everyday substance was changed into a plague of lice?
9. What caused the boils on the Egyptians?
10. What did the Nile waters turn into?
11. What plague was sent upon the Egyptians' cattle?

Supernatural Journeys (Answers)

1. Elijah (1 Kings 19:5-9)
2. His mantle (2 Kings 2:8)
3. Ahab (1 Kings 18:41-46)
4. In a whirlwind (2 Kings 2:11)
5. The Jordan (Joshua 3)
6. The Spirit of the Lord (Acts 8:39-40)
7. Jesus and Peter (Matthew 14:22-32)
8. The devil (Matthew 4:5-7)
9. A lock of Ezekiel's hair (Ezekiel 8:1-3)
10. Jesus (Acts 1:9)
11. Paul (2 Corinthians 12:1-7)

Moses and Miracles (Answers)

1. A brass serpent (Numbers 21:5-9)
2. Quail (Exodus 16:11-13)
3. He struck it twice (Numbers 20:1-11)
4. Frogs (Exodus 8:5-7)
5. It became leprous, then became normal again (Exodus 4:7)
6. It was accompanied by fire that ran along the ground (Exodus 9:22-26)
7. A serpent (Exodus 4:2-4)
8. Dust (Exodus 8:16-17)
9. Ashes that were turned into dust (Exodus 9:8-12)
10. Blood (Exodus 7:19-25)
11. Murrain (Exodus 9:1-7)

12. Who appeared on the Mount of Transfiguration with Moses and Jesus?
13. What did Moses cast into the bitter water at Marah to make it sweet?
14. What happened to Aaron's staff when placed in the Tent of Meeting?
15. What was done to stop the plague that killed 14,700 of the Israelites?
16. What voracious insect was a plague on the Egyptian flora?
17. What happened to the rebellious Korah and his men?
18. What happened to 250 men who offered incense?
19. For how long did the thick darkness hang over the Egyptians?
20. What substance, called bread from heaven, fed the Israelites in the wilderness?
21. What hid the departing Israelites?
22. Who was made leprous and then healed after her rebellious acts?
23. What did the Israelites put on their doorposts so the angel of death would pass over?
24. What did the Lord use to part the Red Sea?
25. What means did the Lord use to halt the Egyptian chariots?
26. What happened to the manna the Israelites tried to hoard?
27. Who was slain by the angel of death?
28. What was Moses supposed to do to the rock at Horeb to bring water from it?
29. What consumed the offering on the altar?
30. What did Moses do at Taberah when the fire of the Lord destroyed many Israelites?
31. What brought the locust plague to a halt?
32. When the plague of hail came, where was the one place it did not fall?
33. Whose rod was turned into a serpent that swallowed the Egyptian sorcerers' serpents?
34. What bit the Israelites, causing Moses to fix a brass figure on a pole?

12. Elijah (Luke 9:28-36)
13. A tree (Exodus 15:23-25)
14. It sprouted and blossomed and bore almonds (Numbers 17)
15. An offering of incense was made (Numbers 16:46-50)
16. Locusts (Exodus 10:12-15)
17. They were swallowed up by the earth (Numbers 16:28-33)
18. They were consumed by fire from the Lord (Numbers 16:16-18)
19. Three days (Exodus 10:21-23)
20. Manna (Exodus 16:14-15)
21. A cloud (Exodus 14:19-20)
22. Miriam (Numbers 12)
23. Lamb's blood (Exodus 12:21-30)
24. A strong east wind (Exodus 14:21)
25. He made their wheels come off (Exodus 14:23-25)
26. It was filled with maggots (Exodus 16:20)
27. The firstborn among the Egyptians (Exodus 12:29-30)
28. Strike it (Exodus 17:1-6)
29. Fire from the Lord (Leviticus 9:22-24)
30. He prayed and the fire died down (Numbers 11:1-2)
31. The Lord blew them away with a strong west wind (Exodus 10:16-20)
32. In Goshen, where the Israelites dwelled (Exodus 9:26)
33. Aaron's (Exodus 7:10-12)
34. Fiery serpents (Numbers 21:5-9)

✦Wonders of Elijah and Elisha

1. What happened to the children who made fun of Elisha's bald head?
2. For whom did Elijah supply meal and oil through miraculous means?
3. What did the bones of Elisha do to a dead man?
4. What did Elisha do to make an ax head float to the surface of the water?
5. Who was healed of leprosy when he followed Elisha's instructions?
6. Who appeared with Jesus and Elijah on the Mount of Transfiguration?
7. What birds fed Elijah in the wilderness?
8. What river did Elijah part by striking it with his mantle?
9. What did Elisha do to make the poisoned pottage edible?
10. What happened to the Syrian soldiers when Elisha prayed?
11. How long was rain withheld after Elijah's prayer?
12. Who conceived a son after Elisha predicted she would?
13. What did Elijah call on to destroy the soldiers sent to arrest him?
14. Who was Elijah up against when fire from the Lord burned up a sacrifice and the water around the altar?
15. How many men did Elisha feed with twenty loaves of barley and some ears of corn?
16. How did Elisha raise the Shunammite woman's son from the dead?
17. What did Elisha's servant see after Elisha prayed that his eyes would be opened?
18. For whom did Elisha supply water miraculously?
19. What took Elijah into heaven?
20. Who fed Elijah after he prayed to the Lord to take his life?
21. What did Elisha do for the Syrian soldiers after leading them to Samaria?
22. What did Elisha supply the poor widow with?
23. How did Elisha purify the bitter water?
24. Who did Elijah miraculously outrun on the way to Jezreel?

Wonders of Elijah and Elisha (Answers)

1. They were torn apart by two bears (2 Kings 2:23-25)
2. A widow and her son (1 Kings 17:13-16)
3. Brought him back to life (2 Kings 13:20-21)
4. He threw a stick into the water (2 Kings 6:4-7)
5. Naaman the Syrian (2 Kings 5:1-14)
6. Moses (Luke 9:28-36)
7. Ravens (1 Kings 17:2-7)
8. The Jordan (2 Kings 2:8)
9. He poured meal into it (2 Kings 4:38-41)
10. They were struck blind (2 Kings 6:18)
11. Three and a half years (1 Kings 17:1)
12. The Shunammite woman (2 Kings 4:14-17)
13. Fire from heaven (2 Kings 1:10-12)
14. The prophets of Baal (1 Kings 18:17-38)
15. A hundred (2 Kings 4:42-44)
16. He stretched his body out on the boy's (2 Kings 4:32-37)
17. An angelic army (2 Kings 6:15-17)
18. The armies of the kings of Judah, Israel, and Edom (2 Kings 3:14-20)
19. A whirlwind (2 Kings 2:11)
20. An angel (1 Kings 19:4-8)
21. Prayed for the healing of their blindness (2 Kings 6:19-20)
22. Large quantities of oil (2 Kings 4:1-7)
23. He threw a container of salt into it (2 Kings 2:19-22)
24. Ahab (1 Kings 18:46)

✦Miracles of Jesus

1. How was the woman with the issue of blood healed by Jesus?
2. What woman got up and started doing household chores after Jesus healed her of a fever?
3. What unproductive tree did Jesus wither by cursing it?
4. Where did Jesus work his first miracle?
5. Who appeared with Jesus at his miraculous Transfiguration?
6. Which apostle did Jesus enable to walk (briefly) on water?
7. What disciples did Jesus call after blessing them with an enormous catch of fish?
8. Who did Jesus send to catch a fish that had a coin in its mouth?
9. When Jesus healed the blind man of Bethsaida, what did the man say people looked like?
10. What widow had her dead son brought to life by Jesus?
11. Where was Jesus when he healed the son of an official from Capernaum?
12. What was the affliction of the man Jesus healed by sending him to the pool of Siloam?
13. Why did the people complain when Jesus healed a woman who had been stooped for eighteen years?
14. Where was Jesus when he miraculously escaped from a crowd that was going to push him off a cliff?
15. What was the other affliction of the deaf man Jesus healed in the Decapolis?
16. How many loaves of bread were used to feed the five thousand?
17. How was Joseph told about Jesus' miraculous conception?
18. Who announced Jesus' conception to Mary?
19. What was the affliction of the man Jesus healed after his famous Sermon on the Mount?
20. What little girl did Jesus raise from the dead after telling people she was only asleep?
21. What did Jesus say to calm the storm on the lake?
22. When Jesus healed a man of dumbness, what did the Pharisees accuse him of?
23. When Jesus healed a paralyzed man, what did the man pick up and carry home?

Miracles of Jesus (Answers)

1. She touched the hem of his garment (Matthew 9:20-22)
2. Peter's mother-in-law (Matthew 8:14-15)
3. A fig tree (Matthew 21:17-20)
4. Cana (John 2:1-11)
5. Elijah and Moses (Matthew 17:1-9)
6. Peter (Matthew 14:28-31)
7. Peter, James, and John (Luke 5:4-11)
8. Peter (Matthew 17:24-27)
9. Like trees walking (Mark 8:22-26)
10. The widow of Nain (Luke 7:11-15)
11. Cana (John 4:46-54)
12. Blindness (John 9:1-7)
13. He healed her on the Sabbath (Luke 13:11-13)
14. His hometown, Nazareth (Luke 4:29-30)
15. Almost mute (Mark 7:31-35)
16. Five (Matthew 14:15-21)
17. In a dream (Matthew 1:18-21)
18. The angel Gabriel (Luke 1:26-38)
19. Leprosy (Matthew 8:1-4)
20. Jairus's daughter (Matthew 9:23-25)
21. "Peace, be still!" (Matthew 8:23-27)
22. Having demonic power (Matthew 9:34)
23. His bed (Matthew 9:1-8)

24. When Jesus healed ten lepers, how many came back to thank him?
25. How many loaves did Jesus use to feed the four thousand?
26. What woman had her daughter healed, even after Jesus told her that he had been sent to the Jews, not to foreigners?
27. Which Gospel records the miraculous catch of fish after Jesus' resurrection?
28. Which apostle cut off a man's ear at Jesus' arrest and then watched Jesus heal the ear?
29. In what town did Jesus heal a demon-possessed man in the synagogue?
30. What man of Bethany did Jesus bring back to life?
31. Which Gospel records the ability of the resurrected Jesus to walk through locked doors?
32. What was the affliction of the man Jesus healed on the Sabbath at the home of a Pharisee?
33. What Roman of Capernaum asked that Jesus heal his servant?
34. When Jesus was healing people, what prophet did he claim to be fulfilling?
35. Where did Jesus send the demons he drove out of the Gadarene demoniacs?
36. According to Matthew's Gospel, what Sabbath healing caused the Pharisees to plot to kill Jesus?
37. What did Jesus tell the two blind men not to do after he healed them?
38. What future disciple did Jesus see, through miraculous means, sitting under a fig tree?
39. When Jesus healed a man who was both blind and dumb, what demon did the Pharisees accuse him of consorting with?
40. When the disciples saw Jesus walking on the water, what did they think he was?
41. What was the affliction of the young boy who was throwing himself into the fire?
42. How did Jesus heal the two blind men who asked for his help?
43. Where was Jesus doing his healing work when he caused the chief priests and the scribes to be angry?

24. One (Luke 17:11-19)
25. Seven (Matthew 15:32-39)
26. The Canaanite woman (Matthew 15:22-28)
27. John (21:3-11)
28. Peter (Luke 22:49-51)
29. Capernaum (Luke 4:31-37)
30. Lazarus (John 11)
31. John (20:19-21)
32. Dropsy (Luke 14:1-4)
33. The centurion (Matthew 8:5-13)
34. Isaiah (Matthew 8:17)
35. Into a herd of pigs (Matthew 8:28-34)
36. The healing of the man with the withered hand (Matthew 12:10-14)
37. Not to tell anyone else (Matthew 9:27-31)
38. Nathanael (John 1:48)
39. Beelzebub (Matthew 12:24)
40. A ghost (Mark 6:45-50)
41. He was demon-possessed (Matthew 17:14-18)
42. He touched their eyes (Matthew 20:30-34)
43. In the temple (Matthew 21:14-16)

44. What miracle in Jesus' life is mentioned most in the New Testament?
45. Where did Jesus heal a man who had been sick for 38 years?

◆Miracles of Paul and Peter

1. What dead man at Troas was raised up by Paul after falling out of a window?
2. Who did Peter heal of long-term palsy?
3. Where did Paul exorcise a spirit from a possessed girl, whose owners then became furious?
4. What woman did Peter raise from the dead?
5. Where did Paul heal a crippled man?
6. Who, with Peter, healed a crippled man at the Beautiful Gate?
7. What sorcerer was blinded at Paul's command?
8. What, placed on Paul's body, brought about healings and exorcisms?
9. On what island did Paul heal the governor's family and many other people?
10. What miraculous occurrence delivered Paul and Silas from prison in Philippi?
11. What happened when Peter and John placed their hands on the believers at Samaria?
12. What part of Peter was supposed to produce healings?
13. What happened when Paul placed his hands on the believers at Ephesus?
14. What dangerous creature did not affect Paul when it bit him?
15. How many times was Peter delivered from prison by an angel?

◆Working Wonders with Water

1. Who made an ax head float on the water?
2. Who walked on the Sea of Galilee?
3. What did Moses do to heal the bitter waters of Marah?

---

44. His resurrection
45. The pool at Bethesda (John 4:46-54)

Miracles of Paul and Peter (Answers)

1. Eutychus (Acts 20:9-10)
2. Aeneas (Acts 9:33-34)
3. Philippi (Acts 16:16-18)
4. Dorcas (Acts 9:36-41)
5. Lystra (Acts 14:8-10)
6. John (Acts 3:1-6)
7. Elymas (Acts 13:8-11)
8. Aprons and handkerchiefs (Acts 19:11-12)
9. Malta (Acts 28:8-9)
10. An earthquake (Acts 16:25-33)
11. They received the Holy Spirit (Acts 8:14-17)
12. His shadow (Acts 5:15-16)
13. They spoke in tongues and proclaimed the gospel (Acts 19:1-7)
14. A viper (Acts 28:3-6)
15. Twice (Acts 5:17-29; 12:1-17)

Working Wonders with Water (Answers)

1. Elisha (2 Kings 2:19-22)
2. Jesus and Peter (Matthew 14:25-31)
3. He cast a tree into the waters (Exodus 15:23-25)

4. Who was healed of leprosy after dipping seven times in the Jordan?
5. What judge wrung out a bowlful of water from a fleece in answer to prayer?
6. What river was turned into blood?
7. Who healed Jericho's water supply by throwing salt into it?
8. Who turned water into wine?
9. Who died when the parted Red Sea became unparted?
10. When the Israelites in the wilderness complained about lack of water, where did the water come from?
11. How did God water the thirsty army of Israel?
12. Who calmed the sea by speaking to it?
13. Who parted the Jordan by striking it with his mantle?
14. What were the Israelite priests carrying when they crossed the Jordan on dry ground?

4. Naaman the Syrian (2 Kings 5:14)
5. Gideon (Judges 6:38)
6. The Nile (Exodus 7:20)
7. Elisha (2 Kings 2:19-22)
8. Jesus (John 2:1-10)
9. The Egyptians (Exodus 14:21-29)
10. A rock (Exodus 17:1-6; 20:1-11)
11. He ordered them to dig trenches, and in the morning they were filled with water (2 Kings 3:14-22)
12. Jesus (Mark 4:39)
13. Elijah (2 Kings 2:8-14)
14. The ark of the covenant (Joshua 3:7-17)

PART 6
Dabbling with the Demonic

✦The Very Devil

1. According to Jude's epistle, who disputed with Satan over the body of Moses?
2. What animal does 1 Peter compare Satan to?
3. In what epistle does Paul refer to Satan as "the god of this world"?
4. What, according to the New Testament, is the final place for Satan?
5. In what Gospel does Jesus refer to Satan as "the prince of this world"?
6. What is Satan the father of?
7. What prophet spoke of the fallen Lucifer, usually taken to refer to Satan as a fallen angel?
8. According to the parable of the sower, what happens when someone hears the word of the kingdom and does not understand it?
9. According to John's Gospel, Satan was from the very beginning both a liar and a _____ .
10. In what epistle does Paul call Satan the "spirit that worketh in the children of disobedience"?
11. What Gospel uses the name Beelzebub?
12. What book of the Bible speaks of the demonic fiend Abaddon and Apollyon, both names for Satan?
13. What apostle spoke of the contrast between Christ and Belial (presumably another name for the devil)?
14. What prophet spoke of "weeping for the king of Tyre" in a passage that has traditionally been interpreted as referring to Satan instead of a human king?
15. In Luke's Gospel, Jesus refers to seeing the fall of Satan. What does he compare the fall to?
16. Who did Satan provoke to do a census in Israel?
17. What disciple did Satan enter into?
18. What disciple was told by Jesus that Satan wanted to sift him like wheat?

The Very Devil (Answers)

1. The archangel Michael (Jude 9)
2. A roaring lion (1 Peter 5:8)
3. 2 Corinthians (4:4)
4. A lake of fire and brimstone (Revelation 20:10)
5. John (14:30; 16:11)
6. Lies (John 8:44)
7. Isaiah (14:12)
8. The wicked one (Satan) snatches from the heart what was sown (Matthew 13:19)
9. A murderer (John 8:44)
10. Ephesians (2:2)
11. Matthew (12:24)
12. Revelation (9:11)
13. Paul (2 Corinthians 6:15)
14. Ezekiel (28:11-19)
15. Lightning (Luke 10:18)
16. David (1 Chronicles 21:1)
17. Judas Iscariot (Luke 22:3-4)
18. Peter (Luke 22:31)

19. What New Testament man did Satan provoke to lie to the Holy Spirit?
20. Who had seven sons that were overcome by an evil spirit they were trying to cast out of a man?
21. What king of Israel was tormented by an evil spirit?
22. In the story of the demon-possessed boy healed by Jesus, what had the evil spirit been doing to the poor child?
23. What did the evil spirit do when Jesus cast him out of the man at Capernaum?
24. What possessed man ran around naked?
25. What was the affliction of the woman who had had an evil spirit for eighteen years?
26. What king had court prophets that had been the agents of a lying spirit?
27. What woman had Jesus driven seven demons out of?
28. In Revelation, for what reason do the demons perform miracles?
29. According to Jesus, when an evil spirit returns to a person, how many companions does it bring with it?
30. What does Satan masquerade as in the present world?

◆Sorcerers, Witches, and So Forth

1. What emperor had a bevy of magicians and psychics who could not interpret his strange dreams?
2. What prophet called the city of Nineveh the mistress of witchcraft?
3. In what city did Paul find many believers who had formerly dabbled in witchcraft?
4. What queen of Israel practiced witchcraft?
5. What prophet claimed that Edom, Moab, Ammon, and Tyre all had sorcerers?
6. Who called on magicians to duplicate the miracles of Moses?
7. Who was the sorcerer Paul encountered on the isle of Paphos?
8. What medium was consulted by a king who had outlawed all mediums?

19. Ananias (Acts 5:3)
20. Sceva (Acts 19:16)
21. Saul (1 Samuel 16:14-23)
22. Throwing him into the fire or water and making him foam at the mouth and grind his teeth (Mark 9:17-29)
23. Gave a loud scream (Mark 1:23-26)
24. The Gerasene demoniac (Luke 8:27)
25. She was bent and could not straighten up (Luke 13:11-16)
26. Ahab (1 Kings 22:2-22)
27. Mary Magdalene (Luke 8:2)
28. To bring the nations to war (Revelation 16:13-14)
29. Seven (Matthew 12:45)
30. An angel of light (2 Corinthians 11:14)

Sorcerers, Witches, and So Forth (Answers)

1. Nebuchadnezzar (Daniel 2:10)
2. Nahum (3:4)
3. Ephesus (Acts 19:19)
4. Jezebel (2 Kings 9:22)
5. Jeremiah (27:3-10)
6. Pharaoh (Exodus 7:11-12)
7. Elymas (Acts 13:6-8)
8. The witch of Endor, who was visited by Saul (1 Samuel 28:7-25)

9. Who amazed the people of Samaria with his conjuring tricks?
10. What book states, "Thou shalt not suffer a witch to live"?
11. What book claims that witchcraft is an "abomination unto the Lord"?
12. Who told Saul that rebellion was as bad as witchcraft?
13. What epistle mentions witchcraft as one of the works of the flesh?
14. Who called on magicians to interpret his dreams about cattle?
15. What names does the New Testament give to the magicians in Pharaoh's court in the time of Moses?

◆A Gallery of Gods

1. What fish-shaped god of the Philistines was disgraced when his statue was broken by the presence of the ark of the covenant?
2. The Ammonites' bloodthirsty god was widely known in Israel because of the horrible practice of children being sacrificed to him. What was the name of this god?
3. The god of the Moabites also had child sacrifice as part of his worship. Solomon erected an altar for him, but Josiah tore it down. What was he called?
4. The people of Lystra were so dazzled by Paul and Barnabas that they called them by the names of two Greek gods. What were the names?
5. This fertility god of Canaan is mentioned more than any other foreign deity in the Bible. The prophet Elijah and, later, King Jehu of Israel, worked hard to stamp out his cult. What was his name?
6. This goddess of Canaan was associated with depraved worship practices. After Saul's death, his armor was placed in her temple by the Philistines. What was her name?
7. This Babylonian god is mentioned by Jeremiah as being filled with terror after the downfall of Babylon. What was his name?
8. This goddess of Asia had a magnificent temple in Ephesus, a city where Paul ran into trouble with some of her followers. Who was she?

9. Simon the sorcerer (Acts 8:9)
10. Exodus (22:18)
11. Deuteronomy (18:9-12)
12. Samuel (1 Samuel 15:23)
13. Galatians (5:20)
14. Pharaoh (Genesis 41:8)
15. Jannes and Jambres (2 Timothy 3:8)

A Gallery of Gods (Answers)

1. Dagon (Judges 16:23; 1 Samuel 5:1-5; 1 Chronicles 10:10)
2. Moloch (Leviticus 18:21; 1 Kings 11:7; 2 Kings 23:10; Amos 5:26)
3. Chemosh (Numbers 21:29; 1 Kings 11:7; 2 Kings 23:13)
4. Zeus and Hermes (also called Jupiter and Mercury in some Bible translations) (Acts 14:12)
5. Baal (Judges 2:11; 1 Kings 16:32; 18:19; 19:18; 2 Kings 10:18)
6. Astaroth, or Ashtoreth (Judges 2:13; 1 Samuel 7:3; 31:10; 1 Kings 11:33; 2 Kings 23:13)
7. Marduk (Jeremiah 50:2)
8. Artemis (called Diana in some translations) (Acts 19:23–20:1)

9. In Paul's speech to the men of Athens, he mentions the altar of a god. What is the altar's inscription?
10. After Gideon's death, what Canaanite god did the Israelites turn to?
11. Ezekiel saw a woman weeping for what god?
12. Who worshiped Succoth-benoth?
13. What gods did the Avites worship?
14. What was the god of Ekron, consulted by King Ahaziah?
15. What was Nehushtan?
16. What god did the Sepharites sacrifice their children to?
17. What nation was Milcom the god of?
18. While in the wilderness, what Moabite god did the Israelites begin to worship?
19. What god did Naaman the Syrian apologize to Elisha for worshiping?
20. What was the god of the men of Hamath?
21. What god did Amos say was symbolized by a star?
22. Who was King Sennacherib worshiping when his sons murdered him?
23. Whose ship had figures of the gods Castor and Pollux?
24. Who was the god of the men of Cuth?
25. What nation was Bel a god of?
26. What prophet mentions Nebo as one of the gods of Babylon?

✦Offerings to Idols

1. When Elijah challenged the priests of Baal, what were they sacrificing to their god?
2. What king of Israel offered sacrifices to the two golden calves he had made?
3. What idol, associated with Moses, was offered sacrifices by later generations?
4. What wicked king, a dabbler in sorcery, sacrificed his son in the fire?
5. What goddess did Jeremiah accuse the people of Judah of making sacrifices to?
6. What idol did the Israelites in the wilderness bring offerings to?

9. "To the Unknown God" (Acts 17:22-23)
10. Baal-berith (Judges 8:33)
11. Tammuz (Ezekiel 8:14)
12. The Babylonians (2 Kings 17:30)
13. Nibhaz and Tartak (2 Kings 17:31)
14. Baal-zebub (2 Kings 1:2)
15. The brass serpent Moses had made, which the Israelites later worshiped as if it were a god (2 Kings 18:4)
16. Adrammelech (2 Kings 17:31)
17. Ammon (1 Kings 11:5)
18. Baal-peor (Numbers 25:1-3)
19. Rimmon (2 Kings 5:17-18)
20. Ashima (2 Kings 17:30)
21. Rephen (Amos 5:26—see Stephen's words in Acts 7:43)
22. Nisroch (2 Kings 19:36-37)
23. Paul's (Acts 28:11)
24. Nergal (2 Kings 17:30)
25. Babylonia (Jeremiah 51:44)
26. Isaiah (46:1)

Offerings to Idols (Answers)

1. A bullock (1 Kings 18:25)
2. Jeroboam (1 Kings 12:32-33)
3. The brazen serpent (2 Kings 18:4)
4. Manasseh (2 Kings 21:6)
5. The queen of heaven (Jeremiah 44:19)
6. The golden calf (Exodus 32:6)

7. What people burnt their children as an offering to the gods Adramelech and Anammelech?
8. What king despaired in the face of battle and offered his oldest son, the heir to the throne, as a sacrifice?
9. What wicked king of Judah built a Syrian style altar and offered up his son as a sacrifice?
10. What was the name of the foreign god that many Israelites had sacrificed their children to?

7. The Sepharvites (2 Kings 17:31)
8. The king of Moab (2 Kings 3:26-27)
9. Ahaz (2 Chronicles 28:1-4, 23)
10. Molech (2 Kings 23:10)

PART 7
Getting It in Writing

✦So Many Versions

1. What book, published in its entirety in 1971, has been the best-selling paraphrase of the Holy Bible?
2. What translation, popular with contemporary evangelicals, was done under the auspices of the New York International Bible Society and published in 1978?
3. What famous Greek version of the Old Testament, usually designated by LXX, was supposed to have been completed by seventy scholars working in Alexandria, Egypt, around 250 B.C.?
4. What are the oldest existing copies of pieces of several Old Testament books called?
5. What Bible, now in the British Museum, is the oldest complete Bible in existence?
6. What famous church scholar made the much-used Latin translation known as the Vulgate?
7. What king of England and Scotland authorized a translation of the Bible that was published in 1611?
8. What, until recent years, was the most popular English Bible used by Roman Catholics?
9. What is the alternate title of the American Bible Society's translation Today's English Version?
10. What English king ordered the execution of Bible translator Tyndale and then had a translation dedicated to him by Tyndale's friend Coverdale?
11. What medieval Englishman translated the Latin Bible's New Testament into English and encouraged further translation work?
12. What large English Bible, published in 1539, was chained to the reading desk in English churches?
13. What widely used revision of the King James Version was published in 1952 under the auspices of the International Council of Religious Education?

So Many Versions (Answers)

1. *The Living Bible*
2. The New International Version
3. The Septuagint
4. The Dead Sea Scrolls
5. Codex Sinaiticus
6. Jerome
7. James I
8. The Douay Version
9. *The Good News Bible*
10. Henry VIII
11. John Wycliffe
12. The Great Bible
13. The Revised Standard Version

14. What text of the Old Testament—the first to include vowel markings along with the Hebrew consonants—is considered the authoritative text for most Bible translators?
15. What English translation was made in Europe by scholars who fled the persecution of Protestants under Bloody Mary?
16. When was the New King James Version published?
17. What fresh translation from the Hebrew and Greek was published in 1970 with the assistance of the university presses of Oxford and Cambridge?
18. What English translation, published in 1965, contains bracketed words intended to explain many difficult phrases?
19. What Bible scholar published a translation of Paul's epistles called *Letters to Young Churches?*
20. What Scottish scholar, famous as the author of the *Daily Study Bible*, published his own translation of the New Testament?
21. What English Bible, prepared during the reign of Elizabeth I, was popular with the clergy but not with the common people?
22. What English Catholic did a popular translation of the Bible in the 1940s?
23. What multi-volume translation, done by a number of Catholics, Protestants, and Jews, began in 1964 and is still incomplete?
24. What version, popular with American evangelicals, was sponsored by the Lockman Foundation and published in 1971?
25. What former monk made a translation of the Bible into German that was loved for centuries?
26. What medieval Archbishop of Canterbury is largely responsible for dividing the Bible into chapters?
27. What French Protestant scholar, riding on horseback from Paris to Lyons, divided the New Testament into verses?
28. What English translation, published in 1966, had notes based on a French translation done in Jerusalem?
29. What English translator died as a martyr before he could complete his translation of the Old Testament?

14. The Masoretic text
15. The Geneva Bible
16. 1982
17. *The New English Bible*
18. *The Amplified Bible*
19. J. B. Phillips
20. William Barclay
21. The Bishops' Bible
22. Ronald A. Knox
23. *The Anchor Bible*
24. *New American Standard Bible*
25. Martin Luther
26. Stephen Langton
27. Robert Estienne
28. *The Jerusalem Bible*
29. William Tyndale

30. What was the name of the New Testament paraphrase, done in the style of Southern black tales, written by Clarence Jordan?

31. What Bible was the one most likely used by Shakespeare, the Pilgrims, and Oliver Cromwell's soldiers?

32. What translation, often called the "Chicago Bible," was completed in 1931 by E. J. Goodspeed, J. M. Powis Smith, and others?

33. What brilliant Dutch scholar produced the *textus receptus,* an edition of the Greek New Testament that was used for centuries as the basis for Bible translating?

34. What modern-day community of Protestant monks in France produced a famous "picture Bible"?

35. What Bible version was the basis for the King James Version?

36. What was the Complutensian Polyglot?

37. What was Taverner's Bible?

38. When the New King James Version (1982) was repackaged in 1984, what was it called?

39. What is the alternative title of *The Modern Language Bible* (1969)?

40. Who translated *The Holy Bible in the Language of Today: An American Translation* (1976)?

41. What was the first Bible to use italics for explanatory and connective words and phrases?

42. In November 1986, a modern English translation became the first to outsell the King James Version. What was it?

43. What was the Treacle Bible?

44. What was the Unrighteous Bible?

45. What was the Place-makers' Bible?

46. What was the Discharge Bible?

47. What was the He Bible?

48. What was the Murderers' Bible?

49. What was the Standing Fishes Bible?

50. What was the Wicked Bible?

51. What was the Rosin Bible?

52. What was the Wife-hater Bible?

53. What was the Printers' Bible?

54. What was the Breeches Bible?

30. *The Cotton Patch Version*
31. The Geneva Bible
32. *The Bible: An American Translation*
33. Erasmus
34. Taize
35. The Bishops' Bible (1568)
36. The massive six-volume work, published in Spain in 1513, that contained the Hebrew and Greek texts, the Septuagint, the Vulgate, and the Chaldee paraphrase of the Pentateuch
37. An independent translation made by Greek scholar Richard Taverner in 1539
38. *The Bible*
39. The New Berkeley Version
40. William Beck
41. The Geneva Bible (1560)
42. The New International Version
43. The Bishops' Bible, so called because Jeremiah 8:22 reads, "Is there no treacle in Gilead?"
44. An edition, printed at Cambridge in 1653, containing the printer's error, "Know ye not that the unrighteous shall inherit the kingdom of God?" (1 Corinthians 6:9)
45. The second edition of the Geneva Bible, printed in 1562, which has a printer's error in Matthew 5:9: "Blessed are the place-makers."
46. An 1806 Bible that substituted "discharge" for "charge" in 1 Timothy 5:21: "I discharge thee before God."
47. The first edition of the King James Bible, which (correctly) reads "He went into the city" (Ruth 3:15). Later versions often incorrectly used "she." The verse refers to Boaz.
48. An edition of 1801 which contained this misprint of Jude 16: "There are murderers, complainers, walking after their own lusts." It should read "murmurers."
49. An 1806 printing in which Ezekiel 47:10 reads, "And it shall come to pass that the fishes shall stand upon it." It should read "fishers."
50. A 1632 English Bible that omitted the word "not" in the seventh commandment. It read, "Thou shalt commit adultery."
51. The Catholic Douay Bible, which has for Jeremiah 8:22, "Is there no rosin in Gilead?"
52. An 1810 Bible in which "life" in Luke 14:26 is printed "wife."
53. A 1702 printing which substitutes "printers" for "princes" in Psalm 119:161: "Printers have persecuted me without a cause."
54. The Geneva Bible, so called because Genesis 3:7 reads, "They sewed fig tree leaves together, and made themselves breeches."

55. What was the Bug Bible?
56. What was the Ear to Ear Bible?
57. What were Poor Man's Bibles?

◆Scripture Translates Itself

(In several places Scripture explains the meaning of phrases or the names of certain people and places. For the meanings listed below, supply the proper name.)

1. Sons of thunder
2. God with us
3. The place of the skull
4. King of peace
5. Teacher
6. Son of encouragement
7. Sorcerer
8. Little girl
9. Be opened
10. Sent
11. King of righteousness
12. Bitter
13. My God, my God, why have you forsaken me?
14. Confused
15. Red
16. Small
17. Shelters
18. Burning
19. Not my people
20. Not loved

◆Who Said That? (I)

1. I have need to be baptized of thee, and comest thou to me?
2. I will not let thee go, except thou bless me.
3. We are all one man's sons; we are true men; thy servants are no spies.

55. Coverdale's Bible (1535), which has this translation for Psalm 91:5: "Thou shalt not need to be afraid for any bugs by night." (The King James Version has "terror by night.")
56. An 1810 printing in which Matthew 13:43 reads, "Who hath ears to ear, let him hear."
57. Picture books widely used in the Middle Ages in place of the Bible. Used by the illiterate, they were probably the earliest books to be printed.

Scripture Translates Itself (Answers)

1. Boanerges (Mark 3:17)
2. Immanuel (Matthew 1:23)
3. Golgotha (Matthew 27:33)
4. King of Salem (Hebrews 7:2)
5. Rabboni or Rabbi (John 1:38; 20:16)
6. Barnabas (Acts 4:36)
7. Elymas (Acts 13:8)
8. Talitha (Mark 5:41)
9. Ephphatha (Mark 7:34)
10. Siloam (John 9:7)
11. Melchizedek (Hebrews 7:2)
12. Marah (Exodus 15:23)
13. Eloi, eloi, lama sabachthani (Mark 15:34)
14. Babel (Genesis 11:9)
15. Edom (Genesis 25:30)
16. Zoar (Genesis 19:22)
17. Succoth (Genesis 33:17)
18. Taberah (Numbers 11:3)
19. Lo-ammi (Hosea 1:9)
20. Lo-ruhamah (Hosea 1:6)

Who Said That? (I) (Answers)

1. John the Baptist (Matthew 3:14)
2. Jacob (Genesis 32:26)
3. Joseph's brothers (Genesis 42:11)

4. Why, what evil hath he done? I have found no cause of death in him; I will therefore chastise him and let him go.
5. Let the day perish wherein I was born, and the night in which it was said, There is a man child conceived.
6. I go the way of all the earth; be thou strong therefore and show thyself a man.
7. Speak, for thy servant heareth.
8. Hath the Lord indeed spoken only by Moses? Hath he not spoken also by us?
9. I saw a dream which made me afraid, and the thoughts upon my bed and the visions of my head troubled me.
10. Let there be fair young virgins sought for the king.
11. Ye men of Athens, I perceive that in all things ye are too superstitious.
12. Behold, Lord, the half of my goods I give to the poor.
13. Set thine house in order; for thou shalt die, and not live.
14. Cursed be Canaan; a servant of servants shall he be unto his brethren.
15. Who am I, that I should go unto Pharaoh?
16. Remember the word which Moses the servant of the Lord commanded you, saying, The Lord your God hath given you rest, and hath given you this land.
17. I am but a little child; I know not how to go out or come in.
18. Oh, that my grief were thoroughly weighed, and my calamity laid in the balances together!
19. Ah, Lord God! Behold, I cannot speak, for I am a child.
20. This is John the Baptist; he is risen from the dead; and therefore mighty works do show forth themselves in him.
21. Ananias, why hath Satan filled thine heart to lie to the Holy Ghost, and to keep back part of the price of the land?
22. As many as I love, I rebuke and chasten; be zealous therefore, and repent.
23. Who is the Lord, that I should obey his voice to let Israel go?
24. Praise ye the Lord for the avenging of Israel, when the people willingly offered themselves.
25. Treason, treason.
26. What peace, so long as the whoredoms of thy mother Jezebel and her witchcrafts are so many?

4. Pilate (Luke 23:22)
5. Job (3:3)
6. David (1 Kings 2:2)
7. Samuel (1 Samuel 3:10)
8. Miriam and Aaron (Numbers 12:2)
9. Nebuchadnezzar (Daniel 4:5)
10. Ahasuerus's servants (Esther 2:2)
11. Paul (Acts 17:22)
12. Zacchaeus (Luke 19:8)
13. Isaiah (2 Kings 20:1)
14. Noah (Genesis 9:25)
15. Moses (Exodus 3:11)
16. Joshua (1:13)
17. Solomon (1 Kings 3:7)
18. Job (6:2)
19. Jeremiah (1:6)
20. Herod (Matthew 14:2)
21. Peter (Acts 5:3)
22. Jesus (Revelation 3:19)
23. Pharaoh (Exodus 5:2)
24. Deborah and Barak (Judges 5:2)
25. Athaliah (2 Kings 11:14)
26. Jehu (2 Kings 9:22)

27. O my son Absalom, O Absalom, my son, my son!
28. Woe is me, for I am undone!
29. I was no prophet, neither was I a prophet's son; but I was a herdman, and a gatherer of sycamore fruit.
30. Depart from me; for I am a sinful man, O Lord.
31. Rabbi, we know that thou art a teacher come from God; for no man can do these miracles that thou doest, except God be with him.
32. Fear not, Mary; for thou hast found favor with God.
33. Ye stiffnecked and uncircumcised in heart and ears, ye do always resist the Holy Ghost.
34. I pray thee, of whom speaketh the prophet this? Of himself, or of some other man?
35. Behold, thou hast mocked me, and told me lies; now tell me, I pray thee, wherewith thou mightest be bound.
36. Why are ye come out to set your battle in array? Am I not a Philistine, and ye servants to Saul?
37. I have found the book of the law in the house of the Lord.
38. Skin for skin, yea, all that a man hath will he give for his life.
39. Thou, O king, art a king of kings; for the God of heaven hath given thee a kingdom, power, and strength, and glory.
40. Where is he that is born King of the Jews?
41. Why should it be thought a thing incredible with you, that God should raise the dead?
42. The Lord is my rock, and my fortress, and my deliverer.
43. If I be a man of God, let fire come down from heaven, and consume thee and thy fifty.
44. Dost thou still retain thine integrity? Curse God and die.
45. It was a true report that I heard in mine own land of thy acts and of thy wisdom.
46. Why is thy countenance sad, seeing thou art not sick? This is nothing else but sorrow of heart.
47. O thou seer, go, flee thee away into the land of Judah, and there eat bread, and prophesy there, but prophesy not again any more at Bethel.
48. Master, we saw one casting out devils in thy name, and he followeth not us; and we forbade him, because he followeth not us.
49. Why was not this ointment sold for three hundred pence, and given to the poor?

27. David (2 Samuel 19:4)
28. Isaiah (6:5)
29. Amos (7:14)
30. Peter (Luke 5:8)
31. Nicodemus (John 3:2)
32. Gabriel (Luke 1:30)
33. Stephen (Acts 7:51)
34. The Ethiopian eunuch (Acts 8:34)
35. Delilah (Judges 16:10)
36. Goliath (1 Samuel 17:8)
37. Hilkiah (2 Kings 22:8)
38. Satan (Job 2:4)
39. Daniel (2:37)
40. The wise men (Matthew 2:2)
41. Paul (Acts 26:8)
42. David (2 Samuel 22:2)
43. Elijah (2 Kings 1:10)
44. Job's wife (Job 2:9)
45. The queen of Sheba (1 Kings 10:6)
46. Artaxerxes (Nehemiah 2:2)
47. Amaziah (Amos 7:12-13)
48. John (Mark 9:38)
49. Judas Iscariot (John 12:5)

50. What shall I do unto this people? They be almost ready to stone me.
51. The sceptre shall not depart from Judah, nor a lawgiver from between his feet, until Shiloh come.
52. The serpent beguiled me, and I did eat.
53. Turn again, my daughters. Why will ye go with me? Are there yet any more sons in my womb, that they may be your husbands?
54. Had Zimri peace, who slew his master?
55. Take heed now; for the Lord hath chosen thee to build an house for the sanctuary; be strong, and do it.
56. Behold, a virgin shall conceive, and bear a son, and shall call his name Immanuel.
57. I heard thy voice in the garden, and I was afraid.
58. Get thee from me, take heed to thyself, see my face no more; for in that day thou seest my face thou shalt die.
59. My punishment is greater than I can bear.
60. How long halt ye between two opinions? If the Lord be God, follow him; but if Baal, then follow him.
61. Out of the eater came forth meat, and out of the strong came forth sweetness.
62. He will take your daughters to be confectionaries, and to be cooks, and to be bakers.
63. What hast thou to do with peace? Turn thee behind me.
64. He must increase, but I must decrease.
65. Therefore let all the house of Israel know assuredly, that God hath made that same Jesus, whom ye have crucified, both Lord and Christ.
66. Lord God, what wilt thou give me, seeing I go childless, and the steward of my house is this Eliezer of Damascus?
67. Shall I go and call to thee a nurse of the Hebrew women, that she may nurse the child for thee?
68. What have I done unto thee, that thou hast smitten me these three times?
69. Master, behold, the fig tree which thou cursedst is withered away.
70. Repent and be baptized every one of you in the name of Jesus Christ for the remission of sins.
71. Behold, I see the heavens opened, and the Son of man standing on the right hand of God.

50. Moses (Exodus 17:4)
51. Jacob (Genesis 49:10)
52. Eve (Genesis 3:13)
53. Naomi (Ruth 1:11)
54. Jezebel (2 Kings 9:31)
55. David (1 Chronicles 28:10)
56. Isaiah (7:14)
57. Adam (Genesis 3:10)
58. Pharaoh (Exodus 10:28)
59. Cain (Genesis 4:13)
60. Elijah (1 Kings 18:21)
61. Samson (Judges 14:14)
62. Samuel (1 Samuel 8:13)
63. Jehu (2 Kings 9:19)
64. John the Baptist (John 3:30)
65. Peter (Acts 2:36)
66. Abraham (Genesis 15:2)
67. Miriam (Exodus 2:7)
68. Balaam's donkey (Numbers 22:28)
69. Peter (Mark 11:21)
70. Peter (Acts 2:38)
71. Stephen (Acts 7:56)

72. What shall be the sign that the Lord will heal me, and that I shall go up into the house of the Lord the third day?
73. Lord God of Abraham, Isaac, and Israel, let it be known this day that thou art God in Israel.
74. Behold now, the Lord hath restrained me from bearing. I pray thee, go in unto my maid; it may be that I may obtain children by her.
75. There shall come a star out of Jacob, and a scepter shall rise out of Israel.
76. Let me die with the Philistines.
77. Let not my lord, I pray thee, regard this man of Belial, even Nabal; for as his name is, so is he; Nabal is his name, and folly is with him.
78. My father made your yoke heavy, and I will add to your yoke.
79. After I am waxed old, shall I have pleasure, my lord being old also?
80. I know that the Lord hath given you the land, and that your terror is fallen upon us, and that all the inhabitants of the land faint because of you.
81. Can the blind lead the blind? Shall they not both fall into the ditch?
82. Cast out this bondwoman and her son; for the son of this bondwoman shall not be heir with my son.
83. Entreat me not to leave thee, or to return from following after thee; for whither thou goest, I will go.
84. My father chastised you with whip, but I will chastise you with scorpions.
85. I know thou canst do everything, and that no thought can be withholden from thee.
86. If it seems good unto the king, let the king and Haman come this day unto the banquet that I have prepared for him.
87. Behold the handmaid of the Lord.
88. Of a truth I perceive that God is no respecter of persons.
89. It is hard for thee to kick against the pricks.
90. This is one of the Hebrews' children.
91. Saul hath slain his thousands, and David his ten thousands.
92. Am I a dog, that thou comest to me with staves?

72. Hezekiah (2 Kings 20:8)
73. Elijah (1 Kings 18:36)
74. Sarah (Genesis 16:2)
75. Balaam (Numbers 24:17)
76. Samson (Judges 16:30)
77. Abigail (1 Samuel 25:25)
78. Rehoboam (1 Kings 12:14)
79. Sarah (Genesis 18:12)
80. Rahab (Joshua 2:9)
81. Jesus (Luke 6:39)
82. Sarah (Genesis 21:10)
83. Ruth (1:16)
84. Rehoboam (1 Kings 12:14)
85. Job (42:2)
86. Esther (5:4)
87. Mary (Luke 1:38)
88. Peter (Acts 10:34)
89. Jesus (Acts 9:5)
90. Pharaoh's daughter (Exodus 2:6)
91. The women of Israel (1 Samuel 18:7)
92. Goliath (1 Samuel 17:43)

93. Behold, the day comes, that all that is in thine house, and that which thy fathers have laid up in store unto this day, shall be carried into Babylon.
94. Wilt thou also destroy the righteous with the wicked?
95. I find no fault in this man.

◆What Gets Quoted Most?

1. What book, one of the prophets, gets quoted in the New Testament more than any Old Testament book (419 times)?
2. What book, the longest in the Old Testament, ranks second with 414 references in the New?
3. What book, part of the Torah, ranks third with 260 references?
4. What book, part narrative and part law, ranks fourth with 250 references?
5. What book, more law than history, ranks fifth with 208 references?
6. What book, a long book of prophecy, ranks sixth with 141 references?
7. What book, with many visions in it, ranks seventh with 133 references?
8. What book, a book by one of the later prophets, ranks eighth with 125 references?
9. What book, probably one of the least read of Old Testament books, ranks ninth with 107 references?
10. What book, mostly history and part law, ranks tenth with 73 references?

◆Everyday Phrases from the Bible

Identify the book and, if possible, the chapter and verse where these commonly used phrases originated.

1. The skin of my teeth
2. Wolf in sheep's clothing

93. Isaiah (2 Kings 20:17)
94. Abraham (Genesis 18:23)
95. Pilate (Luke 23:4)

What Gets Quoted Most? (Answers)

1. Isaiah
2. Psalms
3. Genesis
4. Exodus
5. Deuteronomy
6. Ezekiel
7. Daniel
8. Jeremiah
9. Leviticus
10. Numbers

Everyday Phrases from the Bible (Answers)

1. "I am escaped with the skin of my teeth" (Job 19:20)
2. "Beware of false prophets, which come to you in sheep's clothing, but inwardly they are ravening wolves" (Matthew 7:15)

3. Salt of the earth
4. Holier than thou
5. Woe is me!
6. Can a leopard change his spots?
7. A drop in a bucket
8. Eat, drink, and be merry
9. Pride goeth before a fall
10. Give up the ghost
11. Spare the rod and spoil the child
12. My brother's keeper
13. Fat of the land
14. A lamb for the slaughter
15. The blind leading the blind

✦The Old Testament in the New (I)

Each of these passages from the New Testament is a quotation from the Old Testament. Name the Old Testament book (and, if you're sharp, chapter and verse) where the passage appears.

1. "Behold, a virgin shall be with child, and shall bring forth a son, and they shall call his name Emmanuel" (Matthew 1:23)
2. "Prepare ye the way of the Lord, make his paths straight" (Matthew 3:3)
3. "The people which sat in darkness saw great light; and to them which sat in the region and shadow of death light is sprung up" (Matthew 4:16)
4. "Man shall not live by bread alone, but by every word that proceedeth out of the mouth of God" (Matthew 4:4)
5. "Thou shalt not tempt the Lord thy God" (Matthew 4:7)
6. "Thou shalt worship the Lord thy God, and him only shalt thou serve" (Matthew 4:10)
7. "An eye for an eye, and a tooth for a tooth" (Matthew 5:38)
8. "Thou shalt love thy neighbor, and hate thine enemy" (Matthew 5:43)

3. "Ye are the salt of the earth" (Matthew 5:13)
4. "I am holier than thou" (Isaiah 65:5)
5. "Woe is me! for I am undone" (Isaiah 6:5)
6. "Can the Ethiopian change his skin, or the leopard his spots?" (Jeremiah 13:23)
7. "Behold, the nations are as a drop of a bucket, and are counted as the small dust of the balance" (Isaiah 40:15)
8. "A man hath no better thing under the sun, than to eat, and to drink and to be merry" (Ecclesiastes 8:15)
9. "Pride goeth before destruction, and an haughty spirit before a fall" (Proverbs 16:18)
10. "But man dieth, and wasteth away; yea, man giveth up the ghost, and where is he?" (Job 14:10)
11. "He that spareth the rod hateth his son" (Proverbs 13:24).
12. "Am I my brother's keeper?" (Genesis 4:9)
13. "And ye shall eat the fat of the land" (Genesis 45:18)
14. "He is brought as a lamb to the slaughter" (Isaiah 53:7)
15. "If the blind lead the blind, both shall fall into the ditch" (Matthew 15:14)

The Old Testament in the New (I) (Answers)

1. Isaiah 7:14
2. Isaiah 40:3
3. Isaiah 42:7
4. Deuteronomy 8:3
5. Deuteronomy 6:16
6. Deuteronomy 6:13
7. Exodus 21:24
8. Leviticus 19:18

9. "Himself took our iniquities, and bare our sicknesses" (Matthew 8:17)
10. "I will have mercy, and not sacrifice" (Matthew 9:13)
11. "Behold, I send my messenger before my face, which shall prepare thy way before thee" (Matthew 11:10)
12. "Behold my servant, whom I have chosen; my beloved, in whom my soul is well pleased; I will put my spirit upon him, and he shall show judgment to the Gentiles" (Matthew 12:18)
13. "He shall not strive, nor cry; neither shall any man hear his voice in the streets" (Matthew 12:19)
14. "A bruised reed shall he not break, and smoking flax shall he not quench, till he send forth judgment unto victory" (Matthew 12:20)
15. "And in his name shall the Gentiles trust" (Matthew 12:21)
16. "By hearing ye shall hear, and shall not understand; and seeing ye shall see, and shall not perceive" (Matthew 13:14)
17. "For this people's heart is waxed gross, and their ears are dull of hearing, and their eyes they have closed" (Matthew 13:15)
18. "I will open my mouth in parables; I will utter things which have been kept secret from the foundation of the world" (Matthew 13:35)
19. "This people draweth nigh unto me with their mouth, and honoreth me with their lips; but their heart is far from me" (Matthew 15:8)
20. "My house shall be a house of prayer" (Matthew 21:13)
21. "Out of the mouth of babes and sucklings thou hast perfected praise" (Matthew 21:16)
22. "The stone which the builders rejected, the same is become the head of the corner" (Matthew 21:42)
23. "I am the God of Abraham, and the God of Isaac, and the God of Jacob" (Matthew 22:32)
24. "Thou shalt love the Lord thy God with all thy heart, and with all thy soul, and with all thy mind" (Matthew 22:37)
25. "Thou shalt love thy neighbor as thyself" (Matthew 22:39)
26. "The Lord said unto my Lord, Sit thou on my right hand, till I make thine enemies thy footstool" (Matthew 22:44)

9. Isaiah 53:4
10. Hosea 6:6
11. Malachi 3:1
12. Isaiah 42:1
13. Isaiah 42:2
14. Isaiah 42:3
15. Isaiah 42:4
16. Isaiah 6:9
17. Isaiah 6:10
18. Psalm 78:2
19. Isaiah 29:13
20. Isaiah 56:7
21. Psalm 8:2
22. Psalm 118:22
23. Exodus 3:6
24. Deuteronomy 6:3
25. Leviticus 19:18
26. Psalm 110:1

27. "They parted my garments among them, and upon my vesture did they cast lots" (Matthew 27:35)
28. "He trusted in God; let him deliver him now" (Matthew 27:43)
29. "My God, my God, why hast thou forsaken me?" (Matthew 27:46)
30. "The voice of one crying in the wilderness, Prepare ye the way of the Lord" (Mark 1:3)
31. "That seeing they may see, and not perceive; and hearing they may hear, and not understand; lest at any time they should be converted, and their sins should be forgiven them" (Mark 4:12)
32. "This people honoreth me with their lips, but their heart is far from me" (Mark 7:6)
33. "For this cause shall a man leave his father and mother, and cleave to his wife; and they twain shall be one flesh" (Mark 10:7-8)
34. "Where their worm dieth not, and the fire is not quenched" (Mark 9:48)
35. "For everyone shall be salted with fire, and every sacrifice shall be salted with salt" (Mark 9:49)
36. "Hear, O Israel; The Lord our God is one Lord" (Mark 12:29)
37. "I will smite the shepherd, and the sheep shall be scattered" (Mark 14:27)
38. "Every male that openeth the womb shall be called holy to the Lord" (Luke 2:23)
39. "Every valley shall be filled, and every mountain and hill shall be brought low" (Luke 3:5)
40. "And all flesh shall see the salvation of God" (Luke 3:6)
41. "He shall give his angels charge over thee, to keep thee" (Luke 4:10)
42. "They shall bear thee up, lest at any time thou dash thy foot against a stone" (Luke 4:11)
43. "The Spirit of the Lord is upon me, because he hath anointed me to preach the gospel to the poor" (Luke 4:18)
44. "That seeing they might not see, and hearing they might not understand" (Luke 8:10)
45. "My house is the house of prayer" (Luke 19:46)
46. "Make straight the way of the Lord" (John 1:23)

---

27. Psalm 22:18
28. Psalm 22:8
29. Psalm 22:1
30. Isaiah 40:3
31. Isaiah 6:9
32. Isaiah 29:13
33. Genesis 2:24
34. Isaiah 66:24
35. Leviticus 2:13
36. Deuteronomy 6:4
37. Zechariah 13:7
38. Exodus 13:2
39. Isaiah 40:3-4
40. Isaiah 40:5
41. Psalm 91:11
42. Psalm 91:12
43. Isaiah 61:1
44. Isaiah 6:9
45. Isaiah 56:7
46. Isaiah 40:3

47. "The zeal of thine house hath eaten me up" (John 2:17)
48. "Ye are gods" (John 10:34)
49. "Behold, thy King cometh, sitting on an ass's colt" (John 12:15)
50. "Lord, who hath believed our report? and to whom hath the arm of the Lord been revealed?" (John 12:38)
51. "He hath blinded their eyes, and hardened their heart" (John 12:40)
52. "He that eateth bread with me hath lifted up his heel against me" (John 13:18)
53. "They hated me without a cause" (John 15:25)
54. "They shall look on him whom they pierced" (John 19:37)
55. "A bone of him shall not be broken" (John 19:36)
56. "Let his habitation be desolate, and let no man dwell therein" (Acts 1:20)
57. "And it shall come to pass in the last days, saith God, I will pour out of my Spirit upon all flesh; and your sons and your daughters shall prophesy, and your young men shall see visions, and your old men shall dream dreams" (Acts 2:17)
58. "The sun shall be turned into darkness, and the moon into blood, before that great and notable day of the Lord come" (Acts 2:20)
59. "I foresaw the Lord always before my face, for he is on my right hand, that I should not be moved" (Acts 2:25)
60. "Thou wilt not leave my soul in hell, neither wilt thou suffer thine Holy One to see corruption" (Acts 2:27)
61. "The Lord said unto my Lord, Sit thou on my right hand" (Acts 2:34)
62. "A prophet shall the Lord your God raise up unto you of your brethren, like unto me; him shall ye hear in all things whatsoever he shall say unto you" (Acts 3:22)
63. "This is the stone which was set at nought of you builders which is become the head of the corner" (Acts 4:11)
64. "Why did the heathen rage, and the people imagine vain things?" (Acts 4:25)
65. "Put off thy shoes from thy feet: for the place where thou standest is holy ground" (Acts 7:33)

47. Psalm 69:9
48. Psalm 82:6
49. Zechariah 9:9
50. Isaiah 53:1
51. Isaiah 6:9
52. Psalm 41:9
53. Psalm 35:19
54. Zechariah 12:10
55. Exodus 12:46
56. Psalm 69:25
57. Joel 2:28
58. Joel 2:31
59. Psalm 16:8
60. Psalm 16:10
61. Psalm 110:1
62. Deuteronomy 18:15
63. Psalm 118:22
64. Psalm 2:1
65. Exodus 3:5

66. "I have seen the affliction of my people which is in Egypt, and I have heard their groaning, and am come down to deliver them" (Acts 7:34)
67. "Make us gods to go before us: for as for this Moses, which brought us out of the land of Egypt, we wot not what is become of him" (Acts 7:40)
68. "O ye house of Israel, have ye offered to me slain beasts and sacrifices by the space of forty years in the wilderness?" (Acts 7:42)
69. "He was led as a sheep to the slaughter; and like a lamb dumb before his shearer, so opened he not his mouth" (Acts 8:32).
70. "In his humiliation his judgment was taken away: and who shall declare his generation? for his life is taken from the earth" (Acts 8:33)

◆Books Within the Book

1. What prophet ate a book and found it sweet as honey?
2. What book of the Bible mentions the Lamb's book of life?
3. Which king's acts are said to be recorded in "the book of Jehu the son of Hanani"?
4. Whose acts are recorded in "the book of Shemaiah the prophet"?
5. Whose acts are recorded in "the book of Iddo the seer"?
6. The "book of Gad the seer" records which king's deeds?
7. King David's acts are said to be recorded in the book of which court prophet?
8. What book of the Bible makes reference to "the books of the chronicles of the kings of Media and Persia"?
9. What New Testament writer ate a book that tasted good but gave him indigestion?
10. What Persian king received a letter, asking him to search through the "book of the records" to remind himself how rebellious the Jews had been?
11. What Old Testament prophet mentions the Lord's "book of remembrance"?
12. According to Revelation, who will open the book with seven seals?

66. Exodus 3:7
67. Exodus 32:1
68. Amos 5:25
69. Isaiah 53:7
70. Isaiah 53:8

Books Within the Book (Answers)

1. Ezekiel (Ezekiel 2:9–3:3) or John (Revelation 10:10)
2. Revelation 21:27
3. Jehoshaphat's (2 Chronicles 20:34)
4. Rehoboam (2 Chronicles 12:15)
5. Rehoboam (2 Chronicles 12:15)
6. David's (1 Chronicles 29:29)
7. Nathan (1 Chronicles 29:29)
8. Esther (10:1-2)
9. John (Revelation 10:9-10)
10. Artaxerxes (Ezra 4:15)
11. Malachi 3:16-17
12. The lion of the tribe of Judah (Revelation 5:5)

13. What king cut up Jeremiah's scroll and tossed it piece by piece into a fireplace?
14. In what city in Asia did people burn their valuable books on sorcery?
15. What Old Testament book mentions "the book of the acts of Solomon"?
16. Who described to the people of Israel what life would be like under a king and then wrote down his statements in a book?
17. Who instructed the men of Israel to go through Canaan and write down descriptions of the area?
18. What phenomenal event, described in Joshua, is also said to be described in the "book of Jashar"?
19. What Old Testament book makes reference to "the book of the wars of the Lord"?
20. According to tradition, the "book of the law" found in the temple during Josiah's reign was a form of which Old Testament book?

◆Who Said That? (II)

1. Lord, lay not this sin to their charge.
2. See, here is water; what doth hinder me to be baptized?
3. I die, and God will surely visit you, and bring you out of this land unto the land which he sware to Abraham, to Isaac, and to Jacob.
4. Thou art Peter, and upon this rock I will build my church.
5. Behold, this child is set for the fall and rising again of many in Israel.
6. And put my cup, the silver cup, in the sack's mouth of the youngest, and his corn money.
7. Now shall I be more blameless than the Philistines, though I do them a displeasure.
8. I am a Hebrew, and I fear the Lord, the God of heaven, which hath made the sea and the dry land.
9. There cometh one mightier than I after me, the latchet of whose shoes I am not worthy to stoop down and unloose.
10. The God of our fathers raised up Jesus, whom ye slew and hanged on a tree.

13. Jehoiakim (Jeremiah 36:23)
14. Ephesus (Acts 19:18-19)
15. 1 Kings 11:41
16. Samuel (1 Samuel 10:25)
17. Joshua 18:9
18. The sun standing still (Joshua 10:13)
19. Numbers 21:14-15
20. Deuteronomy

Who Said That? (II) (Answers)

1. Stephen (Acts 7:60)
2. The Ethiopian eunuch (Acts 8:36)
3. Joseph (Genesis 50:24)
4. Jesus (Matthew 16:18)
5. Simeon (Luke 2:34)
6. Joseph (Genesis 44:2)
7. Samson (Judges 15:3)
8. Jonah (1:9)
9. John the Baptist (Mark 1:7)
10. Peter (Acts 5:30)

11. As the Lord liveth, the man that hath done this thing shall surely die.
12. Draw thy sword, and thrust me through therewith, lest these uncircumcised come and thrust me through, and abuse me.
13. Lie with me.
14. I have sinned this time; the Lord is righteous, and I and my people are wicked.
15. Give me thy vineyard, that I may have it for a garden of herbs, because it is near my house; and I will give thee for it a better vineyard.
16. Behold, I have given Esther the house of Haman, and him they have hanged upon the gallows, because he laid his hand upon the Jews.
17. Whoever shall read this writing, and show me the interpretation thereof, shall be clothed with scarlet, and have a chain of gold about his neck, and shall be the third ruler in the kingdom.
18. My soul doth magnify the Lord.
19. All these things will I give thee, if thou wilt fall down and worship me.
20. Repent ye; for the kingdom of heaven is at hand.
21. Men and brethren, I am a Pharisee, the son of a Pharisee; of the hope and resurrection of the dead I am called into question.
22. Silver and gold have I none; but such as I have I give thee: In the name of Jesus Christ of Nazareth, rise up and walk.
23. The voice is Jacob's voice, but the hands are the hands of Esau.
24. How are the mighty fallen, and the weapons of war perished!
25. If now I have found grace in thy sight, then show me a sign that thou talkest with me.
26. Ye have brought this man unto me, as one that perverteth the people; and behold, I, having examined him before you, have found no fault in this man touching those things whereof ye accuse him.
27. Dost thou now govern the kingdom of Israel? Arise, and eat bread, and let thine heart be merry. I will give thee the vineyard of Naboth.

11. David (2 Samuel 12:5)
12. Saul (1 Samuel 31:4)
13. Potiphar's wife (Genesis 39:7)
14. Pharaoh (Exodus 9:27)
15. Ahab (1 Kings 21:2)
16. Ahasuerus (Esther 8:7)
17. Belshazzar (Daniel 5:7)
18. Mary (Luke 1:46)
19. The devil (Matthew 4:9)
20. John the Baptist (Matthew 3:2)
21. Paul (Acts 23:6)
22. Peter (Acts 3:6)
23. Isaac (Genesis 27:22)
24. David (2 Samuel 1:27)
25. Gideon (Judges 6:17)
26. Pilate (Luke 23:14)
27. Jezebel (1 Kings 21:7)

28. Of a truth it is, that your God is a God of gods, and a Lord of kings, and a revealer of secrets, seeing thou couldest reveal this secret.
29. These things have I spoken unto you, that in me ye might have peace.
30. He hath brought in a Hebrew to mock us; he came in unto me to lie with me, and I cried with a loud voice.
31. Entreat the Lord, that he may take away the frogs from me, and from my people.
32. Hearest thou not, my daughter? Go not to glean in another field, neither go from hence, but abide here fast by my maidens.
33. But will God indeed dwell on the earth? Behold, the heaven and heaven of heavens cannot contain thee; how much less this house that I have builded?
34. Have thou nothing to do with that just man; for I have suffered many things this day in a dream because of him.
35. I am he that liveth, and was dead; and behold, I am alive for evermore.
36. Thou art the man.
37. Behold, to obey is better than sacrifice, and to hearken than the fat of rams.
38. I have been a Nazarite unto God from my mother's womb; if I be shaven, then my strength will go from me.
39. I have heard many such things; miserable comforters are ye all.
40. No, my lord, I am a woman of sorrowful spirit; I have drunk neither wine nor strong drink, but have poured out my soul before the Lord.
41. Thy brother came with subtilty, and hath taken away thy blessing.
42. Men and brethren, I have lived in all good conscience before until this day.
43. Will ye that I release unto you the King of the Jews?
44. Yet forty days and Nineveh shall be overthrown.
45. Certainly this was a righteous man.
46. My Lord and my God.
47. Thy people shall be my people, and thy God my God.
48. The Philistines be upon thee, Samson.
49. Go ye, serve the Lord; only let your flocks and your herds be stayed; let your little ones also go with you.

28. Nebuchadnezzar (Daniel 2:47)
29. Jesus (John 16:33)
30. Potiphar's wife (Genesis 39:14)
31. Pharaoh (Exodus 8:8)
32. Boaz (Ruth 2:8)
33. Solomon (1 Kings 8:27)
34. Pilate's wife (Matthew 27:19)
35. Jesus (Revelation 1:18)
36. Nathan (2 Samuel 12:7)
37. Samuel (1 Samuel 15:22)
38. Samson (Judges 16:17)
39. Job (16:2)
40. Hannah (1 Samuel 1:15)
41. Isaac (Genesis 27:35)
42. Paul (Acts 23:1)
43. Pilate (Mark 15:9)
44. Jonah (3:4)
45. The centurion at the crucifixion (Luke 23:47)
46. Thomas (John 20:28)
47. Ruth (1:16)
48. Delilah (Judges 16:20)
49. Pharaoh (Exodus 10:24)

50. The Lord watch between me and thee, when we are absent one from another.
51. O Lord, take, I beseech thee, my life from me; for it is better for me to die than to live.
52. Go and search diligently for the young child; and when ye have found him, bring me word again, that I may come and worship him also.
53. The Lord forbid that I should stretch forth mine hand against the Lord's anointed.
54. Naked came I out of my mother's womb, and naked shall I return thither. The Lord gave, and the Lord hath taken away; blessed be the name of the Lord.
55. Here am I, send me.
56. Prove thy servants, I beseech thee, ten days; and let them give us pulse to eat, and water to drink.
57. We have a father, an old man, and a child of his old age, a little one.
58. Am I my brother's keeper?
59. God that made the world and all things therein, seeing that he is Lord of heaven and earth, dwelleth not in temples made with hands.
60. Lord, it is good for us to be here; if thou wilt, let us make here three tabernacles; one for thee, and one for Moses, and one for Elias.
61. Refrain from these men, and let them alone; for if this counsel or this work be of men, it will come to nought.
62. Lord, now lettest thou thy servant depart in peace, according to thy word; for mine eyes have seen thy salvation.
63. Blessed be the God of Shadrach, Meshach, and Abednego, who hath sent his angel, and delivered his servants that trusted in him.
64. This day is this scripture fulfilled in your ears.
65. Almost thou persuadest me to be a Christian.
66. Now therefore are we all here present before God, to hear all things that are commanded thee of God.
67. Behold, the people of the children of Israel are more and mightier than we.
68. Shall a child be born unto him that is an hundred years old?

50. Laban (Genesis 31:49)
51. Jonah (4:3)
52. Herod (Matthew 2:8)
53. David (1 Samuel 26:11)
54. Job (1:21)
55. Isaiah (6:8)
56. Daniel (1:12)
57. Judah (Genesis 44:20)
58. Cain (Genesis 4:9)
59. Paul (Acts 17:24)
60. Peter (Matthew 17:4)
61. Gamaliel (Acts 5:38)
62. Simeon (Luke 2:29-30)
63. Nebuchadnezzar (Daniel 3:28)
64. Jesus (Luke 4:21)
65. Agrippa (Acts 26:28)
66. Cornelius (Acts 10:33)
67. Pharaoh (Exodus 1:9)
68. Abraham (Genesis 17:17)

69. This will be the manner of the king that shall reign over you: He will take your sons, and appoint them for himself, for his chariots, and to be his horsemen.

70. Give therefore thy servant an understanding heart to judge thy people, that I may discern between good and bad; for who is able to judge this thy so great a people?

71. There is a certain people scattered abroad and dispersed among the people in all the provinces of thy kingdom; and their laws are diverse from all people; neither keep they the king's laws.

72. For before the child shall know to refuse the evil, and choose the good, the land that thou abhorrest shall be forsaken of both her kings.

73. Full well ye reject the commandment of God, that ye may keep your own tradition.

74. Great is Diana of the Ephesians.

75. What is truth?

76. Can there be any good thing come out of Nazareth?

77. Cry aloud, for he is a god; either he is talking, or he is pursuing, or he is in a journey, or peradventure he sleepeth, and must be awaked.

78. Let me, I pray thee, kiss my father and my mother, and then I will follow thee.

79. In what place soever ye enter into an house, there abide till ye depart from that place.

80. How can a man be born when he is old? Can he enter the second time into his mother's womb, and be born?

81. Go, see now this cursed woman, and bury her; for she is a king's daughter.

82. I have heard of thee by the hearing of the ear; but now mine eye seeth thee.

83. God Almighty appeared unto me at Luz in the land of Canaan, and blessed me.

84. The woman whom thou gavest to be with me, she gave me of the tree, and I did eat.

85. Is it true, O Shadrach, Meshach, and Abednego, do not ye serve my gods, nor worship the golden image which I have set up?

86. Not so, Lord, for I have never eaten anything that is common or unclean.

69. Samuel (1 Samuel 8:11)
70. Solomon (1 Kings 3:9)
71. Haman (Esther 3:8)
72. Isaiah (7:16)
73. Jesus (Mark 7:9)
74. The people of Ephesus (Acts 19:34)
75. Pilate (John 18:38)
76. Nathanael (John 1:46)
77. Elijah (1 Kings 18:27)
78. Elisha (1 Kings 19:20)
79. Jesus (Mark 6:10)
80. Nicodemus (John 3:4)
81. Jehu (2 Kings 9:34)
82. Job (42:5)
83. Jacob (Genesis 48:3)
84. Adam (Genesis 3:12)
85. Nebuchadnezzar (Daniel 3:14)
86. Peter (Acts 10:14)

87. He hath regarded the low estate of his handmaiden; for, behold, from henceforth all generations shall call me blessed.
88. Is it not because the Lord hath anointed thee to be captain over his inheritance?
89. And now, my daughter, fear not; I will do to thee all that thou requirest; for all the city of my people doth know that thou art a virtuous woman.
90. Ye men of Judea, and all ye that dwell at Jerusalem, be this known unto you, and hearken to my words; for these are not drunken, as ye suppose, seeing it is but the third hour of the day.
91. Thus saith the king, Let not Hezekiah deceive you; for he shall not be able to deliver you out of his hand.
92. Give me here John [the] Baptist's head in a charger.
93. Truth, Lord, yet the dogs eat of the crumbs which fall from their master's table.
94. What therefore God hath joined together, let not man put asunder.
95. Every man at the beginning doth set forth good wine; and when men have well drunk, then that which is worse; but thou hast kept the good wine until now.

✦Chapter 1, Verse 1

Each of the following is the first verse of a book of the Bible. Name the book in each case.

1. The beginning of the gospel of Jesus Christ, the Son of God.
2. Blessed is the man that walketh not in the counsel of the ungodly.
3. There was a man in the land of Uz.
4. The former treatise have I made, O Theophilus, of all that Jesus began to do and teach.
5. The elder unto the well-beloved Gaius, whom I love in the truth.
6. In the third year of the reign of Jehoiakim king of Judah came Nebuchadnezzar king of Babylon unto Jerusalem and besieged it.

87. Mary (Luke 1:48)
88. Samuel (1 Samuel 10:1)
89. Boaz (Ruth 3:11)
90. Peter (Acts 2:14-15)
91. Rabshakeh (2 Kings 18:29)
92. The daughter of Herodias (Matthew 14:8)
93. The Canaanite woman (Matthew 15:27)
94. Jesus (Mark 10:9)
95. The ruler of the marriage feast at Cana (John 2:10)

Chapter 1, Verse 1 (Answers)

1. Mark
2. Psalms
3. Job
4. Acts
5. 3 John
6. Daniel

7. Now these are the names of the children of Israel, which came unto Egypt; every man and his household came with Jacob.
8. The words of the Preacher, the son of David, king in Jerusalem.
9. God, who at sundry times and in divers manners spake in times past unto the fathers by the prophets.
10. That which was from the beginning, which we have heard, which we have seen with our eyes, which we have looked upon, and our hands have handled, of the Word of life.
11. And the Lord called unto Moses, and spake unto him out of the tabernacle of the congregation.
12. Adam, Seth, Enosh, Kenan, Malahaleel, Jared.
13. The book of the generation of Jesus Christ, the son of David, the son of Abraham.
14. Paul, an apostle of Jesus Christ by the commandment of God our Savior, and Lord Jesus Christ, which is our hope.
15. Now it came to pass in the days of Ahasuerus (this is Ahasuerus which reigned, from India even unto Ethiopia, over an hundred and seven and twenty provinces).
16. How doth the city sit solitary, that was full of people! How is she become as a widow!
17. In the beginning was the Word, and the Word was with God, and the Word was God.
18. Now it came to pass in the thirtieth year, in the fourth month, in the fifth day of the month, as I was among the captives by the river of Chebar, that the heavens were opened, and I saw visions of God.
19. Paul, an apostle (not of men, neither by man, but by Jesus Christ, and God the father, who raised him from the dead).
20. In the beginning God created the heaven and the earth.
21. And the Lord spake unto Moses in the wilderness of Sinai, in the tabernacle of the congregation, on the first day of the second month, in the second year after they were come out of the land of Egypt.
22. And Solomon the son of David was strengthened in his kingdom, and the Lord his God was with him, and magnified him exceedingly.
23. The elder unto the elect lady and her children, whom I love in the truth; and not I only, but also all they that have known the truth.

7. Exodus
8. Ecclesiastes
9. Hebrews
10. 1 John
11. Leviticus
12. 1 Chronicles
13. Matthew
14. 1 Timothy
15. Esther
16. Lamentations
17. John
18. Ezekiel
19. Galatians
20. Genesis
21. Numbers
22. 2 Chronicles
23. 2 John

24. Paul, a servant of Jesus Christ, called to be an apostle, separated unto the gospel of God.
25. Now there was a certain man of Ramathaim-zophim, of mount Ephraim, and his name was Elkanah, the son of Jeroham, the son of Elihu, the son of Tohu, the son of Zuph, an Ephrathite.
26. Now in the first year of Cyrus king of Persia, that the word of the Lord by the mouth of Jeremiah might be fulfilled, the Lord stirred up the spirit of Cyrus king of Persia, that he made a proclamation throughout all his kingdom.
27. Then Moab rebelled against Israel after the death of Ahab.
28. These be the words which Moses spake unto all Israel on this side Jordan in the wilderness, in the plain over against the Red Sea, between Paran and Tophel and Laban and Hazeroth and Dizahab.
29. Paul, a servant of God, and an apostle of Jesus Christ, according to the faith of God's elect, and the acknowledging of the truth which is after godliness.
30. Now it came to pass after the death of Saul, when David was returned from the slaughter of the Amalekites, and David had abode two days in Ziklag.
31. Forasmuch as many have taken in hand to set forth in order a declaration of those things which are most surely believed among us.
32. Paul, called to be an apostle of Jesus Christ through the will of God, and Sosthenes our brother.
33. Now King David was old and stricken in years; and they covered him with clothes, but he got no heat.
34. Now after the death of Joshua it came to pass, that the children of Israel asked the Lord.

◆Beginning at the End

Each of the following is the last verse of a book of the Bible. Name the book in each case.

1. Remember me, O my God, for good.
2. But thou hast utterly rejected us; thou art very wroth against us.

24. Romans
25. 1 Samuel
26. Ezra
27. 2 Kings
28. Deuteronomy
29. Titus
30. 2 Samuel
31. Luke
32. 1 Corinthians
33. 1 Kings
34. Judges

Beginning at the End (Answers)

1. Nehemiah
2. Lamentations

3. And they were continually in the temple, praising and blessing God. Amen.
4. For he served Baal, and worshipped him, and provoked to anger the Lord God of Israel, according to all that his father had done.
5. And Eleazar the son of Aaron died; and they buried him in a hill that pertained to Phinehas his son, which was given him in Mount Ephraim.
6. And for his diet, there was a continual diet given him of the king of Babylon, every day a portion until the day of his death, all the days of his life.
7. The grace of our Lord Jesus Christ be with you all. Amen.
8. So Joseph died, being a hundred and ten years old; and they embalmed him, and he was put in a coffin in Egypt.
9. And David built there an altar unto the Lord, and offered burnt offerings and peace offerings. So the Lord was entreated for the land, and the plague was stayed from Israel.
10. Let every thing that hath breath praise the Lord. Praise ye the Lord.
11. For I will make you a name and a praise among all people of the earth, when I turn back your captivity before your eyes, saith the Lord.
12. For God shall bring every work into judgment, with every secret thing, whether it be good, or whether it be evil.
13. To God only wise, be glory through Jesus Christ forever. Amen.
14. For their worm shall not die, neither shall their fire be quenched; and they shall be an abhorring unto all flesh.
15. Give her of the fruit of her hands; and let her own words praise her in the gates.
16. The salutation by the hand of me Paul. Remember my bonds. Grace be with you. Amen.
17. But go thou thy way till the end be; for thou shalt rest, and stand in thy lot at the end of the days.
18. But I trust I shall shortly see thee, and we shall speak face to face. Peace be to thee. Our friends salute thee. Greet the friends by name.
19. With all his reign and his might, and the times that went over him, and over Israel, and over all the kingdoms of the countries.

---

3. Luke
4. 1 Kings
5. Joshua
6. Jeremiah
7. Philippians, Revelation
8. Genesis
9. 2 Samuel
10. Psalms
11. Zephaniah
12. Ecclesiastes
13. Romans
14. Isaiah
15. Proverbs
16. Colossians
17. Daniel
18. 3 John
19. 1 Chronicles

20. And they went out quickly, and fled from the sepulchre; for they trembled and were amazed; neither said they anything to any man, for they were afraid.

21. For the cloud of the Lord was upon the tabernacle by day, and fire was on it by night, in the sight of all the house of Israel, throughout all their journeys.

22. And they took their bones, and buried them under a tree at Jabesh, and fasted seven days.

23. It was round about eighteen thousand measures; and the name of the city from that day shall be, The Lord is there.

24. To the only wise God our Savior, be glory and majesty, dominion and power, both now and ever. Amen.

25. And he shall turn the heart of the fathers to the children, and the heart of the children to their fathers, lest I come and smite the earth with a curse.

26. Greet ye one another with a kiss of charity. Peace be with you all that are in Christ Jesus. Amen.

27. These are the commandments and the judgments, which the Lord commanded by the hand of Moses unto the children of Israel in the plains of Moab by Jordan near Jericho.

28. Make haste, my beloved, and be thou like a roe or to a young hart upon the mountains of spices.

29. For I will cleanse their blood that I have not cleansed; for the Lord dwelleth in Zion.

30. The Lord Jesus Christ be with thy spirit. Grace be with you. Amen.

31. Let him know, that he which converteth the sinner from the error of his way, shall save a soul from death, and shall hide a multitude of sins.

32. The grace of the Lord Jesus Christ, and the love of God, and the communion of the Holy Ghost, be with you all. Amen.

33. Thou wilt perform the truth to Jacob, and the mercy to Abraham, which thou hast sworn unto our fathers from the days of old.

34. And saviours shall come to up on mount Zion to judge the mount of Esau; and the kingdom shall be the Lord's.

35. All these had taken strange wives; and some of them had wives by whom they had children.

---

20. Mark. (This is probably the real ending of Mark. Many Bibles include verses 9-20, the longer ending.)
21. Exodus
22. 1 Samuel
23. Ezekiel
24. Jude
25. Malachi
26. 1 Peter
27. Numbers
28. Song of Solomon
29. Joel
30. 2 Timothy
31. James
32. 2 Corinthians
33. Micah
34. Obadiah
35. Ezra

36. And his allowance was a continual allowance given him of the king, a daily rate for everyday, all the days of his life.
37. And in that day there shall be no more Canaanite in the house of the Lord of hosts.
38. In those days there was no king in Israel; every man did that which was right in his own eyes.
39. But grow in grace, and in the knowledge of our Lord and Saviour Jesus Christ. To him be glory both now and forever. Amen.
40. And Obed begat Jesse, and Jesse begat David.
41. These are the commandments, which the Lord commanded Moses for the children of Israel in Mount Sinai.
42. And there are also many other things which Jesus did, the which, if they should be written every one, I suppose that even the world itself could not contain the books that should be written. Amen.
43. Little children, keep yourselves from idols. Amen.
44. Who is there among you of all his people? The Lord his God be with him, and let him go up.
45. There is no healing of thy bruise; thy wound is grievous; all that hear the bruit of thee shall clap the hands over thee; for upon whom hath not thy wickedness passed continually?
46. Brethren, the grace of our Lord Jesus Christ be with your spirit. Amen.
47. Which some professing have erred concerning the faith. Grace be with thee. Amen.
48. And I will plant them upon their land, and they shall no more be pulled up out of their land which I have given them, saith the Lord thy God.
49. So Job died, being old and full of days.
50. Who is wise, and he shall understand these things? prudent, and he shall know them? for the ways of the Lord are right, and the just shall walk in them; but the transgressors shall fall therein.
51. And in all that mighty hand, and in all the great terror which Moses showed in the sight of all Israel.
52. And should I not spare Nineveh, that great city, wherein are more than sixscore thousand persons that cannot discern between their right hand and their left hand; and also much cattle?

---

36. 2 Kings
37. Zechariah
38. Judges
39. 2 Peter
40. Ruth
41. Leviticus
42. John
43. 1 John
44. 2 Chronicles
45. Nahum
46. Galatians
47. 1 Timothy
48. Amos
49. Job
50. Hosea
51. Deuteronomy
52. Jonah

53. Preaching the kingdom of God, and teaching those things which concern the Lord Jesus Christ, with all confidence, no man forbidding him.
54. The Lord God is my strength, and he will make my feet like hinds' feet, and he will make me to walk upon mine high places.
55. The children of thy elect sister greet thee. Amen.
56. In that day, saith the Lord of hosts, will I take thee, O Zerubbabel, my servant, the son of Shealtiel, saith the Lord, and will make thee as a signet; for I have chosen thee, saith the Lord of hosts.
57. My love be with you all in Christ Jesus. Amen.
58. For Mordecai the Jew was next unto King Ahasuerus, and great among the Jews, and accepted of the multitude of his brethren, seeking the wealth of his people, and speaking peace to all his seed.
59. Grace be with all them that love our Lord Jesus Christ in sincerity. Amen.
60. Teaching them to observe all things whatsoever I have commanded you and, lo, I am with you always, even unto the end of the world. Amen.

✦The Old Testament in the New (II)

Here are more passages from the New Testament, each of them a quotation from the Old Testament. Name the Old Testament book (and, if you're sharp, chapter and verse) where the passage appears.

1. "Thou art my Son, this day have I begotten thee" (Acts 13:33).
2. "Thou shalt not suffer thine Holy One to see corruption" (Acts 13:35).
3. "After this I will return, and will build again the tabernacle of David, which is fallen down; and I will build again the ruins thereof, and I will set it up" (Acts 15:16).
4. "Go unto this people, and say, Hearing ye shall hear, and shall not understand; and seeing ye shall see, and not perceive" (Acts 28:26).

53. Acts
54. Habakkuk
55. 2 John
56. Haggai
57. 1 Corinthians
58. Esther
59. Ephesians
60. Matthew

The Old Testament in the New (II) (Answers)

1. Psalm 2:7
2. Psalm 16:10
3. Amos 9:11
4. Isaiah 6:9

5. "For the name of God is blasphemed among the Gentiles through you, as it is written" (Romans 2:24).
6. "That thou mightest be justified in thy sayings, and mightest overcome when thou art judged" (Romans 3:4).
7. "They are all gone out of the way, they are together become unprofitable; there is none that doeth good, no, not one" (Romans 3:12).
8. "Their throat is an open sepulchre; with their tongues they have used deceit; the poison of asps is under their lips" (Romans 3:13).
9. "Whose mouth is full of cursing and bitterness" (Romans 3:14).
10. "Their feet are swift to shed blood" (Romans 3:15).
11. "For thy sake we are killed all the day long; we are accounted as sheep for the slaughter" (Romans 8:36).
12. "Jacob have I loved, but Esau have I hated" (Romans 9:13).
13. "I will have mercy on whom I will have mercy, and I will have compassion on whom I will have compassion" (Romans 9:15).
14. "Even for this same purpose have I raised thee up, that I might show my power in thee, that my name might be declared throughout all the earth" (Romans 9:17).
15. "Shall the thing formed say to him that formed it, Why hast thou made me thus?" (Romans 9:20).
16. "I will call them my people, which were not my people; and her beloved, which was not beloved" (Romans 9:25).
17. "Though the number of the children be as the sand of the sea, a remnant shall be saved" (Romans 9:27).
18. "Except the Lord of Sabaoth had left us a seed, we had been as Sodom, and been made like Gomorrah" (Romans 9:29).
19. "Behold, I lay in Zion a stumblingstone and rock of offense; and whosoever believeth on him shall not be ashamed" (Romans 9:33).
20. "Whosoever believeth on him shall not be ashamed" (Romans 10:11).
21. "Lord, who hath believed our report?" (Romans 10:16).
22. "I will provoke you to jealousy by them that are no people, and by a foolish nation I will anger you" (Romans 10:19).

5. Isaiah 52:5
6. Psalm 51:4
7. Psalm 14:3
8. Psalm 5:9
9. Psalm 10:17
10. Isaiah 59:7
11. Psalm 44:22
12. Malachi 1:2-3
13. Exodus 33:19
14. Exodus 9:16
15. Isaiah 29:16
16. Hosea 2:23
17. Isaiah 10:22
18. Isaiah 13:19
19. Isaiah 28:16
20. Isaiah 28:16
21. Isaiah 53:1
22. Deuteronomy 32:21

23. "I was found of them that sought me not; I was made manifest unto them that asked not after me" (Romans 10:20).
24. "All day long I have stretched forth my hands unto a disobedient and gainsaying people" (Romans 10:21).
25. "Hath God cast away his people?" (Romans 11:1).
26. "Lord, they have killed thy prophets, and digged down thine altars; and I am left alone, and they seek my life" (Romans 11:3).
27. "I have reserved to myself seven thousand men, who have not bowed the knee to the image of Baal" (Romans 11:4).
28. "God hath given them the spirit of slumber, eyes that they should not see, and ears that they should not hear" (Romans 11:8).
29. "Let their table be made a snare, and a trap, and a stumblingblock, and a recompense unto them. Let their eyes be darkened, that they may not see, and bow down their back alway" (Romans 11:9-10).
30. "There shall come out of Zion the Deliverer, and shall turn away ungodliness from Jacob. For this is my covenant unto them, when I shall take away their sins" (Romans 11:26-27).
31. "For who hath known the mind of the Lord? or who hath been his counselor?" (Romans 11:34).
32. "Or who hath first given to him, and it shall be recompensed unto him again?" (Romans 11:35).
33. "Vengeance is mine; I will repay" (Romans 12:19).
34. "Therefore if thine enemy hunger, feed him; if he thirst, give him drink: for in so doing thou shalt heap coals of fire on his head" (Romans 12:20).
35. "As I live, saith the Lord, every knee shall bow to me, and every tongue shall confess to God" (Romans 14:11).
36. "The reproaches of them that reproached thee fell on me" (Romans 15:3).
37. "For this cause I will confess to thee among the Gentiles, and sing unto thy name" (Romans 15:9).
38. "Rejoice, ye Gentiles, with his people" (Romans 15:10).
39. "Praise the Lord, all ye Gentiles, and laud him, all ye people" (Romans 15:11).

23. Isaiah 65:1
24. Isaiah 65:2
25. Psalm 94:4
26. 1 Kings 19:10, 14
27. 1 Kings 19:18
28. Isaiah 29:10
29. Psalm 69:22-23
30. Isaiah 27:9
31. Isaiah 40:13
32. Job 41:11
33. Deuteronomy 32:35
34. Proverbs 25:21-22
35. Isaiah 45:23
36. Psalm 69:9
37. Psalm 18:50
38. Deuteronomy 32:43
39. Psalm 117:1

40. "There shall be a root of Jesse, and he that shall rise to reign over the Gentiles; in him shall the Gentiles trust" (Romans 15:12).

41. "To whom he was not spoken of, they shall see: and they that have not heard shall understand" (Romans 15:21).

42. "I will destroy the wisdom of the wise, and will bring to nothing the understanding of the prudent" (1 Corinthians 1:19).

43. "Where is the wise? where is the disputer of the world? hath not God made foolish the wisdom of the world?" (1 Corinthians 1:20).

44. "He that glorieth, let him glory in the Lord" (1 Corinthians 1:31).

45. "Eye hath not seen, nor ear heard, neither have entered into the heart of man, the things which God hath prepared for them that love him" (1 Corinthians 2:9).

46. "Who hath known the mind of the Lord, that he may instruct him?" (1 Corinthians 2:16).

47. "He taketh the wise in their own craftiness" (1 Corinthians 3:19).

48. "The Lord knoweth the thoughts of the wise, that they are vain" (1 Corinthians 3:20).

49. "Therefore put away from among yourselves that wicked person" (1 Corinthians 5:13).

50. "Thou shalt not muzzle the mouth of the ox that treadeth out the corn" (1 Corinthians 9:9).

51. "The people sat down to eat and drink, and rose up to play" (1 Corinthians 10:7).

52. "For the earth is the Lord's, and the fulness thereof" (1 Corinthians 10:26).

53. "With men of other tongues and other lips will I speak unto this people; and yet for all that will they not hear me, saith the Lord" (1 Corinthians 14:21).

54. "Let us eat and drink; for tomorrow we die" (1 Corinthians 15:32).

55. "The first man Adam was made a living soul" (1 Corinthians 15:45).

56. "O death, where is thy sting? O grave, where is thy victory?" (1 Corinthians 15:55).

57. "I believed, and therefore have I spoken" (2 Corinthians 4:13).

40. Isaiah 11:10
41. Isaiah 52:15
42. Isaiah 29:14
43. Isaiah 33:18
44. Jeremiah 9:22-23
45. Isaiah 64:4
46. Isaiah 40:13
47. Job 5:13
48. Psalm 94:11
49. Deuteronomy 13:6
50. Deuteronomy 25:4
51. Exodus 32:6
52. Psalm 24:1.
53. Isaiah 28:11-12
54. Isaiah 22:13
55. Genesis 2:7
56. Hosea 13:14
57. Psalm 116:10

58. "I have heard thee in a time accepted, and in the day of salvation have I succoured thee; behold, now is the accepted time" (2 Corinthians 6:2).
59. "I will dwell in them, and walk in them; and I will be their God, and they shall be my people" (2 Corinthians 6:16).
60. "Wherefore come out from among them, and be ye separate, saith the Lord, and touch not the unclean thing" (2 Corinthians 6:17).
61. "I will receive you, and will be a Father unto you, and ye shall be my sons and daughters, saith the Lord Almighty" (2 Corinthians 6:17-18).
62. "He that had gathered much had nothing over; and he that had gathered little had no lack" (2 Corinthians 8:15).
63. "God loveth a cheerful giver" (2 Corinthians 9:7).
64. "He hath dispersed abroad; he hath given to the poor: his righteousness remaineth for ever" (2 Corinthians 9:9).
65. "But he that glorieth, let him glory in the Lord" (2 Corinthians 10:17).
66. "In the mouth of two or three witnesses shall every word be established" (2 Corinthians 13:1).
67. "Abraham believed God, and it was accounted to him for righteousness" (Galatians 3:6).
68. "In thee shall all nations be blessed" (Galatians 3:8).
69. "Cursed is everyone that continueth not in all things which are written in the book of the law to do them" (Galatians 3:10).
70. "The just shall live by faith" (Galatians 3:11).

◆Author, Author

Who, according to tradition, wrote the following books of the Bible?

1. Exodus
2. Revelation
3. Hebrews
4. Esther
5. Proverbs
6. Ruth
7. 1 and 2 Chronicles

58. Isaiah 49:8
59. Leviticus 26:12; Jeremiah 32:38
60. Isaiah 52:11
61. Isaiah 43:6
62. Exodus 43:6
63. Proverbs 22:8
64. Psalm 112:9
65. Jeremiah 9:23
66. Deuteronomy 19:15
67. Genesis 15:6
68. Genesis 12:3
69. Deuteronomy 27:26
70. Habakkuk 2:4

Author, Author (Answers)

1. Moses
2. The apostle John
3. Not known, though often attributed to Paul, Apollos, and many others
4. Attributed to Ezra, Mordecai, and others
5. Solomon, although the book itself names other contributors
6. Samuel
7. Ezra

8. Lamentations
9. Song of Songs
10. Numbers
11. Nehemiah
12. Judges
13. Psalms
14. Ecclesiastes
15. Ezra
16. Deuteronomy
17. Job
18. 1 and 2 Kings
19. Leviticus
20. Joshua
21. Acts
22. Jude
23. Genesis
24. 1 and 2 Samuel
25. James

✦Curious Quotations

For each of the strange quotations listed, name the book of the Bible where it is found. (If you're really good, name the chapter and verse.)

1. At Parbar westward, four at the causeway, and two at Parbar.
2. Therefore will I discover thy skirts upon thy face.
3. The mountains skipped like rams, and the little hills like lambs.
4. All faces shall gather blackness.
5. The ships of Tarshish did sing of thee in thy market.
6. The herds of cattle are perplexed.
7. The voice of the turtle is heard in our land.
8. And they made two ouches of gold.
9. A bell and a pomegranate, a bell and a pomegranate, round about the hem of the robe to minister in.
10. I have put off my coat; how shall I put it on?
11. Dead flies cause the ointment of the apothecary to send forth a stinking savor.

---

8. Jeremiah
9. Solomon
10. Moses
11. Nehemiah
12. Samuel
13. David, Asaph, and many others
14. Solomon
15. Ezra
16. Moses
17. Moses
18. Jeremiah
19. Moses
20. Joshua
21. Luke
22. Jude, the brother of Jesus
23. Moses
24. Samuel and, possibly, the prophet Nathan
25. James, the brother of Jesus

Curious Quotations (Answers)

1. 1 Chronicles (26:18)
2. Jeremiah (13:26)
3. Psalms (114:4)
4. Joel (2:6)
5. Ezekiel (27:25)
6. Joel (1:18)
7. Song of Solomon (2:12)
8. Exodus (39:16)
9. Exodus (39:26)
10. Song of Solomon (5:3)
11. Ecclesiastes (10:1)

12. Every man shall kiss his lips that giveth a right answer.
13. And kings shall be thy nursing fathers.
14. This thy stature is like to a palm tree, and thy breasts to clusters of grapes.
15. Destruction and death say, We have heard the fame thereof with our ears.
16. Associate yourselves, O ye people, and ye shall be broken in pieces.
17. And the rest of the trees of his forest shall be few, that a child may write them.
18. And on the eighth day she shall take unto her two turtles.
19. Thou shalt not seethe a kid in his mother's milk.
20. Thy lips, O my spouse, drop as the honeycomb; honey and milk are under thy tongue; and the smell of thy garments is like the smell of Lebanon.
21. And it came to pass in the first month in the second year, on the first day of the month, that the tabernacle was reared up.
22. Behold, he formed grasshoppers in the beginning of the shooting up.
23. So two or three cities wandered unto one city to drink water.
24. Let the floods clap their hands; let the hills be joyful together.
25. Every head was made bald, and every shoulder was peeled.
26. Her king is cut off as the foam upon the water.
27. And the sea coast shall be dwellings and cottages for shepherds, and folds for flocks.
28. And it waxed great, even to the host of heaven.
29. Then the king's countenance was changed, and his thoughts troubled him, so that the joints of his loins were loosed, and his knees smote one against the other.
30. He maketh them to skip like a calf; Lebanon and Sirion like a young unicorn.
31. And the wild asses did stand in the high places, they snuffed up the wind like dragons.
32. I have compared thee, O my love, to a company of horses in Pharaoh's chariots.
33. Thy bow was made quite naked.
34. The Lord will smite thee with the botch of Egypt, and with the emerods, and with the scab, and with the itch.

12. Proverbs (24:26)
13. Isaiah (49:23)
14. Song of Solomon (7:7)
15. Job (28:22)
16. Isaiah (8:9)
17. Isaiah (10:19)
18. Leviticus (15:29)
19. Deuteronomy (14:21)
20. Song of Solomon (4:11)
21. Exodus (40:17)
22. Amos (7:1)
23. Amos (4:8)
24. Psalms (98:8)
25. Ezekiel (29:18)
26. Hosea (10:7)
27. Zephaniah (2:6)
28. Daniel (8:10)
29. Daniel (5:6)
30. Psalms (29:6)
31. Jeremiah (14:6)
32. Song of Solomon (1:9)
33. Habakkuk (3:9)
34. Deuteronomy (28:27)

35. Cease ye from man, whose breath is in his nostrils.
36. Behold, I will corrupt your seed, and spread dung upon your faces, even the dung of your solemn feasts.
37. They are all adulterers, as an oven heated by the baker.
38. Feed thy people with thy rod.
39. And the man whose hair is fallen off his head, he is bald; yet is he clean.
40. Ye shall not eat one day, nor two days, nor five days, neither ten days, nor twenty days, but even a whole month, until it come out at your nostrils.
41. I am gone like the shadow when it declineth; I am tossed up and down as the locust.
42. And the unicorns shall come down with them, and the bullocks with the bulls; and their land shall be soaked with blood, and their dust made fat with fatness.
43. Thy teeth are like a flock of sheep that are even shorn, which came up from the washing.
44. The words of a man's mouth are as deep waters.
45. Lift up your heads, O ye gates.
46. Thou shalt suck the breast of kings.
47. Will I eat the flesh of bulls, or drink the blood of goats?
48. When she saw Isaac, she lighted off her camel.
49. Thy neck is like the tower of David builded for an armory, whereon there hang a thousand bucklers.
50. Thou shalt not respect persons, neither take a gift.
51. So and more also do God unto the enemies of David, if I leave of all that pertain to him by the morning light any that pisseth against the wall. (Note: The questionable word here was apparently not considered an obscenity at the time of the King James Bible. It occurs eight times in the KJV.)
52. Moab is my washpot; over Edom will I cast out my shoe.
53. The watchman said, The morning cometh, and also the night; if ye will inquire, inquire ye; return, come.
54. And he will take your menservants, and your maidservants, and your goodliest young men, and your asses, and put them to his work.
55. Their feet are swift to shed blood.
56. Now therefore go, and I will be with thy mouth.

35. Isaiah (2:22)
36. Malachi (2:3)
37. Hosea (7:4)
38. Micah (7:14)
39. Leviticus (13:40)
40. Numbers (11:19-20)
41. Psalms (109:23)
42. Isaiah (34:7)
43. Song of Solomon (4:2)
44. Proverbs (18:4)
45. Psalms (24:7)
46. Isaiah (60:16)
47. Psalms (50:13)
48. Genesis (24:64)
49. Song of Solomon (4:4)
50. Deuteronomy (16:19)
51. 1 Samuel (25:22)
52. Psalms (60:8)
53. Isaiah (21:12)
54. 1 Samuel (8:16)
55. Romans (3:15)
56. Exodus (4:12)

✦Prophecies of the Messiah

Many passages in the Old Testament are prophecies which were fulfilled by events in Jesus' life. For each event listed here, name the Old Testament book that contains the prophecy of the event.

1. Casting lots for Jesus robe.
2. Jesus' crucifixion with two thieves.
3. The thirty pieces of silver.
4. The virgin birth.
5. Jesus' birth in Bethlehem.
6. Jesus' resurrection.
7. The piercing of Jesus' side with a spear.
8. Not breaking the bones of the crucified Jesus.
9. Betrayal by a close companion.
10. Jesus' entry into Jerusalem on a donkey.
11. Giving vinegar to the crucified Jesus.
12. Jesus, Mary, and Joseph leaving Egypt and returning to Galilee.
13. Speaking in parables.

✦Between the Testaments

Name the books described below. Some are part of the Apocrypha and are regarded as Scripture by Catholics and some others. Some are considered Pseudepigrapha and are not accepted as genuine Scripture by either Jews or Christians. Some are translations or commentaries made (or begun) after the close of the Old Testament.

1. A book of wise sayings attributed to a king of Israel.
2. A romantic story of a pious Jew whose son is aided by the angel Raphael.
3. A tale of a brave Jewish woman who saves her city from the army of Nebuchadnezzar by murdering a Babylonian captain.
4. A book of wisdom whose author is identified in the text as Sirach of Jerusalem.
5. A historical work that recounts the story of the Jewish revolt against the evil ruler Antiochus Epiphanes and his successors.

Prophecies of the Messiah (Answers)

1. Psalm 22:18: "They part my garments among them, and cast lots upon my vesture."
2. Isaiah 53:12: "He was numbered with the transgressors."
3. Zechariah 11:12: "So they weighed for my price thirty pieces of silver."
4. Isaiah 7:14: "Behold, a virgin shall conceive, and bear a son."
5. Micah 5:2: "But thou Bethlehem Ephratah, though thou be little among the thousands of Judah, yet out of thee shall he come forth unto me that is to be ruler in Israel; whose goings forth have been from of old, from everlasting."
6. Psalm 16:10: "For thou wilt not leave my soul in hell; neither wilt thou suffer thine Holy One to see corruption."
7. Zechariah 12:10: "They shall look upon me whom they have pierced."
8. Psalm 34:20: "He keepeth all his bones; not one of them is broken."
9. Psalm 41:9: "Yea, mine own familiar friend, in whom I trusted, which did eat of my bread, hath lifted up his heel against me."
10. Zechariah 9:9: "Behold, tny king cometh unto thee . . . lowly, and riding upon an ass, and upon a colt the foal of an ass."
11. Psalm 69:21: "In my thirst they gave me vinegar to drink."
12. Hosea 11:1: "I . . . called my son out of Egypt."
13. Psalm 78:2: "I will open my mouth in a parable."

Between the Testaments (Answers)

1. Wisdom of Solomon (Apocrypha)
2. Tobit (Apocrypha)
3. Judith (Apocrypha)
4. Ecclesiasticus (Apocrypha)
5. 1 Maccabees (Apocrypha)

6. A book of prayers and confessions, supposedly written by the friend of an Old Testament prophet.
7. A tale of a virtuous woman accused of adultery and proved innocent by Daniel.
8. An eloquent prayer reputed to be the work of a repentant king of Judah.
9. A tale of Babylonian idol worship and some conniving priests.
10. An historical work that covers some of the same history chronicled in Ezra, Nehemiah, and 2 Chronicles.
11. This book consists of alleged predictions of Moses, given to Joshua just before Moses' death.
12. These are additions, not found in the Hebrew Bible, to an Old Testament book about the Persian period.
13. This addition to the Book of Daniel contains an eloquent prayer, a miraculous deliverance, and a hymn of praise.
14. This work is a shortened form of a five-volume historical work by Jason of Cyrene. It contains letters to the Jews in Egypt.
15. This apocalyptic work contains bizarre visions, images of the Messiah, and references to the Roman Empire.
16. This book about a famous Judean prophet tells of his martyrdom under wicked King Manasseh.
17. These eighteen poems about the coming Messiah are ascribed to a famous Hebrew poet.
18. This collection of predictions speaks about the downfall of empires and the messianic age.
19. This book of revelations purports to have been written by Enoch and Noah.
20. This book purports to be the dying speeches of Jacob's twelve sons.
21. Written by a Pharisee, this book extols the law and the Hebrew patriarchs and urges Jews not to be influenced by Greek culture.
22. These are loose translations of the Hebrew Scriptures into the Aramaic language, made after Aramaic, not Hebrew, was the common language of Palestine.
23. This collection of laws based on the laws of Moses was not completed until A.D. 500. It consists of the Mishnah and the Gemara and is still widely studied by Jewish scholars today.

6. Baruch (Apocrypha)
7. Susanna (Apocrypha)
8. The Prayer of Manasseh (Apocrypha)
9. Bel and the Dragon (Apocrypha)
10. 1 Esdras (Apocrypha)
11. The Assumption of Moses (Pseudepigrapha)
12. Additions to Esther (Apocrypha)
13. Song of the Three Children (Apocrypha)
14. 2 Maccabees (Apocrypha)
15. 2 Esdras (Apocrypha)
16. Ascension of Isaiah (Pseudepigrapha)
17. Psalms of Solomon (Pseudepigrapha)
18. Sybilline Oracles (Pseudepigrapha)
19. Book of Enoch (Pseudepigrapha)
20. Testament of the Twelve Patriarchs (Pseudepigrapha)
21. Book of Jubilees (Pseudepigrapha)
22. Targums
23. The Talmud

✦Who Said That? (III)

1. The waters compassed me about, even to the soul; the depth closed me round about, the weeds were wrapped about my head.
2. I know that my redeemer liveth, and that he shall stand at the latter day upon the earth.
3. What meaneth then this bleating of the sheep in mine ears, and the lowing of the oxen which I hear?
4. Surely the Lord is in this place.
5. For in him we live, and move, and have our being.
6. Lord Jesus, receive my spirit.
7. While the child was yet alive, I fasted and wept; for I said, Who can tell whether God will be gracious to me, that the child may live?
8. Where thou diest, will I die, and there will I be buried; the Lord do so to me, and more also, if ought but death part thee and me.
9. Within three days ye shall pass over this Jordan, to go in to possess the land, which the Lord your God giveth you to possess it.
10. This is none other but the house of God, and this is the gate of heaven.
11. It was not you that sent me hither, but God; and he hath made me a father to Pharaoh.
12. Be sure your sin will find you out.
13. Shall not the judge of all the earth do right?
14. God forbid that I should sin against the Lord in ceasing to pray for you.
15. Be thou strong, therefore, and show thyself a man; and keep the charge of the Lord thy God, to walk in his ways.
16. Hear, O Israel: The Lord our God is one Lord.
17. Lord, increase our faith.
18. O earth, earth, earth, hear the word of the Lord.
19. If a man die, shall he live again?
20. Lord, it is nothing with thee to help, whether with many, or with them that have no power; help us, O Lord our God.
21. All things come of thee, and of thine own have we given thee.

Who Said That? (III) (Answers)

1. Jonah (2:5)
2. Job (19:25)
3. Samuel (1 Samuel 15:14)
4. Jacob (Genesis 28:16)
5. Paul (Acts 17:28)
6. Stephen (Acts 7:59)
7. David (2 Samuel 12:22)
8. Ruth (1:17)
9. Joshua (1:11)
10. Jacob (Genesis 28:17)
11. Joseph (Genesis 45:8)
12. Moses (Numbers 32:23)
13. Abraham (Genesis 18:15)
14. Samuel (1 Samuel 12:23)
15. David (1 Kings 2:2-3)
16. Moses (Deuteronomy 6:4)
17. The disciples (Luke 17:5)
18. Jeremiah (22:29)
19. Job (14:14)
20. Asa (2 Chronicles 14:11)
21. David (1 Chronicles 29:14)

22. There hath not failed one word of all his good promise, which he promised by the hand of Moses his servant.
23. For the Lord thy God is a consuming fire, even a jealous God.
24. But as for you, ye thought evil against me, but God meant it unto good, to bring to pass, as it is this day, to save much people alive.
25. We are journeying unto the place of which the Lord said, I will give it you. Come thou with us, and we will do thee good; for the Lord hath spoken good concerning Israel.
26. O our God, wilt thou not judge them? For we have no might against this great company that cometh against us; neither know we what to do; but our eyes are upon thee.
27. Though he slay me, yet will I trust in him; but I will maintain mine own ways before him.
28. Is there no balm in Gilead? Is there no physician there?
29. Woe to them that are at ease in Zion.
30. For the earth shall be filled with the knowledge of the glory of the Lord, as the waters cover the sea.
31. And now brethren, I commend you to God, and to the word of his grace, which is able to build you up, among all them which are sanctified.
32. Not by might, nor by power, but by my spirit, saith the Lord of hosts.
33. And it shall come to pass afterward, that I will pour out my spirit upon all flesh.
34. He hath showed thee, O man, what is good; and what doth the Lord require of thee, but to do justly, and to love mercy, and to walk humbly with thy God?
35. Believe in the Lord your God, so shall ye be established; believe his prophets, so shall ye prosper.
36. For the Lord searcheth all hearts, and understandeth all the imaginations of the thoughts; if thou seek him, he will be found of thee.
37. The grass withereth, the flower fadeth, but the word of our God shall stand forever.
38. Behold, I will send you Elijah the prophet before the coming of the great and dreadful day of the Lord.
39. This is the stone which was set at nought of you builders, which is become the head of the corner.

22. Solomon (1 Kings 8:56)
23. Moses (Deuteronomy 4:24)
24. Joseph (Genesis 50:20)
25. Moses (Numbers 10:29)
26. Jehoshaphat (2 Chronicles 20:12)
27. Job (13:15)
28. Jeremiah (8:22)
29. Amos (6:1)
30. Habakkuk (2:14)
31. Paul (Acts 20:32)
32. Zechariah (4:6)
33. Joel (2:28)
34. Micah (6:8)
35. Jehoshaphat (2 Chronicles 20:20)
36. David (1 Chronicles 28:9)
37. Isaiah (40:8)
38. Malachi (4:5)
39. Peter (Acts 4:11)

40. Let judgment run down as waters, and righteousness as a mighty stream.
41. Seek good, and not evil, that ye may live; and so the Lord, the God of hosts, shall be with you.
42. Daughter, be of good comfort; thy faith hath made thee whole.
43. Am I not a Benjamite, of the smallest of the tribes of Israel?
44. But, behold, they will not believe me, nor hearken unto my voice; for they will say, The Lord hath not appeared unto thee.
45. Come near now, and kiss me, my son.
46. What is this dream that thou hast dreamed? Shall I and thy mother and thy brethren indeed come to bow down ourselves to thee to the earth?
47. I did see all Israel scattered upon the mountains, as sheep that have no shepherd; and the Lord said, These have no master.
48. God forbid that I should justify you; till I die I will not remove mine integrity from me.
49. We will go with our young and with our old, with our sons and with our daughters, with our flocks and with our herds will we go; for we must hold a feast unto the Lord.
50. If thou be the king of the Jews, save thyself.
51. Behold, I will send you Elijah the prophet before the coming of the great and dreadful day of the Lord.
52. Ho, everyone that thirsteth, come ye to the waters, and he that hath no money; come ye, buy, and eat.
53. Yet once, it is a little while, and I will shake the heavens, and the earth, and the sea, and the dry land.
54. Whether it be right in the sight of God to hearken unto you more than unto God, judge ye.
55. How beautiful upon the mountains are the feet of him that bringeth good tidings, that publisheth peace.
56. Who am I? And what is my life, or my father's family in Israel, that I should be son-in-law to the king?
57. Give me children, or else I die.
58. What will ye then that I shall do unto him whom ye call the King of the Jews?
59. Behold my servant whom I uphold; my elect, in whom my soul delighteth; I have put my spirit upon him.

40. Amos (5:24)
41. Amos (5:14)
42. Jesus (Matthew 9:22)
43. Saul (1 Samuel 9:21)
44. Moses (Exodus 4:1)
45. Isaac (Genesis 27:26)
46. Jacob (Genesis 37:10)
47. Micaiah (2 Chronicles 18:16)
48. Job (27:5)
49. Moses (Exodus 10:9)
50. The soldiers at the crucifixion (Luke 23:37)
51. Malachi (4:5)
52. Isaiah (55:1)
53. Haggai (2:6)
54. Peter and John (Acts 4:19)
55. Isaiah (52:7)
56. David (1 Samuel 18:18)
57. Rachel (Genesis 30:1)
58. Pilate (Mark 15:12)
59. Isaiah (42:1)

60. Come and let us return unto the Lord; for he hath torn, and he will heal us; he hath smitten, and he will bind us up.

◆Scripture on Scripture

1. According to Paul, who takes away the "veil" over the Old Testament?
2. What group of Christians examined the Scriptures every day to see if Paul was telling the truth?
3. To what young pastor did Paul address his famous words on the divine inspiration of all Scripture?
4. What apostle claimed that the prophets, in writing of the coming Christ, were writing for later generations?
5. Who told the Jews that the Scriptures had testified about him?
6. Where was Jesus when he taught two people how the prophets had predicted his death?
7. To what church did Paul say the Old Testament was written as a set of examples and warnings for the church?
8. In the parable of Lazarus and the rich man, what does Abraham say to the rich man who wants to keep his relatives out of hell?
9. To whom does the writer of Hebrews attribute Psalm 95?
10. What apostle claimed that no Scripture had come about through the prophet's own efforts, but by God's will?
11. In what epistle does Paul promote the public reading of Scripture?
12. To what foreign official did Philip teach the predictions of Jesus contained in the Old Testament?
13. In what gospel does Jesus say that the Scripture cannot be broken?
14. To whom did Peter and John attribute the words of David (Psalm 2)?
15. To whom did Jesus say "Ye do err, not knowing the Scriptures" after they had posed a ridiculous riddle to him?

60. Hosea (6:1)

Scripture on Scripture (Answers)

1. Christ (2 Corinthians 3:14)
2. The Christians at Berea (Acts 17:11)
3. Timothy (2 Timothy 3:15-17)
4. Peter (1 Peter 1:10-12)
5. Jesus (John 5:39-40)
6. The road to Emmaus (Luke 24:25-27)
7. Corinth (1 Corinthians 10:11)
8. He tells him that the people have Moses and the prophets (Luke 16:27-29)
9. The Holy Spirit (Hebrews 3:7)
10. Peter (2 Peter 1:20)
11. 1 Timothy (4:13)
12. The Ethiopian eunuch (Acts 8:32-35)
13. John (10:35)
14. The Holy Spirit (Acts 4:25)
15. The Sadducees (Matthew 22:29)

◆Take a Letter

1. What lost letter of Paul is mentioned in the Letter to the Colossians?
2. Who received a letter from David, telling him to put Uriah in the heat of battle?
3. Who wrote to the churches concerning the Jerusalem council's decision on the issue of circumcision?
4. Who, using John as a scribe, wrote to the seven churches in Asia?
5. Who had enemies that wrote smear letters about him to the Persian king?
6. What mighty king wrote a letter to Hezekiah concerning surrender?
7. Who wrote to the people of Samaria regarding the fate of Ahab's seventy sons?
8. Who wrote a letter recommending Apollos to the Corinthian church?
9. Who wrote a letter to Felix concerning the apostle Paul?
10. Who wrote a letter granting permission to continue construction on the second temple?
11. What king received a letter from Elijah predicting judgment on his sinful reign?
12. What queen wrote to the leaders of Jezreel concerning Naboth?
13. Who asked the high priest for letters of introduction to the synagogues in Damascus?
14. Who sent letters of invitation to the tribes of Ephraim and Manasseh, asking them to join in a Passover celebration?
15. Who sent a letter giving Judah's enemies permission to stop the Jews' work on the temple?
16. What feast did Mordecai prescribe in his letters to the Jews in Persia?
17. What leper carried a letter from the king of Syria to the king of Israel?
18. Who sent a threatening letter designed to discourage Nehemiah from his plans to rebuild Jerusalem?
19. Who, with Paul, penned the First Letter to the Corinthians?
20. Who wrote to Philemon concerning his runaway slave, Onesimus?

Take a Letter (Answers)

1. The Letter to the Laodiceans (Colossians 4:16)
2. Joab (2 Samuel 11:4, 15)
3. James (Acts 15:23)
4. Jesus (Revelation 1-3)
5. Zerubbabel (Ezra 4:6-16)
6. Sennacherib (2 Kings 19:14)
7. Jehu (2 Kings 10:1-2)
8. The Ephesian church (Acts 18:27)
9. Claudius Lysias (Acts 23:25)
10. King Darius (Ezra 6:6-12)
11. Jehoram (2 Chronicles 21:12)
12. Jezebel (1 Kings 21:8)
13. Paul (Acts 9:2)
14. Hezekiah (2 Chronicles 30:1-3)
15. King Artaxerxes (Ezra 4:17-22)
16. Purim (Esther 9:20-21)
17. Naaman (2 Kings 5:5-6)
18. Sanballat (Nehemiah 6:5-7)
19. Sosthenes (1 Corinthians 1:1)
20. Paul (Philemon)

✦The Old Testament in the New (III)

Here are still more passages from the New Testament, each of them a quotation from the Old Testament. Name the Old Testament book (and, if you're sharp, chapter and verse) where the passage appears.

1. "Cursed is every one that hangeth on a tree" (Galatians 3:13)
2. "The man that doeth them shall live in them" (Galatians 3:12)
3. "Rejoice, thou barren that bearest not; break forth and cry, thou that travailest not: for the desolate hath many more children than she which hath a husband" (Galatians 4:27)
4. "Cast out the bondwoman and her son: for the son of the bondwoman shall not be heir with the son of the free woman" (Galatians 4:30)
5. "And [he] hath put all things under his feet" (Ephesians 1:22)
6. "And [he] came and preached peace to you which were afar off, and to them that were nigh" (Ephesians 2:17)
7. "When he ascended up on high, he led captivity captive, and gave gifts unto men" (Ephesians 4:8)
8. "Speak every man truth with his neighbor" (Ephesians 4:25)
9. "Be ye angry, and sin not" (Ephesians 4:26)
10. "For this cause shall a man leave his father and mother, and shall be joined unto his wife, and they two shall be one flesh" (Ephesians 5:31)
11. "Honor thy father and mother: which is the first commandment with promise; that it may be well with thee, and thou mayest live long on the earth" (Ephesians 6:2-3)
12. "The Lord knoweth them that are his" (2 Timothy 2:19)
13. "Thou art my Son, this day have I begotten thee" (Hebrews 1:5)
14. "I will be to him a Father, and he shall be to me a Son?" (Hebrews 1:5)
15. "Let all the angels of God worship him" (Hebrews 1:6)
16. "Who maketh his angels spirits, and his ministers a flame of fire" (Hebrews 1:7)

The Old Testament in the New (III) (Answers)

1. Deuteronomy 21:23
2. Leviticus 18:5
3. Isaiah 54:1
4. Genesis 21:10
5. Psalm 8:6
6. Isaiah 57:19
7. Psalm 68:18
8. Zechariah 8:16
9. Psalm 4:4
10. Genesis 2:24
11. Deuteronomy 5:16
12. Numbers 16:15
13. Psalm 2:7
14. 2 Samuel 7:14
15. Deuteronomy 32:43
16. Psalm 104:4

17. "Thy throne, O God, is for ever and ever: a sceptre of righteousness is the sceptre of thy kingdom. Thou hast loved righteousness, and hated iniquity; therefore God, even thy God, hath anointed thee with the oil of gladness above thy fellows" (Hebrews 1:8-9)
18. "Thou, Lord, in the beginning hast laid the foundation of the earth; and the heavens are the works of thine hands" (Hebrews 1:10)
19. "They shall perish, but thou remainest; and they all shall wax old as doth a garment" (Hebrews 1:11)
20. "But thou art the same, and thy years shall not fail" (Hebrews 1:12)
21. "What is man, that thou art mindful of him? or the son of man, that thou visitest him?" (Hebrews 2:6)
22. "Thou hast put all things in subjection under his feet" (Hebrews 2:8)
23. "I will declare thy name unto my brethren, in the midst of the church will I sing praise unto thee" (Hebrews 2:12)
24. "I will put my trust in him" (Hebrews 2:13)
25. "Behold I and the children which God hath given me" (Hebrews 2:13)
26. "Today if ye will hear his voice, harden not your hearts, as in the provocation, in the day of temptation in the wilderness" (Hebrews 3:7-8)
27. "Wherefore I was grieved with that generation, and said, They do always err in their heart; and they have not known my ways" (Hebrews 3:10)
28. "And God did rest the seventh day from all his works" (Hebrews 4:4)
29. "Thou art a priest forever after the order of Melkizedek" (Hebrews 5:6)
30. "Surely blessing I will bless thee, and multiplying I will multiply thee" (Hebrews 6:14)
31. "I will put my laws into their mind, and write them in their hearts" (Hebrews 8:10)
32. "And they shall not teach every man his neighbour, and every man his brother, saying, Know the Lord: for all shall know me" (Hebrews 8:11)
33. "This is the blood of the testament which God hath enjoined unto you" (Hebrews 9:20)

17. Psalm 45:6-7
18. Psalm 102:25
19. Psalm 102:26
20. Psalm 102:27
21. Psalm 8:4
22. Psalm 8:6
23. Psalm 22:22
24. Isaiah 8:17
25. Isaiah 8:18
26. Psalm 95:7-8
27. Psalm 95:10
28. Genesis 2:2
29. Psalm 110:4
30. Genesis 22:17
31. Jeremiah 31:33
32. Jeremiah 31:34
33. Exodus 24:8

34. "Sacrifice and offering thou wouldest not, but a body hast thou prepared for me: In burnt offerings and sacrifices for sin thou hast had no pleasure" (Hebrews 10:5-6)

35. "Then said he, Lo, I come to do thy will, O God" (Hebrews 10:9)

36. "Vengeance belongeth unto me, I will recompense, saith the Lord" (Hebrews 10:30)

37. "The Lord shall judge his people" (Hebrews 10:30)

38. "In Isaac shall thy seed be called" (Hebrews 11:18)

39. "My son, despise not thou the chastening of the Lord, nor faint when thou art rebuked of him; for whom the Lord loveth he chasteneth" (Hebrews 12:5-6)

40. "Wherefore lift up the hands which hang down, and the feeble knees" (Hebrews 12:12)

41. "Make straight paths for your feet" (Hebrews 12:13)

42. "Yet once more I shake not the earth only, but also heaven" (Hebrews 12:26)

43. "I will never leave thee, nor forsake thee" (Hebrews 13:5)

44. "The Lord is my helper, and I will not fear what man shall do unto me" (Hebrews 13:6)

45. "Abraham believed God, and it was imputed unto him for righteousness" (James 2:23)

46. "God resisteth the proud, but giveth grace unto the humble" (James 4:6)

47. "Be ye holy; for I am holy" (1 Peter 1:16)

48. "For all flesh is grass, and all the glory of man as the flower of grass. The grass withereth, and the flower thereof falleth away: but the word of the Lord endureth forever" (1 Peter 1:24-25)

49. "Behold, I lay in Zion a chief corner stone, elect, precious" (1 Peter 2:6)

50. "A stone of stumbling, and a rock of offense" (1 Peter 2:8)

51. "Who did no sin, neither was any guile found in his mouth" (1 Peter 2:22)

52. "For he that will love life, and see good days, let him refrain his tongue from evil, and his lips that they speak no guile" (1 Peter 3:10)

53. "Let him eschew evil, and do good" (1 Peter 3:11)

34. Psalm 40:6
35. Psalm 40:7-8
36. Deuteronomy 32:35
37. Deuteronomy 32:36
38. Genesis 21:12
39. Proverbs 3:11-12
40. Isaiah 35:3
41. Proverbs 4:26
42. Haggai 2:6
43. Deuteronomy 31:6
44. Psalm 118:6
45. Genesis 15:16
46. Proverbs 3:34
47. Leviticus 19:2
48. Isaiah 40:6-8
49. Isaiah 28:16
50. Isaiah 8:14
51. Isaiah 53:9
52. Psalm 34:12-13
53. Psalm 34:14

54. "The eyes of the Lord are over the righteous, and his ears are open unto their prayers: but the face of the Lord is against them that do evil" (1 Peter 3:12)
55. "Be not afraid of their terror, neither be troubled" (1 Peter 3:14)
56. "If the righteous scarcely be saved, where shall the ungodly and the sinner appear?" (1 Peter 4:18)
57. "The dog is turned to his own vomit again" (2 Peter 2:22)
58. "One day is with the Lord as a thousand years, and a thousand years as one day" (2 Peter 3:8)
59. "And he shall rule them with a rod of iron; as the vessels of a potter shall they be broken to shivers" (Revelation 2:27)
60. "And let him that is athirst come" (Revelation 22:17)

◆Differences of Opinion

(Many readers are puzzled by what seem to be discrepancies in the biblical narratives. Most of these differences can be easily explained by a close reading of the text. Others may be due to errors that occurred in centuries of copying manuscripts. None reflect on the inspiration of the Scriptures. I include these questions here, not to cast doubt on the Bible, but merely to test the reader's knowledge of some of these so-called discrepancies.)

1. According to Genesis 25:1, Abraham's second wife was Keturah. According to 1 Chronicles 1:32, what was Keturah?
2. In Exodus 33:20, God tells Moses that no man can see God's face. According to Exodus 33:11, what man saw God face to face?
3. The Levites entered the service of the sanctuary at age thirty—according to Numbers 4:3. At what age, according to Numbers 8:24, did they enter the service?
4. The mission of the twelve Israelite spies started from Paran—according to Numbers 13:3. In Numbers 20:1, where does the mission start?

54. Psalm 34:15-16
55. Isaiah 8:12-13
56. Proverbs 11:31
57. Proverbs 26:11
58. Psalm 90:4
59. Psalm 2:9
60. Isaiah 55:1

Differences of Opinion (Answers)

1. His concubine
2. Moses
3. Twenty-five
4. Kadesh Barnea

5. According to Deuteronomy 10:6, Aaron died at Moserah. Where, according to Numbers 20:28, did he die?

6. Deuteronomy 15:4 says, "There shall be no poor among you." What does Deuteronomy 15:11 say?

7. According to 1 Samuel 16:10-11, David had eight brothers. How many in 1 Chronicles 2:13-15 did he have?

8. In 1 Samuel 16:19-21, David comes to know Saul by being employed as his harpist. In 1 Samuel 17, how does David come to know Saul?

9. In 1 Samuel 17, David is the slayer of Goliath. According to 2 Samuel 21:19, who killed the giant? (For this question, check a modern translation, not the King James Version.)

10. In 1 Samuel 31:3-4, Saul takes his own life after being wounded. In 2 Samuel 1, who claims he actually killed Saul?

11. Absalom had, according to 2 Samuel 14:27, three sons. How many did he have, according to 2 Samuel 18:18?

12. The Lord moved David to number the people of Israel, according to 2 Samuel 24:1. Who, in the story in 1 Chronicles 21, moved David to do this?

13. According to 2 Kings 24:8, King Jehoiachin was eighteen years old when he began to reign. How old was he in the account in 2 Chronicles 36:9?

14. Samuel was an Ephraimite, according to 1 Samuel 1. What tribe was he from in the account in 1 Chronicles 6?

15. According to 2 Chronicles 33:13-16, evil King Manasseh repented of his sins after being held captive in Babylon. What does the parallel account in 2 Kings 21 say about this repentance?

16. In Matthew's genealogy of the Messiah, Jesus is descended from David's son Solomon. What son of David in Luke's account is Jesus' ancestor?

17. In Luke's account of the temptation of Jesus, the last temptation is to jump from the pinnacle of the temple. What is the last temptation in Matthew's version?

18. According to Matthew 8:5-13, a centurion asks that his servant be healed. In Luke 7:2-11, who does the asking?

5. Mount Hor
6. "The poor shall never cease out of the land."
7. Seven
8. Through the killing of Goliath
9. Elhanan
10. Saul's Amalekite bodyguard
11. None
12. Satan
13. Eight
14. Levi
15. Nothing
16. Nathan
17. The temptation to rule the world
18. The servant

19. In Matthew 8, the maniac lives in Gadara. In Luke 8 and Mark 5, where does he live? (For this question, check a modern translation, not the King James Version.)
20. Matthew 20:20 states that the mother of James and John requested that her sons be appointed to high office in the coming kingdom. In Mark 10:35, who made the request?
21. In Matthew 26:34, Jesus predicts that Peter will betray him before the rooster crows once. In Mark 14:30, how many times is the rooster supposed to crow?
22. According to Matthew 27:3-10, Judas hanged himself. How, according to Acts 1:18, did he kill himself?
23. In John 19:19, we are told that the inscription of the cross read, "Jesus of Nazareth, the King of the Jews." According to Matthew 27:37, what was the inscription?
24. According to John's account of the post-Resurrection appearances, what two disciples ran to Jesus' tomb?
25. In Mark 2:26, Jesus says that Abiathar was priest during David's reign. Who, according to 1 Samuel 21, was priest at that time?
26. Matthew 5:3 has Jesus saying, "Blessed are the poor in spirit." What does he say in Luke 6:20?
27. James 1:13 says God does not tempt men. But Genesis 22:1 says God tempted a certain man. Who?
28. Solomon had 40,000 horses, according to 1 Kings 4:26. How many did he have according to 2 Chronicles 9:25?
29. Matthew 27:6-8 says the priests bought the potter's field, but Acts 1:18-19 says someone else bought it. Who?
30. Matthew 27:9-10 attributes the prophecy about the potter's field to Jeremiah. Where is the prophecy found?
31. Mark 15:26 says the inscription on Jesus' cross read "The King of the Jews." What is it in Luke's account (23:38)?
32. Matthew's genealogy of Jesus says that Joseph's father was Jacob (1:16). According to Luke 3:23, who was it?
33. In what epistle does Paul say "Bear ye one another's burdens" and "Every man shall bear his own burden."
34. What book says, in the same chapter, "Answer not a fool according to his folly" and "Answer a fool according to his folly."
35. David's wife Michal had, according to 2 Samuel 6:23, no children. But according to 2 Samuel 21:8 she had children. How many?

19. Gerasa
20. James and John
21. Twice
22. He fell headlong and burst apart.
23. "This is Jesus, the King of the Jews."
24. Peter and John
25. Ahimelech
26. "Blessed are the poor."
27. Abraham
28. 4,000
29. Judas Iscariot
30. Zechariah 11:12-13. Neither Jeremiah nor Zechariah quotes the prophecy as it is quoted in Matthew.
31. "This is the King of the Jews."
32. Heli
33. Galatians (6:2 and 6:5)
34. Proverbs (26:4 and 26:5)
35. Five. (This apparent scribal error is corrected in some translations, where Merab, not Michal, is the mother of the five children.)

36. Solomon stated in Proverbs 18:22, "Whoso findeth a wife findeth a good thing." Who, in the New Testament, stated, "It is good for a man not to touch a woman"?
37. Acts 9:7 says that the people traveling with Paul heard the heavenly voice Paul heard. But, according to Acts 22:9, who said that the people did not hear the voice?
38. Mark 1:12-13 says that Jesus immediately went into the wilderness after his baptism and was there for forty days. Which Gospel claims that the day after his baptism he called Andrew and Peter to be his disciples?
39. According to 1 Corinthians 15:5, Jesus appeared to the twelve disciples after his resurrection. According to Matthew and Acts, how many apostles were there after his resurrection?

✦The Last Word

Name the persons who said the following as their last words.

1. Lord Jesus, receive my spirit. Lord, lay not this sin to their charge.
2. There they buried Abraham and Sarah his wife; there they buried Isaac and Rebekah his wife; and there I buried Leah.
3. Thou shouldest have smitten five or six times; then hadst thou smitten Syria till thou hadst consumed it; whereas now thou shalt smite Syria but thrice.
4. Draw thy sword, and thrust me through therewith; lest these uncircumcised come and thrust me through, and abuse me.
5. Mine eyes have seen thy salvation, which thou hast prepared before the face of all people: a light to lighten the Gentiles and the glory of thy people Israel.
6. God will surely visit you, and ye shall carry up my bones from hence.
7. Happy art thou, O Israel, who is like unto thee, O people saved by the Lord, the shield of thy help, and who is the sword of thy excellency! And thine enemies shall be found liars unto thee; and thou shalt tread upon their high places.

36. Paul (1 Corinthians 7)
37. Paul
38. John (1:35)
39. Only eleven. Matthew 27:3-5 says that Judas Iscariot hanged himself before Jesus' resurrection, and Acts 1:9-26 says that the new apostle, Matthias, had not yet been chosen at the time of the resurrection.

The Last Word (Answers)

1. Stephen (Acts 7:59-60)
2. Jacob (Genesis 49:31)
3. Elisha (2 Kings 13:19)
4. Saul (1 Samuel 31:4)
5. Simeon (Luke 2:30-32)
6. Joseph (Genesis 50:25)
7. Moses (Deuteronomy 33:29)

8. Behold, this stone shall be a witness unto us; for it hath heard all the words of the Lord which he spake unto us: it shall be therefore a witness unto you, lest ye deny your God.

9. O Lord, remember me, I pray thee, and strengthen me, I pray thee, only this once, O God, that I may be at once avenged of the Philistines for my two eyes.

10. Go ye therefore, and teach all nations, baptizing them in the name of the Father, and of the Son, and of the Holy Ghost, teaching them to observe all things whatsoever I have commanded you: and, lo, I am with you alway, even unto the end of the world.

11. Lord, remember me when thou comest into thy kingdom.

12. Now therefore hold him not guiltless; for thou art a wise man, and knowest what thou oughtest to do unto him; but his hoar head bring thou down to the grave with blood.

13. What is there done, my son?

14. But ye shall receive power, after that the Holy Ghost is come upon you; and ye shall be witnesses unto me, both in Jerusalem, and in all Judea, and in Samaria, and unto the uttermost part of the earth.

15. Thou hast asked a hard thing; nevertheless, if thou see me when I am taken from thee, it shall be so unto thee; but if not, it shall not be so.

16. Had Zimri peace, who slew his master?

17. Come to me, and I will give thy flesh unto the fowls of the air and to the beasts of the field.

18. Turn thine hand, and carry me out of the host; for I am wounded.

19. They shall take up serpents; and if they drink any deadly thing, it shall not hurt them; they shall lay hands on the sick, and they shall recover.

✦Who Said That? (IV)

1. Jesus Christ maketh thee whole; arise, and make thy bed.

2. Why is my pain perpetual, and my wound incurable, which refuseth to be healed?

8. Joshua (Joshua 24:27)
9. Samson (Judges 16:28)
10. Jesus (Matthew 28:19-20)
11. The repentant thief on the cross (Luke 23:42)
12. David (1 Kings 2:9)
13. Eli (1 Samuel 4:16)
14. Jesus (Acts 1:8)
15. Elijah (2 Kings 2:10)
16. Jezebel (2 Kings 9:31)
17. Goliath (1 Samuel 17:44)
18. Ahab (1 Kings 22:34)
19. Jesus (Mark 16:18)

Who Said That? (IV) (Answers)

1. Peter (Acts 9:34)
2. Jeremiah (15:18)

3. And after thee shall arise another kingdom inferior to thee, and another third kingdom of brass, which shall bear rule over all the earth.

4. We have found him, of whom Moses in the law, and the prophets, did write, Jesus of Nazareth, the son of Joseph.

5. Do violence to no man, neither accuse any falsely; and be content with your wages.

6. In the name of Jesus Christ of Nazareth rise up and walk.

7. What I have written, I have written.

8. A man can receive nothing, except it be given him from heaven.

9. God hath numbered thy kingdom, and finished it.

10. But the Lord is in his holy temple; let all the earth keep silence before him.

11. Thy crowned are as the locusts, and thy captains as the great grasshoppers.

12. Lord, trouble not thyself; for I am not worthy that thou shouldest enter under my roof.

13. Will a man rob God?

14. Woe to them that devise iniquity, and work evil upon their beds!

15. My mother and my brethren are these which hear the word of God, and do it.

16. I shall now perish one day by the hand of Saul.

17. Hast thou found me, O mine enemy?

18. Can two walk together, except they be agreed?

19. Sir, I perceive that thou art a prophet.

20. Son, why hast thou thus dealt with us? Behold, thy father and I have sought thee sorrowing.

21. Let us now go even unto Bethlehem, and see this thing which is come to pass, which the Lord hath made known unto us.

22. He shall speak peace unto the heathen; and his dominion shall be from sea even to sea.

23. Why have I found grace in thine eyes, that thou shouldest take knowledge of me, seeing I am a stranger?

24. Have pity upon me, have pity upon me, O ye my friends; for the hand of God hath touched me.

25. But thou Bethlehem Ephratah, though thou be little among the thousands of Judah, yet out of thee shall he come forth unto me that is to be ruler in Israel.

---

3. Daniel (2:39)
4. Philip (John 1:45)
5. John the Baptist (Luke 3:14)
6. Peter (Acts 3:6)
7. Pilate (John 19:22)
8. John the Baptist (John 3:27)
9. Daniel (5:26)
10. Habakkuk (2:20)
11. Nahum (3:17)
12. The centurion of Capernaum (Luke 7:6)
13. Malachi (3:8)
14. Micah (2:1)
15. Jesus (Luke 8:21)
16. David (1 Samuel 27:1)
17. Ahab (1 Kings 21:20)
18. Amos (3:3)
19. The woman at the well (John 4:19)
20. Mary (Luke 2:48)
21. The shepherds (Luke 2:15)
22. Zechariah (9:10)
23. Ruth (2:10)
24. Job (19:21)
25. Micah (5:2)

26. Thou art the Christ, the Son of the living God.
27. At midday, O king, I saw in the way a light from heaven, above the brightness of the sun, shining round about me and them which journeyed with me.
28. As many as I love, I rebuke and chasten; be zealous therefore, and repent.
29. Happy art thou, O Israel; who is like unto thee, O people saved by the Lord, the shield of thy help, and who is the sword of thy excellency!
30. Sing ye to the Lord, for he hath triumphed gloriously; the horse and his rider hath he thrown into the sea.
31. Lord, speakest thou this parable unto us, or even to all?
32. The voice of him that crieth in the wilderness, Prepare ye the way of the Lord, make straight in the desert a highway for our God.
33. Behold, the days come, saith the Lord, that I will sow the house of Israel and the house of Judah with the seed of man, and with the seed of beast.
34. Understandest thou what thou readest?
35. Thy money perish with thee, because thou hast thought that the gift of God may be purchased with money.
36. Which of the prophets have not your fathers persecuted?
37. Hate the evil, and love the good, and establish judgment in the gate; it may be that the Lord God of hosts will be gracious unto the remnant of Joseph.
38. Our father is old, and there is not a man in the earth to come in unto us after the manner of all the earth.
39. Hath Amnon thy brother been with thee?
40. Is there not an appointed time to man upon earth? Are not his days also like the days of a hireling?
41. I have sinned in that I have betrayed the innocent blood.
42. A prophet is not without honor, save in his own country, and in his own house.
43. Ye men of Israel, why marvel ye at this? Or why look ye so earnestly on us, as though by our own power or holiness we had made this man to walk?
44. Bring me up Samuel.
45. For God doth know that in the days ye eat thereof, then your eyes shall be opened, and ye shall be as gods, knowing good and evil.

---

26. Peter (Matthew 16:16)
27. Paul (Acts 26:13)
28. Jesus (Revelation 3:19)
29. Moses (Deuteronomy 33:29)
30. Miriam (Exodus 15:21)
31. Peter (Luke 12:41)
32. Isaiah (40:3)
33. Jeremiah (31:27)
34. Philip (Acts 8:30)
35. Peter (Acts 8:20)
36. Stephen (Acts 7:52)
37. Amos (5:15)
38. Lot's daughters (Genesis 19:31)
39. Absalom (2 Samuel 13:20)
40. Job (7:1)
41. Judas Iscariot (Matthew 27:4)
42. Jesus (Matthew 13:57)
43. Peter (Acts 3:12)
44. Saul (1 Samuel 28:11)
45. The serpent (Genesis 3:5)

46. What evil hath he done? I have found no cause of death in him; I will therefore chastise him and let him go.
47. Whomsoever I shall kiss, that same is he; take him, and lead him away safely.
48. Art thou he that troubleth Israel?
49. Behold, the nations are as a drop of a bucket, and are counted as the small dust of the balance.
50. Lord, how is it that thou wilt manifest thyself unto us, and not unto the world?

46. Pilate (Luke 23:22)
47. Judas Iscariot (Mark 14:44)
48. Ahab (1 Kings 18:17)
49. Isaiah (40:15)
50. Judas (not Iscariot) (John 14:22)

PART 8
Back to Nature

✦Some Amazing Animals

1. What four creatures did God send as plagues upon the Egyptians?
2. What venomous creature bit Paul on the hand but did not harm him?
3. What did Jesus use to feed the five thousand?
4. Where did Jesus send the legion of unclean spirits he had cast out of a man?
5. What did Peter find with a coin in its mouth?
6. What did God send to destroy the vine that shaded the sulking prophet Jonah?
7. When children laughed at Elisha for his baldness, what appeared that mauled the children?
8. What croaking birds fed Elijah in his solitude by the brook Cherith?
9. What two animals owned by the Philistines carried the ark of the covenant back to Israel?
10. What foreign prophet had a talking donkey to ride on?
11. What bird served as food for the Israelites in the wilderness?
12. What animals, considered rather loathsome in Bible times, ate the carcass of Jezebel?
13. What did God provide as a sacrifice in substitute for Isaac?
14. What miraculous animals parted Elijah and Elisha as Elijah was taken by a whirlwind into heaven?

✦Snakes and Other Creepy Things

1. Who amazed his comrades by surviving the bite of a viper?
2. According to Proverbs, what substance affects man like the bite of a snake?

Some Amazing Animals (Answers)

1. Frogs, lice, flies, and locusts (Exodus 8, 10)
2. A viper (Acts 28:3-6)
3. Two fish and five barley loaves (John 6:9-12)
4. Into a herd of swine (Mark 5:13)
5. A fish (Matthew 17:27)
6. A worm (Jonah 4:7)
7. Two she-bears (2 Kings 2:24)
8. Ravens (1 Kings 2:11)
9. Two cows (1 Samuel 6:7-12)
10. Balaam of Moab (Numbers 22:28)
11. Quail (Exodus 16:13)
12. Dogs (2 Kings 9:36)
13. A ram (Genesis 22:13)
14. Horses of fire (2 Kings 2:24)

Snakes and Other Creepy Things (Answers)

1. Paul (Acts 28:3-6)
2. Wine (Proverbs 23:32)

3. Who put a bronze snake on a pole in order to heal snakebite?
4. According to Job, what sort of men suck the poison of snakes?
5. What repulsive creatures bit the Israelites in the wilderness?
6. What did the people of Judah call the bronze snake in the temple?
7. What kind of snake did God promise to Jeremiah as a punishments for Israel's sin?
8. What tribe of Israel was supposed to be like a snake?
9. What animal came out of the Nile in droves as a plague on the Egyptians?
10. What bloodsucking creature is, in Proverbs, held up as an example of something that can never be satisfied?
11. According to Jesus, what would a loveless father give a child who asked for an egg?
12. What destructive creature did the prophet Joel have a vision of?
13. Who had a rod that God turned into a snake?
14. According to the Law, what hopping insects were edible?
15. What did King Rehoboam say he would use to discipline the people?
16. What book makes the pessimistic statement that whoever breaks through a wall may be bitten by a snake?
17. In Revelation, what sort of creatures had tails that were like snakes?
18. Who did Jesus refer to as a brood of vipers?
19. What was the only animal to lie?
20. In Revelation, what was the name of the great serpent?
21. According to Isaiah, what is the food of the serpent?
22. Who had a vision of locusts that were like horses prepared for battle?
23. Could the Israelites eat lizards?
24. According to Psalm 91, what kind of man can tread on a cobra without fear?
25. What did Amos say would happen to a man who rested his hand on the wall of his own house?
26. Who predicted that a child would be able to put his hand over a snake's den?

3. Moses (Numbers 21:8-9)
4. The wicked (Job 20:16)
5. Fiery serpents (Numbers 21:6)
6. Nehushtan (2 Kings 18:4)
7. Vipers that could not be charmed (Jeremiah 8:17)
8. Dan (Genesis 49:17)
9. Frogs (Exodus 8:1-4)
10. The leech (Proverbs 30:15)
11. A scorpion (Luke 11:12)
12. The locust (Joel 1:1-4)
13. Moses (Exodus 4:3)
14. The locust and the grasshopper (Leviticus 11:22)
15. Scorpions (1 Kings 12:11, 14)
16. Ecclesiastes (10:8)
17. Horses (Revelation 9:19)
18. The scribes and Pharisees (Matthew 23:33)
19. The serpent (Genesis 3:1-13)
20. The Devil (Revelation 12:9)
21. Dust (Isaiah 65:25)
22. John (Revelation 9:7)
23. No (Leviticus 11:29)
24. The man who trusts God (verse 13)
25. A snake would bite him (Amos 5:19)
26. Isaiah (11:8)

27. Who told his followers they would have the power to handle deadly snakes?
28. What curse did God put on the lying snakes?
29. What creature supposedly melts away as it moves?
30. What kind of tails did the hideous locusts have in Revelation?
31. What did the author of Proverbs admire the snake for?
32. According to Genesis, what part of man is the snake supposed to strike at?
33. What voracious insect was a plague on the Egyptians?
34. Who described locusts as stretching across the heavens like a dark curtain?
35. According to Ecclesiastes, what gives perfume a bad smell?
36. What prophet referred to the Sadducees and Pharisees as vipers?
37. What tiny insect did David compare himself to when Saul pursued him?
38. To what loathsome creature did Bildad compare man?
39. What swarming, pesky insects were sent as a plague on the Egyptians?
40. What ruler was eaten by worms before he died?
41. According to Jesus, what insect devours the treasures we store up on earth?
42. What creature, according to Isaiah, will not die?
43. What people had a fly god named Baal-zebub?
44. Who ate locusts in the wilderness?
45. What stinging creature did God promise to protect Ezekiel from?
46. What prophet had his vine eaten by a worm?
47. What water creature is the Bible probably referring to when it talks about a dragon?
48. When Israel's spies came back from Canaan, what insect did they compare themselves to when describing the giants in the land?
49. In the Law, what mammal is classified as an unclean bird?
50. According to Jesus, what small insects are strained out by the Pharisees?
51. What industrious insect is held up as an example to the lazy man?

27. Jesus (Mark 16:18)
28. It would have to crawl on its belly and eat dust (Genesis 3:14)
29. The slug (Psalm 58:8)
30. Tails like scorpions (Revelation 9:10)
31. Its grace of movement (Proverbs 30:19)
32. The heel (Genesis 3:15)
33. The locust (Exodus 10:12-19)
34. Isaiah (40:22)
35. Dead flies (Ecclesiastes 10:1)
36. John the Baptist (Matthew 3:7)
37. A flea (1 Samuel 24:14)
38. A worm (Job 25:6)
39. Gnats and flies (Exodus 8:16-32)
40. Herod (Acts 12:23)
41. The moth (Luke 12:33)
42. The worm (Isaiah 66:24)
43. The people of Ekron (2 Kings 1:2)
44. John the Baptist (Mark 1:6)
45. The scorpion (Ezekiel 2:6)
46. Jonah (4:7)
47. The crocodile
48. The grasshopper (Numbers 13:33)
49. The bat (Leviticus 11:19)
50. Gnats (Matthew 23:24)
51. The ant (Proverbs 6:6-8)

52. According to Bildad, what fragile thing is a godless man's trust like?
53. Who imitated Moses' feat of turning a staff into a snake?

✦The Lion's Den

1. What future king claimed that he had grabbed lions by the throat and beat them to death?
2. Who tore a lion apart with his bare hands?
3. Who saw locusts with lions' teeth?
4. What book speaks of the Lion of the tribe of Judah?
5. What father and son did David say were stronger than lions?
6. According to 1 Peter, what person is like a ravenous lion?
7. What brave soldier in David's army went into a pit on a snowy day and killed a lion?
8. Who had a throne with lion statues beside it?
9. What prophet foresaw a time when a lion would eat straw instead of meat?
10. Which of his sons did the dying Jacob compare to a vicious lion?
11. What prophet had a vision of a creature that had, on one of its four sides, a lion's face?
12. What devout young man was placed in a lions' den?
13. According to Ecclesiastes, what is better than being a dead lion?
14. Who saw a lionlike creature near the throne of God?
15. What book has a man asking his loved one to come down from the place where lions dwell?
16. Who had a vision of a lion with eagle's wings?

✦Shepherds and Sheep

1. What wealthy man had fourteen thousand sheep?
2. Who married the shepherd girl Zipporah?
3. What former shepherd boy is supposed to have written, "The Lord is my shepherd"?
4. Who did Jesus command to shepherd his church?

52. A spider web (Job 8:14)
53. The Egyptian court magicians (Exodus 7:11)

The Lion's Den (Answers)

1. David (1 Samuel 17:35)
2. Samson (Judges 14:6)
3. Joel (1:6)
4. Revelation (5:5)
5. Saul and Jonathan (2 Samuel 1:23)
6. Satan (1 Peter 5:8)
7. Benaiah (2 Samuel 23:20)
8. Solomon (1 Kings 10:18-20)
9. Isaiah (11:7)
10. Judah (Genesis 49:9)
11. Ezekiel (1:10)
12. Daniel (6:16)
13. A live dog (Ecclesiastes 9:4)
14. John (Revelation 4:7)
15. The Song of Solomon (4:8)
16. Daniel (7:4)

Shepherds and Sheep (Answers)

1. Job (42:12)
2. Moses (Exodus 2:16-17)
3. David (Psalm 23:1)
4. Peter (John 21:15-17)

5. Who was the first shepherd?
6. Who is the good shepherd?
7. Which prophet said, "All we like sheep have gone astray"?
8. Which Old Testament book compares a lover's teeth to a flock of newly shorn sheep?
9. In which gospel does Jesus speak of separating the sheep from the goats?
10. Who had compassion on the people because they seemed like sheep without a shepherd?
11. Who called Saul on the carpet because he had heard the bleating of sheep taken in Saul's battle with the Amalekites?
12. What book warns against sacrificing a defective sheep to God?
13. In what book does God say, "My people hath been lost sheep; their shepherds have caused them to go astray"?
14. To whom did Jesus say, "I send you forth as sheep in the midst of wolves"?
15. In Jesus' parable of the lost sheep, how many sheep were in the field?
16. Who did God tell Moses would be the new shepherd over Israel?
17. Which psalm says, "We are his people and the sheep of his pasture"?
18. Which epistle says, "We were as sheep going astray"?
19. Which psalm says, "We are counted as sheep for the slaughter"?
20. Who became a shepherd in Midian for his father-in-law?
21. Who paid Jesse a visit when young David was out tending the sheep?
22. What daughter of Laban was a shepherdess?
23. Who was out shearing his sheep when David's servants called on him?
24. What prophet said, "Woe to the idle shepherd"?
25. What prophet said that God would search out his scattered sheep?
26. What prophet told Ahab that Israel was scattered like sheep?
27. What Old Testament book says, "Smite the shepherd and the sheep will be scattered"?

5. Abel (Genesis 4:2)
6. Jesus (John 10:11)
7. Isaiah (53:6)
8. The Song of Solomon (4:2)
9. Matthew (25:32)
10. Jesus (Matthew 9:36)
11. Samuel (1 Samuel 15:14)
12. Deuteronomy (17:1)
13. Jeremiah (50:6)
14. The twelve disciples (Matthew 10:16)
15. A hundred (Matthew 18:12-14)
16. Joshua (Numbers 27:16-18)
17. 100
18. 1 Peter (2:25)
19. 44:22
20. Moses (Exodus 3:1)
21. Samuel (1 Samuel 16:11)
22. Rachel (Genesis 29:9)
23. Nabal (1 Samuel 25:2-9)
24. Zechariah (11:17)
25. Ezekiel (34:11)
26. Micaiah (1 Kings 22:17)
27. Zechariah (13:7)

28. According to Isaiah, whom did God say was his appointed shepherd?
29. Which epistle speaks of the "great shepherd of the sheep"?
30. What prophet talked about a shepherd pulling parts of a sheep from a lion's mouth?
31. In what book do we find the words, "He shall feed his flock like a shepherd"?
32. What almost-slaughtered son asked his father, "Where is the lamb for a burnt offering?"
33. Who said, "Behold, the lamb of God"?
34. What prophet told David a tale about a man with one lamb?
35. What foreign traveler was reading a passage about the Messiah being like a sheep for the slaughter?
36. What book of the Bible describes a lamb with seven horns and seven eyes?
37. What prophet spoke of a wolf dwelling with a lamb?
38. For what festival, instituted during the exodus from Egypt, was a lamb slaughtered?
39. Which epistle refers to Christ as a Passover lamb?
40. Who found a ram caught in a bramble?
41. Who had a vision of a powerful ram on a destructive rampage?
42. Who used a sheep's horn as a container for oil?
43. In front of what Canaanite city did priests blow trumpets made of rams' horns?
44. What did Samuel tell Saul was more important than sacrificing sheep?
45. What king of Moab was noted as a keeper of sheep?

◆Biblical Bird Walk

1. What book says that anyone who scorns his parents will have his eyes pecked out by ravens?
2. In Revelation, what bird went about crying, "Woe! Woe!"?
3. What book portrays God as having wings and feathers?
4. What bird does the lover in Song of Solomon compare his beloved's eyes to?
5. What king instructed people in bird lore?

28. Cyrus (Isaiah 44:28)
29. Hebrews (13:20)
30. Amos (3:12)
31. Isaiah (40:11)
32. Isaac (Genesis 22:7)
33. John the Baptist (John 1:29)
34. Nathan (2 Samuel 12:1-7)
35. The Ethiopian eunuch (Acts 8:27-35)
36. Revelation (5:6)
37. Isaiah (11:6)
38. Passover (Exodus 12:21)
39. 1 Corinthians (5:7)
40. Abraham (Genesis 22:13)
41. Daniel (8:3-4)
42. Samuel (1 Samuel 16:1)
43. Jericho (Joshua 6:4)
44. Obeying God (1 Samuel 15:22)
45. Mesha (2 Kings 3:4)

Biblical Bird Walk (Answers)

1. Proverbs (30:17)
2. An eagle (Revelation 8:13)
3. Psalms (91:4)
4. The dove (Song of Solomon 1:15)
5. Solomon (1 Kings 4:33)

6. Who compared his days to eagles swooping down on their prey?
7. On what day did God create the birds?
8. Who had a dream about birds eating out of a basket on his head?
9. Who boasted to David that he would give David's body to the birds for food?
10. What king's search for his rival is compared with looking for a partridge in the mountains?
11. What bird in great droves fed the Israelites in the wilderness?
12. On Mount Sinai, God told Moses that he had carried the Israelites from Egypt on the wings of a bird. What bird?
13. What father and son were, according to David, swifter than eagles?
14. According to the Law, what must a Nazarite sacrifice if someone dies in his presence during his period of separation?
15. What prophet had a vision of a desolate day when no birds were in the sky?
16. In Ezekiel's vision of the creatures with four faces, what bird's face was on the creatures?
17. What Babylonian king had a dream of a tree where every bird found shelter?
18. Who had a vision of a lion with eagle's wings?
19. What prophet said that Ephraim was as easily deceived as a foolish dove?
20. What nation would, according to Obadiah, be brought down by God even though it had soared like an eagle?
21. Who had a vision of two women with storks' wings?
22. Who prophesied that Assyria would become a roosting place for all sorts of strange night birds?
23. Who had a vision of a sheet filled with all sorts of unclean birds and other animals?
24. What domestic bird signaled Peter's betrayal of Christ?
25. According to Jesus, what inevitably gathers near a dead body?
26. What form did the Holy Spirit assume at Jesus' baptism?
27. In what parable of Jesus do greedy birds play a major role?
28. Who predicted that desert birds would use a ruined Edom as their home?

6. Job (9:26)
7. The fifth day (Genesis 1:20)
8. Pharaoh's baker (Genesis 40:16-17)
9. Goliath (1 Samuel 17:44)
10. Saul's search for David (1 Samuel 26:20)
11. Quails (Exodus 16:13)
12. The eagle (Exodus 19:4)
13. Saul and Jonathan (2 Samuel 1:23)
14. Two doves (Numbers 6:10)
15. Jeremiah (4:25)
16. The eagle's (Ezekiel 1:10)
17. Nebuchadnezzar (Daniel 4:12)
18. Daniel (7:4)
19. Hosea (7:11)
20. Edom (Obadiah 4)
21. Zechariah (5:9)
22. Zephaniah (2:14)
23. Peter (Acts 10:9-13)
24. The rooster (John 13:38; 18:27)
25. Vultures (Luke 17:37)
26. A dove (Mark 1:10)
27. The parable of the sower (Mark 4:1-20)
28. Isaiah (34:11-14)

29. Who called his lover "my dove, my perfect one"?
30. Who warned people that the birds of the air could be tattletales, telling the king who had said bad things about him?
31. In Revelation, who told the birds to gather together to eat the flesh of warriors?
32. According to Psalm 147, what young birds are fed by God when they call to him?
33. What prophet said that God's protection for Jerusalem was like birds circling overhead?
34. According to Leviticus, what must be done to any bird killed for food?
35. According to the Law, what two types of birds comprise the category of unclean fowl?
36. How many of each species of bird was Noah supposed to take into the ark?
37. Who had a vision of a woman with eagle's wings flying to the desert?
38. According to James, what cannot be tamed even though all birds can be tamed?
39. Who said that idolatrous man had exchanged the glory of the true God for images like birds?
40. What bird was being sold in the temple courts when Jesus drove out the salesmen?
41. What bird, according to Jesus, is cared for by God even though it had no barns or storerooms?
42. What kind of bird did Jesus compare to his love for Jerusalem?
43. What prophet warned of a destruction in which all birds would be swept from the earth?
44. What prophet warned that he would wail like an owl and walk about barefoot and naked?
45. Who declared that Nineveh's slave girls would moan like doves when the city was plundered?
46. In what book does God say that he knows all the birds of the air and the beasts of the field?
47. According to Job, what is hidden from the keen-eyed birds of prey?
48. What beautiful bird did Solomon's navy bring to Israel?
49. When the king of Syria besieged Samaria, what unusual substance sold for five shekels in the city?

29. The lover in the Song of Solomon (6:9)
30. The author of Ecclesiastes (10:20)
31. An angel standing in the sun (Revelation 19:17)
32. Ravens (verse 9)
33. Isaiah (31:5)
34. The blood must be drained from it (Leviticus 17:13)
35. Mostly scavengers and birds of prey (Deuteronomy 14:12-18)
36. Seven (Genesis 7:3)
37. John (Revelation (12:14)
38. The tongue (James 3:7)
39. Paul (Romans 1:23)
40. Doves (John 2:14)
41. The raven (Luke 12:24)
42. A hen gathering her chicks (Matthew 23:37)
43. Zephaniah (1:3)
44. Micah (1:8)
45. Nahum (2:7)
46. Psalms (50:11)
47. The whereabouts of jewels and precious metal (Job 28:7)
48. The peacock (2 Chronicles 9:21—some modern translations have "ape" instead of "peacock.")
49. Dove's dung (2 Kings 6:25)

50. What prophet said that Ahab's people would be eaten by birds?
51. According to Psalm 68, what are the dove's feathers covered with?
52. Who said that he had become a companion of owls?
53. According to Psalm 84, what two small birds have a nesting place near the temple?
54. What bird's song is, in the Song of Solomon, a sign of spring?
55. What bird's youth is, according to Psalms, renewable?
56. What bird does Jeremiah compare to a man who gains riches by unjust means?
57. According to Ezekiel, what will the moaning of the survivors sound like?
58. In what book do you find this: "Mine enemies chased me sore, like a bird, without cause"?
59. What was the first bird released from the ark?
60. In the system of sacrifice, what bird was normally offered?
61. What means did the Lord use to bring quail to the Israelites?
62. What concubine of Saul stood by the unburied bodies of her sons in order to keep the birds away?
63. According to the Law, one of the curses of disobedience was the coming of a cruel nation. What bird is that nation compared to?
64. According to the Law, what is an Israelite to do if he finds a mother bird with young or with eggs?
65. What was the dove carrying in its beak when it returned to Noah?
66. Who, according to tradition, said, "Oh, that I had the wings of a dove"?
67. Who asked Job who provided for the feeding of young ravens?
68. According to the Bible, what foolish bird lays its eggs on the ground in the sun?
69. What psalm speaks of the quail the Israelites ate in the wilderness?
70. What king always had choice poultry in his daily provisions?
71. Who did God tell to have dominion over all the birds?

50. Elijah (1 Kings 21:24)
51. Gold (Psalm 68:13)
52. Job (30:29)
53. The sparrow and the swallow (Psalm 84:3)
54. The turtledove (Song of Solomon 2:12)
55. The eagle (Psalm 103:5)
56. A partridge that hatches eggs it does not lay (Jeremiah 17:11)
57. Doves (Ezekiel 7:16)
58. Lamentations (3:52)
59. A raven (Genesis 8:7)
60. A dove or pigeon (Leviticus 1:14-17)
61. A wind from the sea (Numbers 11:31)
62. Rizpah (2 Samuel 21:10)
63. An eagle (Deuteronomy 28:49)
64. He may take the young or the eggs, but must not kill the mother bird (Deuteronomy 22:6-7)
65. An olive leaf (Genesis 8:11)
66. David (Psalm 55:6)
67. God (Job 38:41)
68. The ostrich (Job 39:13-18—some translations have "stork")
69. 78:26-29
70. Solomon (1 Kings 4:23)
71. Noah (Genesis 9:1-7)

72. What greedy king does Isaiah compare to a man grabbing eggs from a bird's nest?
73. What black birds fed Elijah when he lived by Kerith Brook?
74. According to Job, what bird feeds blood to its young?
75. What prophet told Baasha, king of Israel, that the birds would feast on those of his household?
76. What bird does Proverbs compare fleeting riches to?
77. What book speaks of the uselessness of spreading out a net in view of the birds it is supposed to catch?
78. According to the Song of Solomon, what is the male lover's hair like?
79. What nation's women did Isaiah compare to fluttering birds?
80. What book says that the Lord's people have become as heartless as ostriches in the desert?
81. Who told the Moabites to live like doves nesting at the mouth of a cave?
82. According to Isaiah, from what direction does God summon the birds of prey?
83. Who compared Assyria with a cedar of Lebanon that sheltered all the birds in its branches?
84. Who compared Israel with a speckled bird of prey, surrounded and attacked by other birds of prey?
85. According to Isaiah, what will those who hope in the Lord fly like?
86. According to Jeremiah, what large bird knows it has appointed seasons?
87. What prophet asked, "Does a bird fall into a trap on the ground where no snare has been set"? (NIV)
88. According to Jesus, what does not sow nor reap?
89. What seed grows a plant so large that the birds can make nests in it?
90. What did Mary and Joseph sacrifice in the temple when they took the young Jesus there?
91. In John's vision of the four living creatures, what bird does one of the creatures resemble?
92. According to the law, what can be used in place of a lamb as a sin offering?
93. What two birds did Abram sacrifice to God?

72. The king of Assyria (Isaiah 10:14)
73. Ravens (1 Kings 17:6)
74. The eagle (Job 39:30)
75. Jehu (1 Kings 16:4)
76. An eagle (Proverbs 23:5)
77. Proverbs (1:17)
78. A raven (Song of Solomon 5:11)
79. Moab's (Isaiah 16:2)
80. Lamentations (4:3)
81. Jeremiah (48:28)
82. The east (Isaiah 46:11)
83. Ezekiel (31:6)
84. Jeremiah (12:9)
85. Eagles (Isaiah 40:31)
86. The stork (Jeremiah 8:7)
87. Amos (3:5)
88. The birds of the air (Matthew 6:26)
89. The mustard seed (Luke 13:18-19)
90. A pair of doves (Luke 2:24)
91. An eagle (Revelation 4:7)
92. Two doves (Leviticus 5:7)
93. A dove and a pigeon (Genesis 15:9)

94. What prayer of an afflicted man compares him to an owl living among ruins?
95. According to Psalm 104, what bird nests in the pine trees?
96. According to Proverbs, what is an undeserved curse like?
97. What city, according to John, will become a home for every detestable and unclean bird?
98. What book says that in old age the songs of the birds will grow faint?
99. According to Isaiah, what bird honors God for providing streams in the desert?
100. What prophet speaks of God's covenant with the birds of the air?

◆The Lowly Donkey

1. What prophet of Moab had a talking donkey?
2. What future king was looking for lost donkeys when he ran into Samuel?
3. Who gave his irate brother twenty donkeys as a goodwill gesture?
4. What prince was riding a mule (that's a half-donkey) when he got his hair caught in an oak tree?
5. Who took his wife and sons and set them on a donkey when he returned to Egypt, his boyhood home?
6. What future wife of David rode out to meet him on a donkey when she was pleading for her husband's life?
7. Who used a donkey to carry the wood he was using to sacrifice his son on?
8. Who sent her servant on a donkey to inform Elisha that her son had died?
9. What prophet predicted that the Messiah would enter in riding on a donkey?
10. What is the only Gospel to mention Jesus' riding on a donkey?

94. Psalm 102:6
95. The stork (verse 17)
96. A fluttering sparrow or swallow (Proverbs 26:2)
97. Babylon (Revelation 18:2)
98. Ecclesiastes (12:4)
99. The owl (Isaiah 43:20)
100. Hosea (2:18)

The Lowly Donkey (Answers)

1. Balaam (Numbers 22:21-33)
2. Saul (1 Samuel 9:1-6)
3. Jacob (Genesis 32:13-18)
4. Absalom (2 Samuel 18:9)
5. Moses (Exodus 4:20)
6. Abigail (1 Samuel 25:20)
7. Abraham (Genesis 22:1-3)
8. The Shunemite woman (2 Kings 4:18-32)
9. Zechariah (9:9)
10. Matthew (21:1-9)

✦Horses and Horsemen

1. What book of the Old Testament contains a hymn celebrating drowned horses?
2. What New Testament author had a vision of locusts that looked like horses?
3. What evil queen was executed by Jerusalem's Horse Gate?
4. What leader was told by God to cripple his enemies' horses?
5. What king had twelve thousand cavalry horses?
6. What king took his household manager out to look for grass for the royal horses?
7. What two prophets were separated by horses of fire?
8. What queen had her blood spattered on King Jehu's horses?
9. Who removed the horse idols that the kings of Judah had dedicated to the worship of the sun?
10. What prophet had a vision of locusts that run like war horses?
11. Who had a vision of an angel on a red horse?
12. What king had horses imported from Cilicia and Musri?
13. Who ordered seventy horsemen to accompany Paul out of Jerusalem?
14. Who had a vision of the hills filled with horses and chariots of fire?
15. What prophet saw four chariots pulled by horses that represented the four winds?
16. In Revelation, what horse represents Death?
17. Who had horsemen accompany him as he went to bury his father?

✦The Biblical Greenhouse

1. What plant sprang up miraculously to give shade to the prophet Jonah?
2. What woman used mandrakes to gain a night in bed with Jacob?
3. Who used rods of poplar, hazel, and chestnut tree to make genetic changes in his cattle?
4. What kind of tree did the weary Elijah sit under?

Horses and Horsemen (Answers)

1. Exodus (chapter 15, Miriam's song)
2. John (Revelation 9:7)
3. Athaliah (2 Chronicles 23:15)
4. Joshua (11:6)
5. Solomon (1 Kings 4:26)
6. Ahab (1 Kings 18:5)
7. Elijah and Elisha (2 Kings 2:11)
8. Jezebel (2 Kings 9:33)
9. Josiah (2 Kings 23:11)
10. Joel (2:4)
11. Zechariah (1:8)
12. Solomon (1 Kings 10:29)
13. Claudius Lysias (Acts 23:23)
14. Elisha's servant (2 Kings 6:17)
15. Zechariah (6:1-5)
16. The pale horse (Revelation 6:8)
17. Joseph (Genesis 50:9)

The Biblical Greenhouse (Answers)

1. A gourd (Jonah 4:6)
2. Leah (Genesis 30:14-16)
3. Jacob (Genesis 30:37-39)
4. A broom tree (1 Kings 19:4)

5. What plant had such a bitter taste that it became a symbol for sorrow and disaster?
6. What, according to the New Testament, produces the smallest seed of any plant?
7. Which book mentions the rose of Sharon and the lily of the valley?
8. What mythical creature eats grass—according to the Book of Job?
9. What is the only book of the Bible to mention the apple tree?
10. What kind of tree did Zacchaeus climb in order to see Jesus?
11. What tree was a symbol of grace, elegance, and uprightness?
12. What kind of wood was Noah's ark made of?
13. What miraculous event was the eating of bitter herbs supposed to commemorate?
14. What unusual food was said to have resembled coriander seed?
15. What tree's spice was used in making oil for anointing?
16. What grain did not suffer from the plague of hail in Egypt because it had not grown enough?
17. What did Jacob send as a gift to Joseph in Egypt?
18. What massive trees were brought to make the beams and pillars in the Jerusalem temple?
19. What expensive wood is mentioned in the Book of Revelation?
20. What vine is mentioned in the Old Testament as bearing poisonous berries?
21. What kind of tree does Psalms compare a wicked man to?
22. What prophet complained about the people making sacrifices under spreading oaks, poplars, and elms?
23. What kind of weed does Jesus say will be separated from the wheat at the last judgment?
24. What kind of wood was the Ark of the Covenant made of?
25. What prophet was a "dresser of sycamore trees"?
26. What kind of trees did the exiled Jews hang their harps upon?
27. What did Delilah use to bind the sleeping Samson?

5. Wormwood (Proverbs 5:4; Amos 5:7)
6. Mustard (Matthew 13:31)
7. Song of Solomon (2:1)
8. Behemoth (Job 40:15-22)
9. Song of Solomon (2:3)
10. A sycamore (Luke 19:1-4)
11. The palm (Psalm 92:12; Jeremiah 10:5)
12. Gopherwood (Genesis 6:14)
13. The Passover (Exodus 12:8)
14. Manna (Exodus 16:31)
15. The cassia tree (Exodus 30:24)
16. Rye (Exodus 9:32)
17. Almonds (Genesis 43:11)
18. The cedars of Lebanon (1 Kings 5:6)
19. Thyine (Revelation 18:12)
20. The vine of Sodom (Deuteronomy 32:32)
21. A green bay tree (Psalm 37:35)
22. Hosea (4:13)
23. Tares (Matthew 13:25)
24. Acacia (Exodus 25:10)
25. Amos (7:14)
26. Willows (Psalm 137:2)
27. "Green withs"—probably tree bark or twigs (Judges 16:11)

28. What defeated king was buried with his sons under an oak tree?
29. Which tree does Jesus say can be uprooted and thrown into the sea—if one has enough faith?
30. What city was the "city of palm trees"?
31. What tree's foliage was found in the carvings inside the temple?
32. What king appointed an overseer to watch after the fruits of the olive trees and sycamores?
33. Who was killed after his hair was caught in an oak's branches?
34. What man met the Lord at the oaks of Mamre?
35. What prophet had a vision of a branch of an almond tree?
36. To what king did Jesus compare the lilies of the field?
37. What plant was used to purify lepers?
38. When Rahab hid the Israelite spies on her rooftop, what did she hide them under?
39. What did Noah's dove bring back in its beak?
40. What kind of tree was withered by Jesus because it bore no fruit?
41. What tree's leaves were used to cover the naked Adam and Eve?
42. What tree's fruit was used to make a plaster to heal the diseased King Hezekiah?
43. What furnishings in the temple were made of olive wood?
44. What epistle uses the grafting of the olive tree as a symbol of God choosing the Gentiles in addition to the Jews?
45. What prophet mentions a gift of ebony wood sent to Tyre?
46. In what land did Moses see a burning bush that was not consumed?
47. On what day of Creation did God make the plants?
48. What kind of flowers were supposed to be carved into the sacred lampstands?
49. What were Solomon's chariots made of?
50. What book mentions "apples of gold"?
51. In the parable of the sower, what unwanted plant causes some of the seeds to die?
52. What was Moses' basket made of?
53. What plant was used to lift up a sponge to the dying Jesus?
54. What plant was given to Jesus as a mock scepter by the Roman soldiers?

28. Saul (1 Chronicles 10:12)
29. The sycamine (Luke 17:6)
30. Jericho (2 Chronicles 28:15)
31. The palm (1 Kings 6:29)
32. David (1 Chronicles 27:28)
33. Absalom (2 Samuel 18:9-10)
34. Abraham (Genesis 18:1)
35. Jeremiah (1:11)
36. Solomon (Luke 12:27)
37. Hyssop (Leviticus 14:4-6)
38. Stacks of flax (Joshua 2:6)
39. An olive twig (Genesis 8:11)
40. A fig tree (Mark 11:12-14)
41. The fig's (Genesis 3:7)
42. The fig's (2 Kings 20:7)
43. The cherubim (1 Kings 6:23)
44. Romans (11:17)
45. Ezekiel (27:15)
46. Midian (Exodus 3:2)
47. The third day (Genesis 1:9-13)
48. Almond blossoms (Exodus 25:33)
49. Cedar wood (Song of Solomon 3:9)
50. Proverbs (25:11)
51. Thorns (Matthew 13:7)
52. Bulrushes (Exodus 2:3)
53. Hyssop (John 19:29)
54. A reed (Mark 15:19)

55. What plant food, given to pigs, was wanted by the prodigal son?
56. What flower were the capitals on the temple columns shaped like?
57. What plant, according to Isaiah, would not be broken by the Messiah?
58. What tree's fruit was symbolically represented on the clothing of Israel's high priest?
59. What leaves were thrown down in front of Jesus on his entry into Jerusalem?
60. What wood was used to make the table in the tabernacle for holding the sacred bread?
61. What wood was used for building the temple after the exile in Babylon?
62. What two herbs does Jesus say the Pharisees would tithe?

◆Some Earthquakes

1. What famous mountain smoked like a furnace and quaked greatly?
2. An earthquake at Philippi eventually led to the release of two Christians from prison there. Who were they?
3. Which Gospel mentions an earthquake in connection with the resurrection of Jesus?
4. An earthquke during King Uzziah's reign was so remarkable that one of the Hebrew prophets dates his book "two years before the earthquake." Which prophet?
5. According to Matthew's Gospel, an earthquke occurred when Jesus died on the cross. What other spectacular event occurred at that time in the temple?
6. What Hebrew prophet experienced an earthquake, a strong wind, and a supernatural fire all in one day?
7. During Saul's reign an earthquake occurred during the attack on the Philistines at Michmash. Who led the attack?
8. During a rebellion under Moses, 250 people rebelled and were swallowed up in an earthquake. Who led the rebellion?

55. Husks (Luke 15:16)
56. Lilies (1 Kings 7:19)
57. A bruised reed (Isaiah 42:3)
58. The pomegranate's (Exodus 28:33)
59. Palm leaves (John 12:13)
60. Acacia (Exodus 25:23-30)
61. Cedar (Ezra 3:7)
62. Mint and rue (Luke 11:42)

Some Earthquakes (Answers)

1. Sinai (Exodus 19:17-18)
2. Paul and Silas (Acts 16:25-27)
3. Matthew (28:2)
4. Amos (1:1)
5. The temple veil (curtain) was torn in half from top to bottom (Matthew 27:51)
6. Elijah (1 Kings 19:9-12)
7. Jonathan (1 Samuel 14:15)
8. Korah (Numbers 16:31-33)

✦Blowing in the Wind

1. What Old Testament book speaks of life as a "chasing after the wind"?
2. Where were the disciples when they heard a noise that sounded like a mighty wind filling the house they had gathered in?
3. Who had a dream of seven heads of grain being scorched by a hot east wind?
4. What loathsome creatures did God drive into Egypt with an east wind?
5. What prophet was told to cut off his hair and scatter a third of it in the wind?
6. How long did the wind that parted the Red Sea blow?
7. According to James, what sort of person is like a wave tossed by the wind?
8. What prophet experienced a furious wind that split the hills and shattered the rocks?
9. Whose children were destroyed when a strong wind struck the house they were banqueting in?
10. According to the Book of Job, what directional wind will inevitably strike down the wicked?
11. What epistle compares false teachers to rainless clouds blown about by the wind?
12. According to Psalms, what sort of people are like chaff that the wind blows away?
13. Who did God address from a whirlwind?
14. According to Jesus, what sort of man sees his house fall when the winds beat against it?
15. What was blown out of Egypt by a strong west wind?
16. Who had a dream about a statue that crumbled into dust that was driven away by the wind?
17. What prophet spoke of people who sow a wind and reap a whirlwind?
18. What runaway boarded a ship that the Lord struck with a strong wind?
19. What prophet suffered from a hot east wind after his shade plant was eaten by a worm?
20. Who lost faith and began to flounder when he noticed the strong wind on a lake?

Blowing in the Wind (Answers)

1. Ecclesiastes (chapters 1 and 2)
2. Jerusalem (Acts 2:2)
3. Pharaoh (Genesis 41:6)
4. Locusts (Exodus 10:13)
5. Ezekiel (5:2)
6. All night (Exodus 14:21)
7. A doubter (James 1:6)
8. Elijah (1 Kings 19:11)
9. Job's (Job 1:19)
10. East (Job 27:21)
11. Jude (12)
12. The wicked (Psalm 1:4)
13. Job (38:1)
14. The foolish man who builds on the sand (Matthew 7:26-27)
15. Locusts (Exodus 10:19)
16. Nebuchadnezzar (Daniel 2:35)
17. Hosea (8:7)
18. Jonah (1:4)
19. Jonah (4:8)
20. Peter (Matthew 14:30)

21. Who was saved from being a full-time sailor when God sent a wind to dry up the flood waters?
22. What food did God bring to the Israelites by using a wind?
23. According to the Book of Job, which directional wind punishes the land with its heat?
24. According to Revelation, what sort of creatures held back the winds from blowing on the earth?
25. What prophet had a vision of the four winds lashing the surface of the oceans?
26. In what book does a woman call on the north wind and south wind to blow on her garden?
27. According to Proverbs, what kind of woman is as hard to restrain as the wind itself?

◆Under a Cloud

1. What two long-dead men were with Jesus when a shining cloud covered them?
2. What sign did God set in the clouds to indicate that he would never again flood the world?
3. Did the pillar of cloud in the wilderness lead the Israelites by day or by night?
4. What prophet saw a little cloud like a man's hand?
5. What epistle talks about a "cloud of witnesses"?
6. At what critical spot did the pillar of cloud separate the Egyptians from the Israelites?
7. What epistle mentions believers being caught up in the clouds to meet the Lord?
8. According to Jesus, what person will appear coming in glory on the clouds of heaven?
9. In Revelation, what two unfortunate men are raised by God and then taken to heaven in a cloud?
10. On what mountain did God appear in the form of a cloud?
11. What object of the Israelites was notable for having the cloud of God's glory upon it?
12. What king, seeing the cloud in the temple, said that God had chosen to live in clouds and darkness?
13. What portable object did the cloud of God's glory appear over?

21. Noah (Genesis 8:1)
22. Quails (Numbers 11:31)
23. South (Job 37:17)
24. Four angels (Revelation 7:1)
25. Daniel (7:2)
26. Song of Solomon (4:16)
27. A nagging wife (Proverbs 27:16)

Under a Cloud (Answers)

1. Moses and Elijah (Matthew 17:5)
2. The rainbow (Genesis 9:13)
3. By day (Exodus 13:21-22)
4. Elijah (1 Kings 18:44)
5. Hebrews (12:1)
6. By the Red Sea (Exodus 14:20)
7. 1 Thessalonians (4:17)
8. The Son of man (Matthew 24:30)
9. The two witnesses (Revelation 11:12)
10. Sinai (Exodus 19:9)
11. The tabernacle (Exodus 40:34)
12. Solomon (1 Kings 8:10-11)
13. The ark of the covenant (Leviticus 16:2)

14. What epistle compares false teachers to clouds that bring no rain?
15. At what event did a cloud hide Jesus from the apostles' sight?
16. According to Zephaniah, what special day will be a day of clouds and blackness?

✦Rivers, Brooks, Lakes, Seas

1. What body of water was the first victim of the plague in Egypt?
2. What river did the Israelites cross when they entered Canaan?
3. What are the four rivers connected with the garden of Eden?
4. According to the Song of Solomon, what is so powerful that rivers cannot quench it?
5. Who lived by Kerith Brook?
6. Who proclaimed a fast at the river Ahava?
7. Who had a dream about cows standing by the riverside?
8. Who spoke of a river flowing with honey?
9. According to God's covenant with Abraham, how far did Abraham's land extend?
10. Who ordered the casting of the Israelite boys into the river?
11. In John's vision, what caused a third of the rivers on earth to become bitter?
12. What lake is called the Salt Sea in Genesis 14:3?
13. What apostle noted that he had been endangered by the sea and by rivers?
14. Who prophesied to the Jews by the Kebar River?
15. Who had a vision of a river of fire?
16. Who spoke about justice rolling down like a river?
17. Where did John baptize the repentant people?
18. What Christian woman worshiped with a group that met by a river?
19. In John's vision, what happened to the sea when the second angel poured out his bowl on it?
20. Who found a baby while down by the riverside?

14. Jude (verse 12)
15. The Ascension (Acts 1:9)
16. The day of the Lord (Zephaniah 1:15)

Rivers, Brooks, Lakes, Seas (Answers)

1. The Nile (Exodus 7:7-15)
2. The Jordan (Joshua 1:1-2)
3. Gihon, Pison, Tigris, and Euphrates (Genesis 2:10-14)
4. Love (Song of Solomon 8:7)
5. Elijah (1 Kings 17:1-4)
6. Ezra (8:21)
7. The Pharaoh (Genesis 41:3)
8. Zophar (Job 20:17)
9. From the river of Egypt to the Euphrates (Genesis 15:18)
10. Pharaoh (Exodus 1:22)
11. A star (Revelation 8:10-11)
12. The Dead Sea
13. Paul (2 Corinthians 11:26)
14. Ezekiel (1:1)
15. Daniel (7:10)
16. Amos (5:24)
17. In the Jordan (Mark 1:5)
18. Lydia (Acts 16:13-14)
19. It turned to blood (Revelation 16:3)
20. Pharaoh's daughter (Exodus 2:5)

21. By what river did Nebuchadnezzar defeat Pharaoh Neco of Egypt?
22. Who had a vision of a deep river that could not be passed over?
23. Who spoke of the Lord being displeased with "ten thousand rivers of oil"?
24. In Revelation, what is the fiery lake composed of?
25. Who fled across Kidron Brook to escape from Absalom?
26. Where were Pharaoh and his men drowned?
27. In Revelation, where does the pure river of the water of life flow out from?
28. According to James, what kind of man is like the waves of the sea?
29. Who lodged at the home of a tanner who lived by the sea?
30. What name is the Sea of Galilee called in the Gospel of John?
31. What were the seafaring people west of Israel known as?
32. What was the Mediterranean usually called in Bible times?
33. What was the Sea of Galilee called in Old Testament times?
34. What happens to the sea in the world to come?
35. Who had a vision of a sea of glass?
36. Who asked his shipmates to cast him into the sea?
37. By what lake did Jesus appear to his disciples after the Resurrection?
38. By what other name is the Salt Sea (Dead Sea) known in the Old Testament?
39. What Syrian army man had his leprosy washed away in the Jordan River?

✦Cave Men, Cave Women

1. Who lived in a cave with his daughters after Sodom and Gomorrah were destroyed?
2. Who trapped five Canaanite kings in the cave where they were hiding?
3. What friend of Jesus was buried in a cave?
4. What prophet, fleeing from Jezebel, hid in a cave?

21. The Euphrates (Jeremiah 46:2)
22. Ezekiel (47:5)
23. Micah (6:7)
24. Burning sulfur (Revelation 19:20)
25. David (2 Samuel 15:13-23)
26. The Red Sea (Exodus 15:4)
27. The throne of God (Revelation 22:1)
28. A doubting man (James 1:6)
29. Peter (Acts 10:6)
30. The Sea of Tiberias (John 6:1)
31. The Philistines
32. The Great Sea
33. The Sea of Chinnereth
34. It does not exist (Revelation 21:1)
35. John (Revelation 4:6)
36. Jonah (1:12)
37. The Sea of Tiberias (John 21:1)
38. The Sea of the Arabah
39. Naaman (2 Kings 5:10-14)

Cave Men, Cave Women (Answers)

1. Lot (Genesis 19:30)
2. Joshua (10:16-27)
3. Lazarus (John 11:38)
4. Elijah (1 Kings 19:9)

5. In the time of the judges, what tribe did the Israelites hide from in caves?
6. What hero hid in caves to avoid the wrath of Saul?
7. Who hid a hundred prophets in a cave when Jezebel was trying to kill them?
8. In Saul's time, what marauding people drove the Israelites into caves?
9. Who was buried in the cave of Machpelah?
10. Who hid in a cave while God passed by?

✦From the Mountains

1. On what mountain did Elijah challenge the priests of Baal?
2. What mountain did Balaam plan to curse Israel from?
3. What mountain did Moses see the promised land from?
4. What mountain did Deborah and Barak descend to defeat Sisera?
5. Where did Noah's ark land?
6. Where did Jesus' Transfiguration occur?
7. Where did the Samaritans build their temple?
8. Where did Moses see the burning bush?
9. On what mountain did Solomon build the temple?
10. Where did Jesus weep over Jerusalem?
11. What mountain range did the wood for Solomon's temple come from?
12. Where were Saul and Jonathan killed by the Philistines?
13. Where was Moses buried?
14. Where did Jacob and Laban make their covenant?
15. Where did Elijah go when he fled from Jezebel?
16. Where did Aaron die?
17. Where did Abraham take Isaac to be sacrificed?
18. Where did Moses bring water out of the rock?
19. What mountain did David cross on his flight from Absalom?
20. What mountain in Jerusalem is mentioned over 160 times in the Bible?
21. On what smoke-covered mountain did Moses meet God?
22. What leader built an altar on Mount Ebal?
23. What prophet criticized the people who felt secure on Mount Samaria?

5. The Midianites (Judges 6:2)
6. David (1 Samuel 22:1-2; 23:14, 29)
7. Obadiah (1 Kings 18:4)
8. The Philistines (1 Samuel 13:5-7)
9. Sarah, Abraham, Isaac, Rebekah, Leah, and Jacob (Genesis 23:19; 25:9; 35:29; 49:30-31)
10. Moses (Exodus 33:21-23)

From the Mountains (Answers)

1. Carmel (1 Kings 18:19)
2. Pisgah (Numbers 22–24)
3. Nebo (Deuteronomy 34:1-4)
4. Tabor (Judges 4:6-15)
5. Ararat (Genesis 8:4)
6. Harmon (Matthew 17)
7. Gerizim (John 4:20-21)
8. Horeb (Exodus 3:1)
9. Moriah (2 Chronicles 3:1)
10. The Mount of Olives (Luke 19:41)
11. Lebanon (1 Kings 5:6-14)
12. Gilboa (1 Samuel 31:1-6)
13. Pisgah (Deuteronomy 34:5-6)
14. Gilead (Genesis 31:20-49)
15. Horeb (1 Kings 19:8)
16. Mount Hor (Numbers 20:25-29)
17. Moriah (Genesis 22:2)
18. Horeb (Exodus 17:6)
19. The Mount of Olives (2 Samuel 15:30-32)
20. Zion
21. Sinai (Exodus 31:18)
22. Joshua (8:30)
23. Amos (6:1)

24. Where did Jesus deliver his final discourse?
25. In what country is Mount Seir?
26. According to Paul, what country is the site of Mount Sinai?

24. The Mount of Olives (Matthew 24–25)
25. Edom (Ezekiel 35:1-7)
26. Arabia (Galatians 4:25)

PART 9

Cities and Other Constructions

✦Builders of Cities

1. Who built ancient Babylon?
2. Who built a city called Enoch east of Eden?
3. Who built the Egyptian treasure cities of Pithom and Raamses?
4. Who rebuilt Gezer, which had been given as a wedding gift to his Egyptian wife by her father?
5. Who built Nineveh?
6. What king of Israel built Penuel?
7. Who rebuilt Ramah in order to keep people from entering or leaving Judah?
8. What king of Judah built up the defenses of Bethlehem?
9. What king of Israel built the nation's capital at Samaria?
10. What man of Bethlehem rebuilt Jericho during Ahab's reign?
11. Who rebuilt Elath and restored it to Judah?
12. Who rebuilt Babylon on a grand scale?

✦Cities Great and Small

1. What city, a seaport on the western coast of Asia Minor, was the second of the seven churches mentioned by John?
2. What city was Paul's hometown?
3. To what city in Macedonia did Paul send at least two letters?
4. What Asian city was the home of Lydia?
5. What city on the Euphrates did Abram leave?
6. What Canaanite city, destroyed by the Israelites has a name that means "ruin"?
7. What Pisidian city was visited by Paul and Barnabas on the first missionary journey?
8. In what city were the followers of Jesus first called Christians?

Builders of Cities (Answers)

1. Nimrod (Genesis 10:8-10)
2. Cain (Genesis 4:17)
3. The enslaved Israelites (Exodus 1:11)
4. Solomon (1 Kings 9:1-17)
5. Nimrod (Genesis 10:11)
6. Jeroboam (1 Kings 12:25)
7. Baasha, king of Israel (1 Kings 15:17)
8. Rehoboam (2 Chronicles 11:6)
9. Omri (1 Kings 16:23-24)
10. Hiel (1 Kings 16:34)
11. Azariah (2 Kings 14:22)
12. Nebuchadnezzar (Daniel 4:30)

Cities Great and Small (Answers)

1. Smyrna (Revelation 2:8-11)
2. Tarsus (Acts 21:39)
3. Thessalonica
4. Thyatira (Acts 16:14)
5. Ur (Genesis 15:7)
6. Ai (Joshua 8:3-29)
7. Antioch (Acts 13:14)
8. Antioch of Syria (Acts 11:26)

9. In what Italian city was Paul met by Christians from Rome?
10. What city is usually mentioned as the southern limit of Israel?
11. In what Greek city did Silas and Timothy stay while Paul went on to Athens?
12. What city was home to Mary, Martha, and Lazarus?
13. What city was the site of Jacob's famous dream?
14. What city was the birthplace of both David and Jesus?
15. What seaport in Asia did Paul walk to from Troas?
16. In what city did Paul address some of the most brilliant men of his time?
17. What famous city had Nebuchadnezzar as a ruler?
18. What Israelite city was built by Omri as his capital?
19. What Asian city was the fifth of the seven churches mentioned by John?
20. In what Canaanite city were Joseph's bones finally laid to rest?
21. What city was the home of Peter, Andrew, and Philip?
22. Where was Cornelius converted?
23. Near what city did Peter profess his faith in Jesus?
24. Where did Jesus perform his first miracle?
25. Where did Jesus stay when John the Baptist was in prison?
26. What city was home to Philemon?
27. What sinful Greek city had a church that received two letters from Paul?
28. In what Syrian city did Paul have his sight restored at the hands of Ananias?
29. What city, usually grouped with Iconium and Lystra, did Paul visit on his first and third missionary journeys?
30. What Asian city did Paul avoid so he could hurry back to Jerusalem?
31. What ancient city is associated with Joshua and the blowing of trumpets?
32. Where did Jonah board a ship bound for Tarshish?
33. What was Solomon's seaport at the head of the Gulf of Elath?
34. What Philistine city was home to Goliath?
35. What Philistine city did Amos curse for its slave trade with Edom?

9. Appii Forum (Acts 28:15)
10. Beersheba
11. Berea (Acts 17:10-14)
12. Bethany (John 11)
13. Bethel (Genesis 28:10-22)
14. Bethlehem
15. Assos (Acts 20:13-14)
16. Athens (Acts 17)
17. Babylon (2 Kings 25)
18. Samaria (1 Kings 16:23-24)
19. Sardis (Revelation 3:1-6)
20. Shechem (Joshua 24:32)
21. Bethsaida (John 1)
22. Caesarea (Acts 10:24-48)
23. Caesarea Philippi (Matthew 16:13-18)
24. Cana (John 2:1-11)
25. Capernaum (Matthew 4:12-13)
26. Colossae (Colossians 4:9)
27. Corinth
28. Damascus (Acts 9)
29. Derbe (Acts 14:20)
30. Ephesus (Acts 19)
31. Jericho (Joshua 6)
32. Joppa (Jonah 1:3)
33. Ezion-Geber (1 Kings 9:26)
34. Gath (1 Samuel 17:4)
35. Gaza (Amos 1:6-7)

36. Where did Solomon have a dream when he asked for wisdom?
37. Where did Abram go after leaving Ur?
38. What city, identified with Mamre, was the place where Sarah died?
39. In what Asian city did Paul and Barnabas make many converts on the second missionary journey?
40. Where were Paul and Barnabas deserted by Mark?
41. What city was said by John to have "Satan's seat"?
42. What city receives the most praise of all the seven cities of Asia?
43. Where did Paul and Silas make their first European converts?
44. Where was Paul's longest epistle sent?
45. Where did Assyrian king Sennacherib receive tribute from Hezekiah?
46. What city was said to have Christians that were neither hot nor cold?
47. Where was Paul mistaken for the god Hermes?
48. Where was King Josiah killed?
49. Where did Paul bid farewell to the elders of Ephesus?
50. What was Jesus' hometown?
51. What port was the site of Paul's first European landing?
52. What city was, according to tradition, founded by Nimrod?
53. What city of Cyprus did Paul and Barnabas visit on their first journey?
54. In what city did Paul, on his way to Jerusalem, board a ship sailing for Phoenicia?
55. What two cities of the plain were destroyed by God for their wickedness?
56. According to the New Testament, in what city will there be no night?
57. What city was Melchizedek king of?
58. Where did tax collector Zacchaeus live?
59. Where did Peter have his vision of a sheet filled with unclean animals?
60. What city is often referred to simply as Zion?
61. What was Jeremiah's hometown?
62. When the captive Paul was taken from Jerusalem to Caesarea, where did his guards stop for the night?
63. What city was home to the harlot Rahab?

36. Gibeon (1 Kings 3:5-15)
37. Haran (Genesis 12)
38. Hebron (Genesis 23)
39. Iconium (Acts 13-14)
40. Perga (Acts 13:13-14)
41. Pergamos (Revelation 2:13)
42. Philadelphia (Revelation 3:7-13)
43. Philippi (Acts 16)
44. Rome
45. Lachish (2 Kings 18:13-16)
46. Laodicea (Revelation 3:14-22)
47. Lystra (Acts 14:6-20)
48. Megiddo (2 Kings 23:29)
49. Miletus (Acts 20:17-38)
50. Nazareth (Luke 2:51)
51. Neapolis (Acts 16:11)
52. Nineveh (Genesis 10:11)
53. Paphos (Acts 13:6-13)
54. Patara (Acts 21:1, 20)
55. Sodom and Gomorrah (Genesis 19)
56. The New Jerusalem (Revelation 22:5)
57. Salem (Genesis 14:18)
58. Jericho (Luke 19:1)
59. Joppa (Acts 10:5-20)
60. Jerusalem
61. Anathoth (Jeremiah 1:1)
62. Antipatris (Acts 23:31)
63. Jericho (Joshua 2)

64. At what town was Saul publicly proclaimed king?
65. In what Syrian city did Elisha visit a sick king?
66. What city was home to Philemon and Onesimus?
67. In what two cities did King Jeroboam erect his golden calves?
68. In what town did Saul massacre eighty-five priests?
69. What city was Esau's home base?
70. What city of Cyprus was a site of Paul's preaching?
71. What city was the home of Naboth, whose vineyard Ahab wanted?
72. What was King Saul's hometown?
73. What city was punished by Gideon for refusing to feed his hungry troops?
74. What prophet hailed from the town of Tekoa?
75. Where was Paul when he received his famous "Macedonian vision"?
76. What city was home to the man who gave Jesus a burial place?
77. What was the site of Moses' burial place?
78. Where were the bodies of Saul and Jonathan nailed to a wall?
79. Where were a number of men slain for looking into the ark of the covenant?
80. Where did Elisha strike Syrian soldiers with blindness?
81. What Philistine city worshiped the god Baal-zebub?
82. Where was the witch Saul consulted?
83. What city was home to the most-praised church mentioned in Revelation?
84. Where was Samuel buried?
85. Where did Peter cure Aeneas?
86. What was the site of the Israelites great victory, led by Jonathan, over the Philistines?
87. What was the place where Jacob and Laban parted company?
88. Where did Jesus raise a widow's son from the dead?
89. What Phoenician city was home to Hiram, who helped construct Solomon's temple?
90. In what Samaritan town did Jesus meet the woman at the well?

64. Gilgal (1 Samuel 11:14-15)
65. Damascus (2 Kings 8:7)
66. Colossae (Colossians 4:9)
67. Dan and Bethel (1 Kings 12:29)
68. Nob (1 Samuel 22:18)
69. Petra (Genesis 36:1)
70. Salamis (Acts 13:4-5)
71. Jezreel (1 Kings 21:1-29)
72. Gibeah (1 Samuel 10:26)
73. Succoth (Judges 8:5-16)
74. Amos (1:1)
75. Troas (Acts 16:11)
76. Arimathea (Matthew 27:57-60)
77. Beth-peor (Deuteronomy 34:1-6)
78. Beth-shan (1 Samuel 31:8-13)
79. Beth-shemesh (1 Samuel 6:19-21)
80. Dothan (2 Kings 6:13)
81. Ekron (2 Kings 1:2)
82. Endor (1 Samuel 28:7-14)
83. Philadelphia (Revelation 3:7-13)
84. Ramah (1 Samuel 25:1)
85. Lydda (Acts 9:32-35)
86. Michmash (1 Samuel 14:1-23)
87. Mizpah (Genesis 31:49)
88. Nain (Luke 7:11-18)
89. Tyre (1 Kings 5:1-11)
90. Sychar (John 4:7)

91. What city was home to the tabernacle after the Israelites conquered Canaan?
92. What Phoenician city was home to evil Jezebel?

◆Palatial Living

1. Whose palace had a hand that wrote on the wall?
2. What king of Tyre sent materials for David's palace?
3. Who burned the royal palace of Israel with himself inside?
4. What Babylonian went insane while walking on the roof of his palace?
5. Who took thirteen years to build his palace?
6. What nation's envoys were taken on a tour of the palace by King Hezekiah?
7. Who had a coveted vineyard close to Israel's royal palace?
8. Who referred to the future Jerusalem temple as a "palace for the Lord God"?
9. Who served as a cupbearer in Persia's royal palace?
10. What king was assassinated in his palace by Pekah?
11. Who had a palace with marble pillars and beds of gold and silver?

◆Up on the Roof

1. When Samson pulled the building down, how many people had been sitting on the rooftop?
2. Who had a vision of unclean animals while in prayer on a housetop?
3. In the days of Ezra, what did some of the Jews build on their rooftops?
4. Who prophesied judgment on the people of Jerusalem because they burned incense to idols on their roofs?
5. Who hid two Israelite spies up on her rooftop among stalks of flax?
6. What king saw his nude neighbor on a rooftop?
7. Who had intercourse on a rooftop with all his father's concubines?

91. Shiloh (Joshua 18:1)
92. Sidon (1 Kings 16:31-33)

Palatial Living (Answers)

1. Belshazzar's (Daniel 5:5)
2. Hiram (2 Samuel 5:11)
3. Zimri (1 Kings 16:15-18)
4. Nebuchadnezzar (Daniel 4:28-33)
5. Solomon (1 Kings 7:1-12)
6. Babylon's (2 Kings 20:16-18)
7. Naboth (1 Kings 21:1-19)
8. David (1 Chronicles 29:1, 19)
9. Nehemiah (1:1; 2:1)
10. Pekahiah (2 Kings 15:25)
11. Ahasuerus (Esther 1:5-6)

Up on the Roof (Answers)

1. About three thousand (Judges 16:27)
2. Peter (Acts 10:9-16)
3. Booths in commemoration of the Feast of Tabernacles (Nehemiah 8:14-16)
4. Jeremiah (19:13)
5. Rahab (Joshua 2:6)
6. David (2 Samuel 11:2-4)
7. Absalom (2 Samuel 16:22)

8. What was the ailment of the man who was let down through a roof in Capernaum so he could be healed by Jesus?
9. Who slept on Samuel's roof when he visited with him?

✦Collapsible Buildings

1. Who caused thousands of deaths by toppling the two main pillars in a large building?
2. In Jesus' parable about houses, who had a house that collapsed when the rains came?
3. Whose children perished when the house they were feasting in collapsed in a storm?
4. What judge tore down the tower of Penuel and slaughtered the people of the city?
5. What building, mentioned by Jesus, killed eighteen people when it collapsed?
6. According to Jesus, what building would be so thoroughly destroyed that there would not be one stone left on another?

✦Up Against the Wall

1. What perfectly square city is described as having walls made of jasper?
2. What prophet was trapped against a wall by an angel with a drawn sword?
3. Who escaped through the wall of Damascus by being let down in a basket?
4. Whose body was fastened to the wall of Beth-shan by the Philistines?
5. Who sacrificed his son on the city wall when the Moabites were losing the battle to Israel?
6. What city was famous for its fallen walls?
7. What prophet measured the wall of the temple district?
8. Who built the walls of Jerusalem?
9. What foreign invader tore down the walls of Jerusalem?

8. He was paralyzed (Mark 2:3-4)
9. Saul (1 Samuel 25-26)

Collapsible Buildings (Answers)

1. Samson (Judges 16:23-30)
2. The foolish man (Matthew 7:26-27)
3. Job's (Job 1:18-19)
4. Gideon (Judges 8:17)
5. The tower of Siloam (Luke 13:4)
6. The temple (Mark 13:1-2)

Up Against the Wall (Answers)

1. The New Jerusalem (Revelation 21:18)
2. Balaam (Numbers 22:24)
3. Paul (Acts 9:25)
4. Saul's (1 Samuel 31:10)
5. Mesha, king of Moab (2 Kings 3:27)
6. Jericho (Joshua 6:20)
7. Ezekiel (42:20)
8. Solomon (1 Kings 9:15)
9. Nebuchadnezzar (2 Kings 25:10)

10. What rebel against David was beheaded, with his head thrown over the wall of Abel to Joab?
11. Who stuck his spear in the wall when it failed to strike its intended target, David?
12. What warrior, the victim of a king's scheming, was killed when shot by arrows from the wall of Rabbah?
13. In what besieged city did the king, walking on the city wall, meet a woman who told him she had eaten her son for dinner?
14. What wine steward sat down and wept when he learned the walls of Jerusalem had not been rebuilt?

✦Opening Windows

1. Who died after falling out of a window during Paul's sermon?
2. What prophet ordered a king to shoot arrows out of a window?
3. What king looked out of his window and saw Isaac and Rebekah wooing?
4. What wicked queen was thrown out of a window by her servants?
5. Who knelt toward Jerusalem and prayed looking out of his eastern window in Babylon?
6. Who let birds fly out of his ship's window?
7. Who let spies escape through a window by using a rope?
8. Who looked out her window and was ashamed to see her husband dancing in the street?
9. In what city did Paul escape a plot by going through a window in the city wall?
10. According to Malachi, what windows would be opened for people who tithed?
11. Who looked out his window and saw a young man being enticed by a prostitute?
12. Whose wife helped him escape from Saul by letting him down through a window?

10. Sheba (2 Samuel 20:22)
11. Saul (1 Samuel 19:10)
12. Uriah the Hittite (2 Samuel 11:24)
13. Samaria (2 Kings 6:26-29)
14. Nehemiah (1:3-4)

Opening Windows (Answers)

1. Eutychus (Acts 20:9)
2. Elisha (2 Kings 13:17)
3. Abimelech (Genesis 26:8)
4. Jezebel (2 Kings 9:30, 32)
5. Daniel (6:10)
6. Noah (Genesis 8:6)
7. Rahab (Joshua 2:15-21)
8. Michal, wife of David (2 Samuel 6:16)
9. Damascus (2 Corinthians 11:33)
10. The windows of heaven (Malachi 3:10)
11. Solomon, or whoever wrote Proverbs (7:6-10)
12. David (1 Samuel 19:12)

✦Wells, Cisterns, and Other Large Containers

1. Who had a miraculous well opened up for him after he worked up a thirst in battle?
2. What king dug wells in the desert?
3. What king ordered the construction of the Sea, the great basin in the temple court?
4. What exiled woman was approached by an angel at a well?
5. What army man was at the well of Sirah when he was summoned to his death by Joab's men?
6. Who escaped from Absalom's men by hiding in a well?
7. Who met his future wife at a well in Midian?
8. Who found a wife for Isaac at the well of Nahor?
9. Who longed for a drink from the well at Bethlehem?
10. What book contains laws telling owners of cisterns what to do if a person or animal accidentally falls in?
11. What prophet was imprisoned in a cistern?
12. Who met his future wife by a well when she came to water her sheep?
13. Where did God pare down Gideon's troops to three hundred men?
14. Who had servants who named their wells Esek, Sitnah, Rehoboth, and Beersheba?
15. What son of Jacob nearly perished in a cistern?
16. Who promised the citizens of Jerusalem that they could be free to drink from their own cisterns if they would surrender to Assyria?
17. In what country did Jesus talk with an immoral woman beside a well?
18. Who tried to take the well of Beersheba away from Abraham?

✦Gates, Doors, and Other Openings

1. Who did God speak to about the "gates of death"?
2. What gate of Jerusalem was rebuilt under Nehemiah's leadership?

Wells, Cisterns, and Other Large Containers
(Answers)

1. Samson (Judges 15:18-20)
2. Uzziah (2 Chronicles 26:10)
3. Solomon (1 Kings 7:23)
4. Hagar (Genesis 16:7-14)
5. Abner (2 Samuel 3:26-27)
6. Ahimaaz and Jonathan (2 Samuel 17:17-21)
7. Moses (Exodus 2:15-21)
8. Abraham's servant (Genesis 24)
9. David (2 Samuel 23:14-17)
10. Exodus (21:33-34)
11. Jeremiah (38:6)
12. Jacob (Genesis 29:1-12)
13. The well of Harod (Judges 7:1-7)
14. Isaac (Genesis 26:17-33)
15. Joseph (Genesis 37:22)
16. Rabshakeh (2 Kings 18:31)
17. Samaria (John 4:5-15)
18. Abimelech (Genesis 21:22-32)

Gates, Doors, and Other Openings (Answers)
1. Job (38:17)
2. The Sheep Gate (Nehemiah 3:1)

3. What faithful soldier, home on furlough, chose to sleep in front of the king's palace door instead of going home to his wife?
4. Who removed the massive doors from the gate of Gaza and carried them to a hill at Hebron?
5. According to what Moses told the Israelites, where were the words of God to be written?
6. Who shut up the door of Noah's ark?
7. What king removed the gold from the doors of the temple and gave it to the king of Assyria?
8. When Lot's two angelic visitors blinded the lecherous men of Sodom, what were the men scrambling to do?
9. At the first Passover, what were the Israelites told to apply to their doorposts?
10. According to Psalm 24, what is to be lifted up so that the king of glory may enter in?
11. Who rolled back the stone from Jesus' tomb?
12. According to Revelation, which of the seven churches in Asia did the Lord say that he had set before it an open door that no man could shut?
13. Who healed a lame man at the temple's Beautiful Gate?
14. In John's vision of the New Jerusalem, how many gates does the city have, and what are they made of?

✦Portable Places to Dwell

1. Who accepted an invitation to hide in a tent, and was then murdered by the woman who invited him?
2. What famous ship captain lived in a tent?
3. What, in the dream of a Midianite soldier, tumbled into the Midianite camp and flattened a tent?
4. Who took spoils from the fallen Jericho and buried them inside his tent?
5. Who took his wife to his mother's tent on their wedding night?
6. Who was "the father of such as dwell in tents"?
7. Who stored Goliath's armor in his tent?
8. What tent was made according to God's specifications?
9. Who plundered the tents of the Syrians after the army fled their camp?

3. Uriah, the husband of Bathsheba (2 Samuel 11:9)
4. Samson (Judges 16:3)
5. On the doorposts of their houses and on their gates (Deuteronomy 11:20)
6. God (Genesis 7:16)
7. Hezekiah (2 Kings 18:16)
8. Finding the door to Lot's home (Genesis 19:11)
9. Lamb's blood (Exodus 12:7)
10. The gates and the everlasting doors (Psalm 24:7-9)
11. The angel of the Lord (Matthew 28:2)
12. Philadelphia (Revelation 3:8)
13. Peter and John (Acts 3:2-7)
14. Twelve, made of pearl (Revelation 21)

Portable Places to Dwell (Answers)

1. Sisera (Judges 4:17-21)
2. Noah (Genesis 9:21)
3. A cake of barley (Judges 7:13-14)
4. Achan (Joshua 7:21)
5. Isaac (Genesis 24:67)
6. Jabal (Genesis 4:20)
7. David (1 Samuel 17:54)
8. The tabernacle (Exodus 26:1-4)
9. The Samaritans (2 Kings 7:3-16)

10. Who commanded his descendants to always live in tents?
11. Who pitched a tent in Jerusalem to house the ark of the covenant?
12. Who killed an Israelite man and a Moabite woman inside the man's tent?
13. Who lived in tents in the wilderness of Sin?
14. Who did Noah say would dwell in the tents of Shem?
15. What rebel against David said, "Every man to his tents, O Israel"?
16. What prophet said, "The Lord shall save the tents of Judah"?
17. What king were the people of Israel rebelling against when they said, "To your tents, O Israel"?
18. Who compares her dark skin to the blackness of the "tents of Kedar"?
19. What prophet saw "the tents of Cushan in affliction"?

10. Jonadab (Jeremiah 35:6-10)
11. David (1 Chronicles 15:1)
12. Phinehas, Aaron's grandson (Numbers 25:6-8)
13. The Israelites (Exodus 33:10)
14. Japheth (Genesis 9:27)
15. Sheba (2 Samuel 20:1)
16. Zechariah (12:7)
17. Rehoboam (2 Kings 12:16)
18. The woman in the Song of Solomon (1:5)
19. Habakkuk (3:7)

PART 10
The Finer Things

✦Makers of Music

1. What stringed instruments did John hear in his vision of the heavenly throne?
2. Who is mentioned as the father of those who play the harp and organ?
3. What prophetess played a timbrel and led the women of Israel in a victory song after the Red Sea incident?
4. What caused Saul's "evil spirit" to leave him?
5. Who wrote over a thousand songs?
6. What is the only book of the Bible that contains numerous directions for musical accompaniment?
7. At the dedication of Solomon's temple, 120 priests played what instruments?
8. What king of Israel had 4,000 musicians who praised the Lord with instruments the king made?
9. What prophet prophesied while accompanied by a minstrel?
10. When the foundation for the second temple was laid, the priests played trumpets. What did the Levites play?
11. What king, who was also a poet and musician, embarrassed his wife by dancing in the streets?
12. What prophetic book of the Old Testament contains musical directions?

✦Artsy, Craftsy Types

1. What notorious opponent of Paul was a silversmith in Ephesus?
2. What leader fashioned a brass snake?
3. Who was the first metal craftsman in the Bible?
4. What Israelite, a worker in gold, silver, brass, stone, and wood, had responsibility for furnishing the tabernacle?
5. Who built a huge ship of gopherwood?

Makers of Music (Answers)

1. Harps (Revelation 14:2-3)
2. Jubal (Genesis 4:21)
3. Miriam (Exodus 15:20-21)
4. David's harp playing (1 Samuel 16:23)
5. Solomon (1 Kings 4:32)
6. Psalms
7. Trumpets (2 Chronicles 5:11-14)
8. David (1 Chronicles 23:5)
9. Elisha (2 Kings 3:15-16)
10. Cymbals (Nehemiah 12:35-36)
11. David (2 Samuel 6:16, 20)
12. Habakkuk (3:1, 3, 9, 13, 19)

Artsy, Craftsy Types (Answers)

1. Demetrius (Acts 19:24)
2. Moses (Numbers 21:9)
3. Tubal-cain (Genesis 4:22)
4. Bezaleel (Exodus 31:1-6)
5. Noah (Genesis 6:13-22)

6. What coppersmith had, according to Paul, done him great harm?
7. Who fashioned a golden calf?
8. What was the trade of Paul, Aquila, and Priscilla?
9. What craftsman from Tyre was put in charge of all the temple's bronze work?
10. What son of a goldsmith was involved in rebuilding the walls of Jerusalem?
11. What engraver and embroiderer helped construct materials for the tabernacle?

✦Looking Good, Smelling Good

1. Who had a harem with women that were "purified" with perfumes?
2. What evil queen "painted her face" before meeting with the rebel king Jehu?
3. What book mentions a woman using such perfumes as spikenard, saffron, calamus, cinnamon, frankincense, myrrh, aloes, and many others?
4. What prophet refused to use anointing oils during three weeks of mourning?
5. Who anointed Jesus' head with an expensive ointment known as spikenard?
6. What sweet-smelling substances were brought to the infant Jesus?
7. What Hebrew officials were anointed with holy oil perfumed with aromatic spices?
8. According to Proverbs 27:9, what do ointment and perfume do?
9. What two prophets speak critically of women putting on eye makeup?
10. What woman, portrayed in Proverbs 7, perfumed her bed with myrrh, aloes, and cinnamon?
11. Where was Jesus when a sinful woman poured an alabaster jar of perfume on his feet?
12. What man uses myrrh, frankincense, and other spices as perfumes?

6. Alexander (2 Timothy 4:14)
7. Aaron (Exodus 32:4)
8. Tentmaking (Acts 18:1-3)
9. Hiram (1 Kings 7:13-14)
10. Uzziel (Nehemiah 3:8)
11. Aholiab (Exodus 38:23)

Looking Good, Smelling Good (Answers)

1. King Ahasuerus (Esther 2:12)
2. Jezebel (2 Kings 9:30)
3. The Song of Solomon
4. Daniel (10:3)
5. Mary, Lazarus' sister (John 12:3)
6. Frankincense and myrrh (Matthew 2:11)
7. Israel's priests (Exodus 30:23-33)
8. "Rejoice the heart"
9. Jeremiah (4:30) and Ezekiel (23:40)
10. The adulteress
11. At the home of Simon the Pharisee (Luke 7:36-50)
12. The male lover in the Song of Solomon

✦Rings on Their Fingers

1. What dreaming ruler gave Joseph his own ring?
2. In which of Jesus' parables does a ring play a part?
3. Who did King Ahasuerus of Persia give his ring to?
4. When Daniel was sealed up in the lions' den, who placed his signet ring on the stone?
5. For what did the Israelites give up their rings and other jewelry?
6. After the death of Haman, who received the Persian king's signet ring?

✦Glad Rags

1. Who wore a camel's hair tunic?
2. What king of Israel is mentioned as wearing a crown and a gold bracelet?
3. What Egyptian official was given fine linen, the pharaoh's ring, and a gold chain for his neck?
4. What people had such well-made clothes that years of wilderness wandering did not even wear out their shoes?
5. Whose eye-catching cloak caused murderous envy in his brothers?
6. The best-dressed man in Israel wore fine colored linen with embroidered bells and pomegranates, a linen breastplate with gold and precious stones, and a gold-studded hat. Who was he?
7. What down-and-out man is mentioned as having worn a gold earring in his better days?
8. Only one person is mentioned in the Bible as having worn gloves. Who?
9. What warriors were so extravagant that even their camels wore necklaces?
10. What people wore fine Egyptian linen and purple robes?

Rings on Their Fingers (Answers)

1. The Pharaoh (Genesis 41:42)
2. The parable of the prodigal son (since the son was given a ring by his father upon returning home) (Luke 15:22)
3. Haman (Esther 3:10-13)
4. The king (Daniel 6:17)
5. As a freewill offering for the tabernacle (Exodus 35:22)
6. Mordecai (Esther 8:2-13)

Glad Rags (Answers)

1. John the Baptist (Matthew 3:4)
2. Saul (2 Samuel 1:10)
3. Joseph (Genesis 42:42)
4. The Israelites (Deuteronomy 29:5)
5. Joseph's (Genesis 37:3)
6. The high priest (Exodus 28)
7. Job (42:11)
8. Jacob (Genesis 27:16)
9. The Midianites (Judges 8:24-26)
10. The "princes of the sea" (Phoenicians) (Ezekiel 26:16)

PART 11
The Domestic Scene

✦So Many Children

1. What judge had 70 sons?
2. Who is the first child mentioned in the Bible?
3. Who was Noah's youngest son?
4. What king was the youngest of eight brothers?
5. Who was Joseph's younger son?
6. Who is the youngest son of Adam mentioned by name?
7. Who were the first twins mentioned in the Bible?
8. Which disciple was probably a twin?
9. Who died giving birth to Benjamin?
10. Was the prodigal son the older or younger son?
11. What wicked king of Israel had 70 sons?
12. Who had 19 sons and 1 daughter by his legitimate wives?
13. Who was older, Moses or Aaron?
14. Who was Jacob's youngest son?
15. Who was born first, Jacob or Esau?
16. What king of Judah had 28 sons and 60 daughters?
17. What court prophet of David's had 14 sons and 3 daughters?
18. What prophet spoke of a time of peace when a little child would lead the wild beasts?
19. Who made sacrifices in case any of his children had sinned?
20. Which epistle advises, "Children, obey your parents in the Lord"?
21. According to Malachi, who will come to turn the hearts of the children to their fathers?
22. What little-known judge of Israel had 30 sons?
23. Who did Paul advise that a bishop must be able to control his own children?
24. In which Gospel did Jesus predict that children rebelling against their parents would be a sign of the end times?
25. Which of the Ten Commandments states that children will be punished for their parents' sins?

So Many Children (Answers)

1. Gideon (Judges 8:30)
2. Cain (Genesis 4:1)
3. Ham (Genesis 9:18-24)
4. David (1 Samuel 17:12-14)
5. Ephraim (Genesis 41:51-52)
6. Seth (Genesis 4:25)
7. Jacob and Esau (Genesis 25:23-26)
8. Thomas (John 11:16)
9. Rachel (Genesis 35:16-18)
10. The younger (Luke 15:11-32)
11. Ahab (2 Kings 10:1)
12. David (1 Chronicles 3:1-9)
13. Aaron (Exodus 7:7)
14. Benjamin (Genesis 35:16-18)
15. Esau (Genesis 25:25-26)
16. Rehoboam (2 Chronicles 11:21)
17. Heman (1 Chronicles 25:5)
18. Isaiah (11:6)
19. Job (1:5)
20. Ephesians (6:1)
21. Elijah (Malachi 4:6)
22. Jair (Judges 10:3-4)
23. Timothy (1 Timothy 3:4)
24. Mark (13:12)
25. The second (against graven images) (Exodus 20:4)

26. Which Gospel does not mention the little children coming to Jesus?
27. Who advised young Christians to stop thinking like children?
28. Which Gospel says that the child Jesus grew up strong?
29. What prophet advised people to tell their children about the locust plague?
30. Which epistle advises fathers not to exasperate their children?
31. What book says that a child raised up in the right way will never depart from it?
32. What priest was too indulgent toward his spoiled sons?
33. What prophet had dishonest sons who took bribes?
34. Which son was Isaac partial to?
35. What king grieved and wailed over his wayward son?
36. Who was Jacob's favorite son?
37. Who made a little coat for her son every year when she went to offer the annual sacrifice?
38. Which psalm says that children are like arrows in the hands of a warrior?
39. What book mentions how wonderful grandchildren are?
40. What prophet named his sons Maher-shalal-hash-baz and Shear-jashub?
41. According to the Law, what is the penalty for anyone who attacks his mother or father?
42. What prophet talks about children dishonoring their parents, so that a man's enemies are in his own household?
43. According to Deuteronomy, what must be done to a rebellious son who will not submit to discipline?
44. What judge of Israel had 40 sons and 30 grandsons?
45. What Old Testament man almost sacrificed his beloved son?
46. What judge of Israel sacrificed his daughter?
47. Who did Paul say had known the Scriptures from his infancy?
48. Which of Gideon's 70 sons (the youngest) was the only one to escape the plot of his scheming brother Abimelech?
49. Who were Perez and Zerah?
50. Who died after giving birth to a son named Ichabod?
51. Who said that we must change and become like children?

26. John
27. Paul (1 Corinthians 14:20)
28. Luke (1:80)
29. Joel (1:3)
30. Ephesians (6:4)
31. Proverbs (22:6)
32. Eli (1 Samuel 3:13)
33. Samuel (1 Samuel 8:3)
34. Esau (Genesis 25:28)
35. David (2 Samuel 18:33)
36. Joseph (Genesis 37:3)
37. Hannah (1 Samuel 2:19)
38. 127:4
39. Proverbs (17:6)
40. Isaiah (7:3; 8:1-4)
41. Death (Exodus 21:15)
42. Micah (7:6)
43. He must be stoned (Deuteronomy 21:18-21)
44. Abdon (Judges 12:13-14)
45. Abraham (Genesis 22)
46. Jephthah (Judges 11:30-40)
47. Timothy (2 Timothy 3:15)
48. Jotham (Judges 9:1-5)
49. Twin sons of Judah and Tamar (Genesis 38:29-30)
50. The wife of Phinehas (1 Samuel 4:19-22)
51. Jesus (Matthew 18:3)

52. Which book says that children will not be put to death for their parents' sins?
53. Who told believers that the promises of God were for their children as well as themselves?
54. Which epistle says that parents are to provide for their children, not vice versa?
55. What prophet said, "Great shall be the peace of thy children"?
56. What prophet said that the son would not share the guilt of the father?
57. What prophet said he was neither a prophet nor a prophet's son?
58. Who envisioned a time when sons and daughters would prophesy?
59. Who asked his childless wife if he was not worth more to her than ten sons?
60. Who was told that she had a daughter-in-law who treated her better than seven sons could?
61. What king made a wise decision about a child claimed by two prostitutes?
62. Who was adopted by Mordecai as his own daughter?
63. What psalm advises dashing the babies of Babylon against stones?

✦Multiple Marriages

1. What king had 700 wives and 300 concubines?
2. Who was the first man in the Bible mentioned as having more than one wife?
3. Who married sisters Rachel and Leah?
4. Who fathered 70 sons by his many wives?
5. Whose father had two wives named Hannah and Peninnah?
6. What hairy man had three wives named Judith, Bashemath, and Mahalath?
7. What early king had two wives named Ahinoam and Rizpah?
8. What woman was married to two of Judah's sons?
9. What New Testament woman had had at least five husbands?

52. Deuteronomy (24:16)
53. Peter (Acts 2:39)
54. 2 Corinthians (12:14)
55. Isaiah (54:13)
56. Ezekiel (18:20)
57. Amos (7:14)
58. Joel (2:28)
59. Elkanah (1 Samuel 1:8)
60. Naomi (Ruth 4:15)
61. Solomon (1 Kings 3:16-28)
62. Esther (2:7)
63. Psalm 137:8-9

Multiple Marriages (Answers)

1. Solomon (1 Kings 11:3)
2. Lamech (Genesis 4:19)
3. Jacob (Genesis 29:15-25)
4. Gideon (Judges 8:30)
5. Samuel (1 Samuel 1:1-2)
6. Esau (Genesis 26:24; 28:9)
7. Saul (1 Samuel 14:50; 2 Samuel 3:7)
8. Tamar (Genesis 38:6-10)
9. The woman at the well (John 4:6-19)

10. Who asked Jesus a ridiculous question about a woman who successively married seven brothers?
11. Who had Mahlon and Boaz for husbands?
12. What woman, given to Phaltiel by her father Saul, was later reclaimed by David?
13. What king of Judah had 14 wives?
14. What Persian king had wives named Vashti and Esther?
15. What son of Solomon had 18 wives and 60 concubines?
16. Whose wives included Abigail, Maacah, Haggith, and Eglah?
17. What patriarch took Keturah as his third wife?
18. Who had two wives, one of them named Zipporah?
19. What king, much influenced by his dominating wife, also had other wives?
20. What judge of Israel lost his Philistine wife to his friend?

◆Widow Women

1. Who probably left more widows than anyone else?
2. What lying woman was a widow for only about three hours?
3. What book of the Old Testament is named for a famous widow who became an ancestress of David?
4. Who became a widow because of King David's lust?
5. What aged prophetess in Jerusalem was a widow?
6. Who posed to Jesus a foolish riddle about a woman who was a widow several times over?
7. What commendable deed was done by a poor widow Jesus saw in the temple?
8. Which church in Greece is mentioned by Paul as having widows in need of care?
9. Which of Paul's proteges had widows under his jurisdiction?
10. What woman of Joppa gave away clothing to the widows?
11. What city was home to the widow whose son Jesus raised from the dead?
12. What parable of Jesus has a widow as the main character?
13. What infamous widow was thrown from a window after she had put on makeup?
14. What prophet revived the son of the widow of Zarephath?

10. The Sadducees (Mark 12:18-25)
11. Ruth (Ruth 4:10, 13)
12. Michal (2 Samuel 3:13-16)
13. Abijah (2 Chronicles 13:21)
14. Ahasuerus (Esther 1:10-12; 2:1-17)
15. Rehoboam (2 Chronicles 11:21)
16. David (2 Samuel 12:8)
17. Abraham (Genesis 16:3; 23:19; 25:1)
18. Moses (Exodus 18:2; Numbers 12:1)
19. Ahab (1 Kings 20:7)
20. Samson (Judges 14:20)

Widow Women (Answers)

1. Solomon, since he had 700 wives (1 Kings 11:3)
2. Sapphira, who conspired with her husband Ananias to lie to Peter about the property they had sold (Acts 5:5-10)
3. Ruth
4. Bathsheba (2 Samuel 11:26)
5. Anna (Luke 2:36-37)
6. The Sadducees (Mark 12:22)
7. She put two mites (coins) in the temple treasury (Mark 12:42)
8. The church at Corinth (1 Corinthians 7:8)
9. Timothy (1 Timothy 5:3)
10. Tabitha (Acts 9:39)
11. Nain (Luke 7:12-15)
12. The parable of the unjust judge (Luke 18:2-5)
13. Jezebel (2 Kings 9:30-37)
14. Elijah (1 Kings 17:8-24)

15. What widow had a husband whom the Lord killed and, later, had an affair with her father-in-law?
16. What widow, the daughter-in-law of the priest Eli, had a baby named Ichabod?
17. What king was almost fooled by the conniving woman of Tekoa who pretended to be a poor widow?
18. Whose mother was a widow named Zeruah?
19. Which widows in Jerusalem were neglected in the daily distribution of funds?
20. What king forced ten of his concubines to live as widows for the rest of their lives?
21. Who married King David after her drunken husband suffered a stroke and died?
22. Who suggested that Christian widows were better off not to remarry?
23. What prophet issued dire warning against people who took advantage of widows?
24. Who did Jesus accuse of "devouring widows' houses"?
25. What New Testament epistle mentions kindness to widows as a mark of true religion?
26. What great city does Isaiah predict will become like a helpless widow?

◆Weddings, Dowries, and Divorces

1. Who made a wedding feast before giving the wrong bride to Jacob?
2. What gruesome objects did Saul require from David as dowry for his daughter?
3. Who prompted the Jews after the Babylonian exile to divorce their foreign wives?
4. Where was the first wedding Jesus attended?
5. Who, according to John, is the bride of Christ?
6. Who made a seven-day marriage feast but never married the woman he intended?
7. Who gave the bride away at the first wedding?
8. How did Boaz obtain Ruth as his wife?

15. Tamar, wife of Er (Genesis 34:25)
16. The unnamed wife of Phinehas (1 Samuel 4:19)
17. David (2 Samuel 14:1-20)
18. King Jeroboam of Israel (1 Kings 11:26)
19. The Greek-speaking (Hellenic) Jews (Acts 6:1)
20. David (2 Samuel 20:3)
21. Abigail (1 Samuel 25:37-39)
22. Paul (1 Corinthians 7:8-9)
23. Malachi (3:5)
24. The Pharisees (Mark 12:40)
25. James (1:27)
26. Babylon (Isaiah 47:8)

Weddings, Dowries, and Divorces (Answers)

1. Laban (Genesis 29:22-25)
2. A hundred Philistine foreskins (1 Samuel 18:25, 27)
3. Ezra (Ezra 10)
4. Cana (John 2:1-11)
5. The church (Revelation 19:7-9)
6. Samson (Judges 14:10-20)
7. God (Genesis 2:22-24)
8. He purchased the property of Naomi, her mother-in-law (Ruth 3–4)

9. When Shechem the Hivite asked to marry Dinah, what did her brothers ask as a dowry?
10. What did Jacob have to do to marry Rachel?
11. Which Gospel records Jesus' parable of a king's wedding feast for his son?
12. Who sent the servant woman Hagar away at his wife's urging?
13. What unscrupulous king divorced his first wife to marry his brother's wife?
14. In Jesus' parable, how many virgins were to accompany the bride and groom?
15. Who arranged Ishmael's marriage?
16. Who was the first polygamist?
17. Who said that Moses allowed divorce because of people's hardness of heart?
18. Where does the Bible prohibit polygamy?
19. What prophet spoke about Jews divorcing their wives to marry pagan woman?
20. What was the levirate law?
21. What was considered proof of the bride's virginity?
22. Which Gospel states that Jesus considered adultery to be grounds for divorce?
23. According to Jeremiah, who did God divorce?
24. What morally upright man wanted to quietly break off his engagement?
25. Which of Elkanah's wives was his favorite?
26. Who was thrown into prison for criticizing the marriage of a king?
27. Which of Paul's epistles gives the most information about marriage?
28. What Egyptian woman did Joseph marry?
29. Who was Naomi's husband?
30. What wife of David was also married to Nabal?
31. What king of Judah married a daughter of Ahab?
32. What emperor married a Jewish girl?
33. What godly priest had a wife named Jehosheba?
34. What prophet married a prostitute named Gomer?
35. Who was married to Zebedee, father of James and John?
36. What childless woman was married to the priest Zacharias?
37. What wicked Persian official had a wife named Zeresh?

9. That all of Shechem's men be circumcised (Genesis 34:1-16)
10. Serve Laban for fourteen years (Genesis 29:16-30)
11. Matthew (22:1-14)
12. Abraham (Genesis 21:9-14)
13. Herod (Matthew 14:3-4)
14. Ten (Matthew 25:1-13)
15. Hagar, his mother (Genesis 21:21)
16. Lamech (Genesis 4:19)
17. Jesus (Matthew 19:8)
18. It doesn't.
19. Malachi (2:10-16)
20. When a man died without children, his brother was expected to take his wife so as to provide descendants for the dead man (Genesis 38:8-10)
21. A blood-stained cloth (Deuteronomy 22:13-21)
22. Matthew (19:3-12)
23. Israel (Jeremiah 3:8)
24. Joseph (Matthew 1:19)
25. Hannah (1 Samuel 1:1-8)
26. John the Baptist (Matthew 14:3-4)
27. 1 Corinthians (ch. 7)
28. Asenath (Genesis 41:45)
29. Elimelech (Ruth 1:2)
30. Abigail (1 Samuel 25:3)
31. Joram, who married Athaliah (2 Kings 8:21, 26)
32. Ahasuerus (Esther 2:16)
33. Jehoiada (2 Chronicles 22:11)
34. Hosea (Hosea 1)
35. Salome (Matthew 4:21; Mark 16:1)
36. Elisabeth (Luke 1:5)
37. Haman (Esther 5:14; 6:13)

38. What saintly woman was the wife of Cuza, the head of Herod's household?
39. What Jewish-Christian couple were probably Paul's closest married friends?
40. What husband and wife lied to Peter about their finances?
41. What Roman governor had a Jewish wife named Drusilla?
42. Who took a wife that was not only nameless but ancestor-less?
43. What unknown wife turned into a pillar of salt?
44. What judge had a Philistine wife?
45. What unnamed wife urged her husband to curse God?
46. What leprous Syrian soldier had a faithful wife?
47. What prophet was married to a prophet?
48. What prophet had a wife who died suddenly?
49. What wicked priest had a harlot wife?
50. Whose wife insisted that her husband have nothing to do with Jesus?
51. Who was Moses' first wife?
52. Who was the only disciple that we know for sure was married?

✦Miraculous Pregnancies

1. Who gave birth to a son when she was 90 years old?
2. What beloved wife of Jacob gave birth after many years to Joseph and Benjamin?
3. What elderly couple produced a child, in accordance with the words of an angel?
4. Who prophesied to the Shunammite woman that, though her husband was too old, she would bear a child?
5. Why did God cause barrenness among the women of Abimelech's household?
6. What woman, long barren, gave birth to twins?
7. Who was taunted by her husband's other wife for being childless, though she later bore a son?
8. Whose astounded mother called herself the "handmaiden of the Lord" when told she would bear a child?
9. Whose mother was told by an angel that she would bear a son who would deliver Israel from the Philistines?

38. Joanna (Luke 8:3)
39. Aquila and Priscilla (Acts 18:2)
40. Ananias and Sapphira (Acts 5)
41. Felix (Acts 24:24)
42. Cain (Genesis 4:17)
43. Lot's wife (Genesis 19:26)
44. Samson (Judges 14)
45. Job's wife (Job 2:9-10)
46. Naaman (2 Kings 5:1-4)
47. Isaiah, whose wife was called a prophetess (Isaiah 8:3)
48. Ezekiel (24:18)
49. Amaziah (Amos 7:10-17)
50. Pilate's (Matthew 27:19)
51. Zipporah (Exodus 2:21)
52. Peter (Mark 1:30)

Miraculous Pregnancies (Answers)

1. Sarah (Genesis 21:1-5)
2. Rachel (Genesis 30:22-24; 35:18)
3. Elisabeth and Zacharias (Luke 1:7-9, 13, 18)
4. Elisha (2 Kings 4:13-17)
5. Abimelech had taken Sarah for himself (Genesis 20:17-18)
6. Rebekah (Genesis 25:21-26)
7. Hannah, mother of Samuel (1 Samuel 1:1-19)
8. Jesus' (Luke 1:26-38)
9. Samson's (Judges 13:3, 5)

10. What very old man remarried after his wife's death and continued to father children?

✦Brother Against Brother

1. Whose older brother refused to attend the welcome home party?
2. What son of Gideon killed seventy of his brothers at once?
3. What judge, an illegitimate son, was thrown out of the house by his brothers?
4. Who hated his brother for taking away his birthright?
5. What did Moses rebuke Aaron for?
6. Who was the first man to murder his brother?
7. Who hated his brother Ammon for what he had done to Tamar?
8. What dreamy boy was hated for being his father's favorite?
9. What older brother of David chewed him out for coming to watch the Israelites fighting the Philistines?

✦Menservants, Maidservants

1. What runaway servant was the main subject of one of Paul's epistles?
2. Who sent two of his servants to fetch Peter from Joppa?
3. To whose servant did Peter deny any knowledge of Jesus?
4. Who, with 318 of his servants, defeated the captors of Sodom and Gomorrah?
5. Who was Elisha's servant?
6. What Egyptian official had Joseph as a servant?
7. Who was permanently crippled because a servant woman dropped him as a baby?
8. Who cut off the ear of Malchus, the high priest's servant?
9. Who had a servant girl who advised him to go to Elisha to be cured of leprosy?
10. What servant woman was the mother of Ishmael?
11. Who did Abraham's eldest servant find a wife for?
12. Where did Jesus heal a centurion's servant?
13. Who was a servant to the Persian king Artaxerxes?

10. Abraham (Genesis 25:1-6)

Brother Against Brother (Answers)

1. The prodigal son's (Luke 15:28)
2. Abimelech (Judges 9:1-5)
3. Jephthah (Judges 11:1-2)
4. Esau (Genesis 27:41)
5. Making the golden calf (Exodus 32:19-22)
6. Cain (Genesis 4:8)
7. Absalom (2 Samuel 13:22)
8. Joseph (Genesis 37:4)
9. Eliab (1 Samuel 17:28-30)

Menservants, Maidservants (Answers)

1. Onesimus (Philemon)
2. Cornelius (Acts 10:7-8)
3. The high priest's (John 18:26)
4. Abraham (Genesis 14:14-15)
5. Gehazi (2 Kings 4:12)
6. Potiphar (Genesis 39)
7. Mephibosheth (2 Samuel 4:4)
8. Peter (John 18:10)
9. Naaman the Syrian (2 Kings 5:2-3)
10. Hagar (Genesis 16:1)
11. Isaac (Genesis 24)
12. Capernaum (Matthew 8:13)
13. Nehemiah (1:11)

14. What two servants of Pharaoh were in prison with Joseph?
15. Who was Laban's servant for many years?
16. Whose servant woman took Moses from the river?
17. What judge's servant killed him at his own request?
18. What two servant women bore children to Jacob?
19. Who made the Israelites into slaves?
20. In what parable are the servants of a landowner beaten up?
21. In what parable are servants given money to invest?
22. At whose house did Peter deny Christ to a servant girl?
23. Who was Elijah's personal servant?
24. What people were, in the time of Joshua, cursed to be Israel's servants?
25. Who was Moses' personal servant?
26. Who was Jesus responding to when he told the parable of the unmerciful servant?

◆Speaking of Beds

1. Who had a huge bed made of iron?
2. What king sulked in bed because he couldn't acquire a certain piece of property?
3. What church was threatened with being thrown on a "bed of suffering"?
4. Whose bedridden mother-in-law was healed by Jesus?
5. What son of a king was murdered and decapitated while lying asleep in bed?
6. Who blessed the twelve tribes while lying in bed?
7. What book of the Old Testament speaks fondly of a "verdant bed"?
8. What prophet condemned the idle rich on their beds of ivory?
9. What bedridden palsied man was healed by Peter?
10. What was Jesus trying to prove when he told the lame man to take up his bed and walk?
11. According to Hebrews, what bed should be kept pure?
12. What scheming son of a king took to his bed in order to take advantage of his sister?
13. What king of Judah was murdered in his bed by his servants?

14. The chief butler and chief baker (Genesis 41)
15. Jacob (Genesis 29–31)
16. Pharaoh's daughter's (Exodus 2:5)
17. Abimelech's (Judges 9:54)
18. Bilhah and Zilpah (Genesis 30)
19. The Egyptians (Exodus 1:13)
20. The parable of the tenants (Mark 12:1-5)
21. The parable of the talents (Matthew 25:14-30)
22. The high priest's (John 18:17)
23. Elisha (2 Kings 3:11)
24. The Hivites (Joshua 9:23)
25. Joshua (Exodus 33:11)
26. Peter (Matthew 18:21-35)

Speaking of Beds (Answers)

1. Og, king of Bashan (Deuteronomy 3:11)
2. Ahab (1 Kings 21:4)
3. The church of Thyatira (Revelation 2:22)
4. Peter's (Mark 1:30)
5. Ishbosheth, son of Saul (2 Samuel 4:7)
6. Jacob (Genesis 47–49)
7. The Song of Solomon (1:16)
8. Amos (6:4)
9. Aeneas (Acts 9:33-34)
10. That the Son of man had authority to forgive sins (Matthew 9:1-8)
11. The marriage bed (Hebrews 13:4)
12. Amnon (2 Samuel 13:5)
13. Joash (2 Chronicles 24:25)

14. Who raised a dead boy by laying him on a bed and lying on top of him?
15. Who saved her husband's life by putting an idol in his bed, covering it, and pretending it was he?
16. Who tried to coax Joseph into going to bed?
17. What king of Israel was told by Elijah that he would never get up from the bed he was lying on?
18. Who put a bed in her home for the prophet Elisha?

14. Elijah (1 Kings 17:19)
15. Michal, wife of David (1 Samuel 19:11-17)
16. Potiphar's wife (Genesis 39:7)
17. Ahaziah (2 Kings 1:4)
18. The rich woman of Shunem (2 Kings 4:10)

PART 12

Things to Eat and Drink

✦Food, Food, Food

1. Who was famous as an eater of locusts?
2. What four faithful young men refused to eat the rich foods of the king of Babylon?
3. Who traded his bread-and-lentil stew for his brother's birthright?
4. Who had a baker who made pastries for him?
5. What incident in David's life caused people to bring him all manner of foods to eat?
6. According to the Law, what was the Passover meal to be composed of?
7. What old man was deceived when his son dressed in goatskin gloves and presented him with a meal of cooked goat?
8. Who served cheese, milk, and veal to the Lord when he made his appearance in the form of three men?
9. What did Ezekiel's edible scroll taste like in his mouth?
10. What judge of Israel cooked an angel a meal that included a pot of broth?
11. In what book of the Bible is Canaan first described as a land flowing with milk and honey?
12. What prized animal was killed for food when the prodigal son returned home?
13. In what country did the Hebrews feed on cucumbers, melons, leeks, onions, and garlic?
14. When Jacob's sons made a second trip to Egypt, what food did they bring with them as a gift for Joseph?
15. What prophet, who was a herdsman and fruit picker by trade, had a vision of a basket of ripe fruit?
16. Who ate honey out of a lion's carcass?
17. What miraculous food resembled coriander seed?
18. What prophet purified some deadly stew and a water supply?
19. Who cursed a fig tree for not bearing fruit?

Food, Food, Food (Answers)

1. John the Baptist (Matthew 3:4)
2. Daniel, Shadrach, Meshach, and Abednego (Daniel 1:3-16)
3. Jacob (Genesis 25:29-34)
4. The pharaoh of Joseph's time (Genesis 40:16-17)
5. His flight from the rebellious Absalom (2 Samuel 17:22-29)
6. A cooked lamb, unleavened bread, and bitter herbs (Exodus 12:3-10)
7. Isaac (Genesis 27:14-18)
8. Abraham (Genesis 18:1-8)
9. Honey (Ezekiel 3:3)
10. Gideon (Judges 6:19)
11. Exodus (3:8)
12. The fatted calf (Luke 15:23)
13. Egypt (Numbers 11:5)
14. Almonds (Genesis 43:11)
15. Amos (8:1)
16. Samson (Judges 14:5-9)
17. Manna (Exodus 16:31)
18. Elisha (2 Kings 2:19-22; 4:38-41)
19. Jesus (Matthew 21:14)

20. What ominous winged creature is described as unclean in the Law?

◆Sweet, Sour, Bitter, Poison

1. What prophet ate a book and found it sweet?
2. According to Jeremiah, what kind of grape sets the children's teeth on edge?
3. What kind of herbs were the Israelites supposed to eat with the Passover meal?
4. Who posed a riddle about finding something sweet in a lion's carcass?
5. According to Jesus after the Resurrection, what would his followers be able to drink?
6. What substance—probably very bitter—did Moses make the people of Israel drink?
7. Who ate a book that was sweet at first but turned bitter afterwards?
8. According to Proverbs, what kind of water is sweet?
9. What sweet substance was part of John the Baptist's diet?
10. What prophet made some poison stew edible by pouring meal into it?
11. According to Proverbs, what kind of bread is sweet to a man?
12. What did Moses do to make the bitter waters of Marah drinkable?
13. Who told the repentant people of Israel to go home and enjoy sweet drinks?
14. In Revelation, what falls on the earth's waters to make them bitter?
15. According to Proverbs, what sort of person thinks even bitter things are sweet?

◆Starvation Dieting

1. Which of the four horsemen in Revelation spreads famine on the earth?
2. Who moved with Naomi to Moab to escape famine?

20. The bat (Leviticus 11:13-19)

Sweet, Sour, Bitter, Poison (Answers)

1. Ezekiel (2:9–3:3)
2. Sour (Jeremiah 31:29)
3. Bitter herbs (Exodus 12:8)
4. Samson (Judges 14:14)
5. Poison (Mark 16:17-18)
6. Gold dust from the golden calf Moses had destroyed (Exodus 32:20)
7. John (Revelation 10:9-10)
8. Stolen water (Proverbs 9:17)
9. Honey (Matthew 3:4)
10. Elisha (2 Kings 4:41)
11. Bread of deceit (Proverbs 20:17)
12. Threw a piece of wood into the water (Exodus 15:25)
13. Nehemiah and Ezra (Nehemiah 8:10)
14. A star (Revelation 8:10)
15. A hungry person (Proverbs 27:7)

Starvation Dieting (Answers)

1. The rider on the black horse (Revelation 6:5-6)
2. Elimelech (Ruth 1:1-2)

3. Who was food storage supervisor in Egypt when famine came?
4. What nation was the victim of a seven-year famine during Elisha's ministry?
5. Where did Abram go when famine struck?
6. What New Testament prophet predicted a worldwide famine?
7. Who went to live with the Philistines during a famine?
8. What two plagues probably caused famine in Egypt?
9. What king's reign saw a three-year famine, which ended when Elijah said rain was coming?
10. What figure in a parable found himself the victim of famine?
11. What king endured famine because Saul had slain the Gibeonites?
12. In the time of the judges, what marauders plundered so many crops and livestock that they probably caused famine in Israel?
13. What Babylonian king caused famine in Jerusalem?
14. Who sent his sons to Egypt because of famine in the land?

◆Spreading a Feast

1. What king had a feast where a mysterious hand wrote on the wall?
2. Who threw a royal feast where his wife disobeyed him?
3. Who spread a meal for some angels at the oaks of Mamre?
4. Who gave a wedding feast and then pulled a trick on his son-in-law?
5. Whose children were killed while attending a feast?
6. Who told a bizarre riddle at his wedding feast?
7. What Pharisee had a feast that Jesus attended?
8. In Revelation, what holy figure has a wedding feast?
9. Where did Jesus have a post-Resurrection fish dinner with seven of his disciples?
10. What dweller in Sodom had a meal prepared for angelic visitors?
11. What Egyptian official had a feast prepared for his kinsmen from back home?

3. Joseph (Genesis 41)
4. Israel (2 Kings 8:1-2)
5. Egypt (Genesis 12:10)
6. Agabus (Acts 11:28)
7. Isaac (Genesis 26:1)
8. Locusts and hail (Exodus 10:14-15)
9. Ahab's (1 Kings 17:1; 18:44-45)
10. The prodigal son (Luke 15:14)
11. David (2 Samuel 21:1)
12. The Midianites (Judges 6:3-6)
13. Nebuchadnezzar (2 Kings 25:1-3)
14. Jacob (Genesis 42:1-2)

Spreading a Feast (Answers)

1. Belshazzar (Daniel 5)
2. Ahasuerus (Esther 1:3-12)
3. Abraham (Genesis 18:1-8)
4. Laban (Genesis 29:22-23)
5. Job's (Job 1:13)
6. Samson (Judges 14:10-14)
7. Simon (Luke 7:36-50)
8. The Lamb (Revelation 19:9)
9. By Lake Tiberias (John 21:1-13)
10. Lot (Genesis 19:3)
11. Joseph (Genesis 43:16-34)

12. What ruler threw a lavish feast where his wife's daughter danced?
13. At the last feast mentioned in the Bible, what is to be the gruesome food?
14. In what village did Jesus have his first dinner after his Resurrection?
15. What child was given a feast on the day he was weaned?
16. What city had a wedding feast where Jesus' first miracle was done?
17. What prophet served his team of oxen at his ordination feast?
18. What tax collector had a feast for Jesus?
19. What army man was given a feast when he joined the side of David?
20. Who gave a feast for the evil Haman?
21. Who was given a three-day feast when he began to reign over all Israel?
22. Who held a long feast when the Jerusalem temple was dedicated?
23. In the parable of the wedding feast, what is the fate of the man who did not put his best clothes on?
24. What town was the scene of the feast where Jesus was anointed with expensive perfume?
25. Who was given a banquet by King Ahasuerus when his beauty contest was over?
26. Who was given a feast where the entree was a fatted calf?
27. Who gave his officials a feast after God had spoken to him in a dream?

◆Fasts and Breaking of Fasts

1. What did Jesus eat after his resurrection to prove he was not a mere phantom?
2. Who fasted for forty days on Mount Sinai?
3. Who had a Passover meal with his followers in the upper room?
4. Who received meals at the hands of birds?
5. Who was raped after bringing a meal to her supposedly sick brother?

12. Herod (Mark 6:21)
13. The flesh of people and horses (Revelation 19:17-18)
14. Emmaus (Luke 24:30)
15. Isaac (Genesis 21:8)
16. Cana (John 2:1-12)
17. Elisha (1 Kings 19:21)
18. Levi (Luke 5:29)
19. Abner (2 Samuel 3:20)
20. Esther (7:1-10)
21. David (1 Chronicles 12:39)
22. Solomon (1 Kings 8:65)
23. He is tied up and thrown outside (Matthew 22:1-13)
24. Bethany (John 12:1-8)
25. Esther (2:17-18)
26. The prodigal son (Luke 15:23)
27. Solomon (1 Kings 3:15)

Fasts and Breaking of Fasts (Answers)

1. Fish (Luke 24:38-43)
2. Moses (Exodus 34:27-28)
3. Jesus (Matthew 26:1-30)
4. Elijah, fed by ravens (1 Kings 17:3-6)
5. Tamar (2 Samuel 13:1-14)

6. What meat was eaten at the Passover meal?
7. Who sold his birthright for a bowl of soup?
8. Who humbled himself and fasted when accused of Naboth's murder?
9. Who fasted after his child by Bathsheba died?
10. How many men had bound themselves by an oath to fast until they had killed Paul?
11. Who prepared a meal for two angels in Sodom?
12. Who obtained his father's blessing by preparing him a meal and pretending to be his brother?
13. What was the first sinful meal?
14. Who fasted for forty days after his baptism?
15. Who was on a ship with 275 passengers who fasted for fourteen days?
16. What Roman official was fasting and praying when an angel told him to send for Peter?
17. Who read the prophecy of Jeremiah when the people of Jerusalem gathered for a fast?
18. What prophet's preaching drove the people of Nineveh to fast?
19. Who fasted before leaving Babylonia for Jerusalem?
20. Who angered his father by unwittingly breaking a fast while pursuing the Philistines?
21. What two apostles prayed and fasted as they chose elders for the churches?
22. What king of Judah proclaimed a fast when the Moabites attacked?
23. What pagan king fasted after Daniel had been thrown into the lions' den?
24. Who proclaimed a day of fasting as part of the scheme to get Naboth's vineyard?
25. What, according to Jesus, do prayer and fasting accomplish?
26. Who was Paul waiting for while he fasted three days in Damascus?
27. What king fasted all day and night while unsuccessfully inquiring of the Lord?
28. What official in the Persian court fasted before presenting his case to the king?
29. Who fasted and wore sackcloth as he prayed for the liberation of his people from Persia?

6. Lamb (Exodus 12:1-20)
7. Esau (Genesis 25:29-34)
8. Ahab (1 Kings 21:27)
9. David (2 Samuel 12:15-16)
10. Forty (Acts 23:20-21)
11. Lot (Genesis 19:1-3)
12. Jacob (Genesis 27:1-29)
13. The forbidden fruit (Genesis 3:6)
14. Jesus (Matthew 4:1-2)
15. Paul (Acts 27:33)
16. Cornelius (Acts 10:1-3)
17. Baruch (Jeremiah 36:9-10)
18. Jonah (3:4-10)
19. Ezra (8:21-23)
20. Jonathan (1 Samuel 14:24-27)
21. Paul and Barnabas (Acts 14:23)
22. Jehoshaphat (2 Chronicles 20:1-4)
23. Darius (Daniel 6:18)
24. Jezebel (1 Kings 21:8-10)
25. Driving out demons (Matthew 17:21)
26. Ananias (Acts 9:9)
27. Saul (1 Samuel 28:20)
28. Nehemiah (1:1-4)
29. Daniel (9:3-4)

30. What church's elders fasted before sending Paul and Barnabas out as missionaries?
31. Where were the Israelites when Samuel had them fasting because of their idolatry?
32. In what country were the Jews when they fasted after learning of an executive order to have them all killed?
33. Whose death caused the people of Jabesh-Gilead to fast for seven days?
34. After Ezra had read the law to the people, what was the main sin that caused them to fast?

✦Fruit of the Vine

1. What did Paul recommend as a substitute for wine?
2. Who was called a glutton and a wine guzzler?
3. What prophet spoke of God putting Israel into a winepress?
4. What part of the body did Paul recommend wine for?
5. Where was the one place the priest could not enter after drinking wine?
6. What group of Israelites was never supposed to drink wine?
7. According to Paul's advice, what church official must not be a wine drinker?
8. What was mingled with the wine Jesus was offered on the cross?
9. What judge threshed wheat by his winepress to hide it from the Midianites?
10. According to Jesus, what do people prefer, old wine or new wine?
11. What kind of person, according to Proverbs, should be given wine?
12. According to what Jesus said at the Last Supper, when would he drink wine again with his disciples?
13. Who murdered the Midianite Zeeb at his winepress?
14. How many jars of water did Jesus turn into wine?
15. What, according to Jesus, happens when new wine is put into old wineskins?
16. What drinkers did Isaiah condemn?

30. Antioch's (Acts 13:1-3)
31. Mizpah (1 Samuel 7:3-6)
32. Persia (Esther 4:1-3, 15-16)
33. Saul's and Jonathan's (1 Samuel 31:13)
34. Marrying foreigners (Nehemiah 9:1-3)

Fruit of the Vine (Answers)

1. The Holy Spirit (Ephesians 5:18)
2. Jesus (Matthew 11:19)
3. Isaiah (63:1-4)
4. The stomach (1 Timothy 5:23)
5. The tabernacle (Leviticus 10:8-9)
6. The Nazarites (Numbers 6:2-3)
7. A bishop (or overseer) (1 Timothy 3:2-3)
8. Myrrh (Mark 15:23)
9. Gideon (Judges 6:11)
10. Old wine (Luke 5:39)
11. The sad or afflicted person (Proverbs 31:6-7)
12. When the kingdom had come (Matthew 26:27-29)
13. Gideon's army (Judges 7:25)
14. Six (John 2:1-10)
15. The wineskins burst (Luke 5:37-38)
16. Those who start early in the morning (Isaiah 5:11)

17. According to Romans, what good reason is there to avoid wine?

◆Under the Influence

1. What husband, the victim of David's adulterous scheming, was made drunk by the king?
2. What man was seduced by his daughters while he was drunk?
3. Who dropped dead as a stone on hearing bad news the morning after being drunk?
4. What virtuous man, who later married a virtuous woman, fell asleep in a heap of grain after eating and drinking?
5. Absalom wanted to avenge the rape of his sister, Tamar, so he waited until the rapist was very drunk. Who was this drunk, later slain by Absalom's men?
6. This king of Israel, who ruled barely two years, was assassinated while drunk. Who was he?
7. What Syrian king was getting drunk at a time when he was supposed to be making war on the Samaritans?
8. Nehemiah waited until this Persian king was softened up with wine before he asked the king to let the Jews return to their homeland. Who was the king?
9. What Persian queen refused to obey her drunken husband's order that she appear before his besotted guests?
10. Job's sons and daughters were so busy eating and drinking that they failed to notice that disaster was about to strike. What killed them?
11. The arrogant Babylonian king Belshazzar, drunk at his feast, committed an outrage when he asked for new drinking vessels to be brought in. What were these vessels that led to so much trouble for the king?

17. It might cause a brother to stumble (Romans 14:21)

Under the Influence (Answers)

1. Uriah, the husband of Bathsheba (2 Samuel 11:13)
2. Lot (Genesis 19:30-36)
3. Nabal, Abigail's husband (1 Samuel 25:36-37)
4. Boaz, husband of Ruth (Ruth 3:7-14)
5. Amnon, Absalom's half-brother (2 Samuel 13:28)
6. Elah (1 Kings 16:9)
7. Ben-hadad (1 Kings 20:12-19)
8. Artaxerxes (Nehemiah 2:1)
9. Vashti (Esther 1:3-12)
10. A great wind storm (Job 1:13-18)
11. Vessels from the temple of Jerusalem (Daniel 5:1-5)

PART 13

Matters of Life and Death

✦Strange Ways to Die

1. Who is the first individual who is killed by God for being wicked?
2. What devoured Aaron's sons, Nadab and Abihu, when they offered "strange fire" to the Lord?
3. What Canaanite captain was killed when Jael, a Hebrew woman, drove a tent peg through his skull?
4. Who was killed for touching the ark of the covenant?
5. The Lord sent a pestilence on Israel that killed 70,000 people. What act of King David brought this on?
6. God sent fire from heaven to kill the soldiers who came to capture what prophet?
7. What husband and wife dropped dead after it was revealed they had lied about the price of the possessions they had sold?
8. Who was hanged on the very gallows he had prepared for Mordecai?
9. What people were killed by great hailstones from heaven?
10. Who, along with his household, was swallowed up by the earth for rebelling against Moses?
11. What man, reluctant to produce children with his widowed sister-in-law, was slain by God?
12. What two cities were rained on by fire and brimstone?
13. What did God do when the Israelites began to complain about the death of Korah and his followers?
14. What was the last plague sent upon the Egyptians?
15. What son of Saul was murdered by two servants who stabbed him in the belly and carried his severed head to David?

Strange Ways to Die (Answers)

1. Er (Genesis 38:7)
2. Fire from God (Leviticus 10:1-2)
3. Sisera (Judges 4:18-21)
4. Uzzah (2 Samuel 6:6-7)
5. He numbered the people of Israel (2 Samuel 24:1-5)
6. Elijah (2 Kings 1:10, 12)
7. Ananias and Sapphira (Acts 5:1-10)
8. Haman (Esther 7:10—8:2)
9. Amorites (Joshua 10:8-14)
10. Korah (Numbers 16)
11. Onan (Genesis 38:9-10)
12. Sodom and Gomorrah (Genesis 19:24-25)
13. He sent a plague that killed 14,700 Israelites (Numbers 16:41-50)
14. The death of the firstborn (Exodus 12:29)
15. Ishbosheth, slain by Recab and Baanah (2 Samuel 4:5-8)

✦Back from the Dead

1. What prominent leader of Israel was summoned up from the dead by a witch?
2. Eutychus, who died after falling out of a window during a sermon, was raised from the dead by whom?
3. What prophet revived the son of the Zarephath widow?
4. Who raised Dorcas from the dead?
5. What man of Bethany was raised from his tomb by Jesus?
6. A man came to life again when his body came into contact with the buried bones of what prophet?
7. What was the name of the town where Jesus raised a widow's son from the dead?
8. Who did Elisha raise from the dead?
9. According to Matthew, what marvelous event occurred in conjunction with Jesus' death on the cross?
10. Whose daughter did Jesus bring back to life?

✦Seven Suicides

1. What judge of Israel had his armor-bearer kill him so he would avoid the disgrace of being killed by a woman?
2. According to Matthew's account, Judas committed suicide by hanging himself. How, according to Acts, did Judas die?
3. What wicked king committed suicide by burning down his palace?
4. What king killed himself by falling on his own sword?
5. What strong man killed himself along with a houseful of Philistines?
6. What friend of Absalom was so disgraced when Absalom did not follow his advice that he went and hanged himself?
7. Who refused to obey the king's request to kill him, then followed the king in committing suicide?

Back from the Dead (Answers)

1. Samuel (1 Samuel 28:7-20)
2. Paul (Acts 20:9-10)
3. Elijah (1 Kings 17:17-22)
4. Peter (Acts 9:36-41)
5. Lazarus (John 11:1-44)
6. Elisha (2 Kings 13:20-21)
7. Nain (Luke 7:11-15)
8. The son of the Shunammite woman (2 Kings 4:32-35)
9. Many holy people came out of their graves (Matthew 27:52-53)
10. Jairus' (Luke 8:41-42, 49-55)

Seven Suicides (Answers)

1. Abimelech, who had a millstone dropped on his head by a woman of Thebez (Judges 9:54)
2. He fell headlong in a field and burst open (Acts 1:18)
3. Zimri (1 Kings 16:18)
4. Saul (1 Samuel 31:5)
5. Samson (Judges 16:30)
6. Ahithophel (2 Samuel 17:23)
7. Saul's armor-bearer (1 Samuel 31:5)

✦People Getting Stoned

1. Who pelted David and his men with stones while he accused David of being a violent man?
2. What son of a priest was stoned to death by order of King Joash?
3. What owner of a vineyard was stoned after being falsely accused in front of Ahab?
4. Who was stoned by an irate mob while trying to carry out the orders of King Rehoboam?
5. Which of Jesus' parables talks about the stoning of a landowner's servant?
6. Who was in danger of being stoned after the Amalekites dragged off the wives and children of Ziklag?
7. What shepherd boy felled a giant with a single stone?
8. Who stoned the Amorites while Joshua led an attack on them?
9. Who was stoned for holding back some of the loot from Jericho?
10. For what seemingly minor offense did the Israelites stone a man while in the wilderness?
11. In what city did some Jews persuade the people to stone Paul?
12. Who fled from Iconium when they heard of a plot to stone them?
13. What deacon became the first Christian martyr when the Jews stoned him?
14. What Gospel mentions Jesus miraculously passing through a crowd that intended to stone him?
15. Who intended to stone the woman caught in adultery?

✦All of These Diseases

1. What afflicted the Philistines when they captured the ark of the covenant?
2. Where did Jesus encounter a woman who had hemorrhaged for many years?
3. What king of Judah suffered from a painful boil?
4. What apostle's mother-in-law had a fever?

People Getting Stoned (Answers)

1. Shimei (2 Samuel 16:5-6)
2. Zechariah (2 Chronicles 24:20-22)
3. Naboth (1 Kings 21:13)
4. Adoniram (1 Kings 12:18)
5. The parable of the tenants (Matthew 21:35)
6. David (1 Samuel 30:6)
7. David (1 Samuel 17:49)
8. The Lord (Joshua 10:11)
9. Achan and his family (Joshua 7:24-25)
10. Gathering sticks on the sabbath (Numbers 15:36)
11. Lystra (Acts 14:19)
12. Paul and Barnabas (Acts 14:5-6)
13. Stephen (Acts 7:59)
14. John (10:31, 39; 8:59)
15. The scribes and the Pharisees (John 8:3-11)

All of These Diseases (Answers)

1. Tumors (1 Samuel 5:6)
2. Capernaum (Matthew 9:20)
3. Hezekiah (2 Kings 20:7)
4. Peter's (Matthew 8:14-15)

5. What was the affliction of the government official's son healed by Jesus?
6. What righteous man suffered from boils?
7. According to Revelation, what afflicts those who have the mark of the beast?
8. What king of Judah suffered from a crippling foot disease?
9. In the parable of Lazarus and the rich man, what was Lazarus's affliction?
10. What son of Jonathan was crippled because he had been dropped by his nurse as a baby?
11. What man was healed of dysentery by Paul?
12. Who healed Aeneas of paralysis?
13. What was the affliction of the man let down through a roof by his friends?
14. What prophet said that all of Israel was covered with sores, wounds, and bruises?
15. What did Moses toss in the air to produce boils on the Egyptians?

✦Some Lepers

1. What leper of Bethany entertained Jesus in his home?
2. What king of Judah was a leper until the day of his death?
3. What captain of the armies of Syria was a leper?
4. What prophetess became a snow-white leper for a short time?
5. Who put his hand into his bosom and, drawing it out, found it leprous?
6. Who became a leper after he lied to the prophet Elisha?
7. Who told Moses to send lepers away from the Israelite camp?
8. What is the greatest number of lepers Jesus healed at any one time?

✦Bodies Not Fully Functional

1. Who healed the crippled man at the Beautiful Gate in Jerusalem?

5. Fever (John 4:52)
6. Job (2:7)
7. Painful sores (Revelation 16:2)
8. Asa (1 Kings 15:23)
9. Running sores (Luke 16:20)
10. Mephibosheth (2 Samuel 4:4)
11. Publius's father (Acts 28:8)
12. Peter (Acts 9:33)
13. Paralysis (Luke 5:18)
14. Isaiah (1:6)
15. Ashes (Exodus 9:9-10)

Some Lepers (Answers)

1. Simon (Mark 14:3)
2. Uzziah (2 Chronicles 26:21)
3. Naaman (2 Kings 5:1)
4. Miriam (Numbers 12:10)
5. Moses (Exodus 4:6)
6. Gehazi (2 Kings 5:27)
7. The Lord (Numbers 5:1-4)
8. Ten (Luke 17:12)

Bodies Not Fully Functional (Answers)

1. Peter and John (Acts 3:2)

2. Where was Jesus when a handicapped man's friends lowered him through the roof?
3. What grandson of Saul was crippled in both feet?
4. Which gospel mentions the healing of the man by the pool at Bethesda?
5. Whose servant did Jesus heal without even being physically near the man?
6. Who did Jesus heal in a synagogue on the sabbath?
7. Who healed the paralytic Aeneas?
8. What apostle healed the man in Lystra who had been crippled since birth?
9. What was the affliction of the man Jesus healed in a Galilean synagogue?
10. Who had so much faith in Jesus' healing power that she touched the hem of his robe?
11. What blind man of Jericho did Jesus heal?
12. What was the affliction of the man at the pool of Siloam?
13. When Jesus healed the blind man of Bethsaida, what did the man say was the first thing he saw?
14. What person, suffering from deafness, was healed by Jesus after the disciples failed to heal?
15. What healing led to Jesus being accused of demon possession?
16. What patriarch became so blind he couldn't tell his sons apart?
17. What sinful city entertained visitors that struck the men with blindness?
18. What priest, ninety-eight years old, was blind?
19. What army did Elisha strike with blindness?
20. What sorcerer, an opponent of Paul, was struck blind?
21. Who was blind for three days after seeing a great light?
22. What judge was blinded by the Philistines?
23. Who had King Zedekiah of Judah blinded?
24. What father of twelve sons was blind in his old age?
25. What did Jesus put in the eyes of blind man at the pool of Siloam?
26. What blind prophet received the wife of King Jeroboam?
27. What book says that blind animals must not be sacrificed to God?
28. What righteous man claimed that he acted as eyes to the blind?

2. Capernaum (Mark 2:5-12)
3. Mephibosheth (2 Samuel 4:4)
4. John (5:8)
5. The centurion's (Matthew 8:13)
6. A crippled woman (Luke 13:10-13)
7. Peter (Acts 9:33)
8. Paul (Acts 14:8)
9. He had a withered hand (Matthew 12:13)
10. The woman with the issue of blood (Matthew 9:22)
11. Bartimaeus (Matthew 20:34)
12. Blind from birth (John 9:7)
13. Men, who looked like trees walking (Mark 8:25)
14. The boy near Mount Hermon (Mark 9:25)
15. The healing of a mute man in Galilee (Luke 11:14)
16. Isaac (Genesis 27:1)
17. Sodom (Genesis 19:11)
18. Eli (1 Samuel 4:15)
19. The Syrians (2 Kings 6:18)
20. Elymas (Acts 13:7-12)
21. Paul (Acts 9:9)
22. Samson (Judges 16:21)
23. Nebuchadnezzar (Jeremiah 39:7)
24. Jacob (Genesis 48:10)
25. Mud (John 9:1-7)
26. Ahijah (1 Kings 14:4)
27. Leviticus (22:22)
28. Job (29:15)

✦A Time to Weep

1. Who wept at thinking her son would die of thirst in the desert?
2. Who wept over the death of his rebellious son, Absalom?
3. What Old Testament woman is pictured as "weeping for her children and refusing to be comforted"?
4. At whose death did Abraham weep?
5. Who wept at seeing the new temple that was built after the exiles' return from Babylon?
6. Whose second husband, Phaltiel, wept as he watched her return to her first husband, David?
7. What caused Nehemiah to weep?
8. Who cried as he begged Isaac for his rightful blessing?
9. Who wept because her husband's other wife taunted her for being childless?
10. Who wept because he realized David had a chance to kill him but chose not to?
11. Who said, "Oh, that my head were waters, and mine eyes a fountain of tears"?
12. Who wept when he thought Joseph was dead?
13. Jacob wept with love and joy over what beautiful woman?
14. Who cried in Egypt when his brothers did not recognize him?
15. What judge's wife wept in front of him?
16. What three men wept when they saw Job's misery?
17. What prophet mentions women weeping for the god Tammuz?
18. What New Testament epistle mentions the priest Melchizedek weeping?
19. Who did Jesus tell not to weep for him?
20. What king's decree for extermination caused the Jews to weep?
21. Who said, "Mine eye poureth out tears to God"?
22. What king of Israel wept in front of the prophet Elisha?
23. What two male friends wept together?
24. When Saul was king, what caused the people of Gibeah to wail in despair?
25. What prophet cried when he realized what Hazael of Syria would do to the people of Israel?
26. What king of Judah cried because of his terrible illness?

A Time to Weep (Answers)

1. Hagar, mother of Ishmael (Genesis 21:16)
2. David (2 Samuel 18:33)
3. Rachel (Jeremiah 31:15)
4. Sarah's (Genesis 23:2)
5. Old men who remembered the glory of Solomon's temple (Ezra 3:12)
6. Michal's (2 Samuel 3:16)
7. He heard the walls of Jerusalem were still in ruins (Nehemiah 1:4)
8. Esau (Genesis 27:38)
9. Hannah (1 Samuel 1:7)
10. Saul (1 Samuel 24:16)
11. Jeremiah (9:1)
12. Jacob (Genesis 27:35)
13. Rachel (Genesis 29:11)
14. Joseph (Genesis 42:24)
15. Samson's (Judges 14:16)
16. Eliphaz, Bildad, and Zophar (Job 2:12)
17. Ezekiel (8:14)
18. Hebrews (5:6-7)
19. The daughters of Jerusalem (Luke 23:28)
20. Ahasuerus's (Esther 4:3)
21. Job (16:20)
22. Joash (2 Kings 13:14)
23. David and Jonathan (1 Samuel 20:41)
24. The threat of attack by the Ammonites (1 Samuel 11:4)
25. Elisha (2 Kings 8:11)
26. Hezekiah (2 Kings 20:3)

27. Who wept with relief when he realized all his sons had not been killed?
28. The elders of what church wept over Paul?
29. Where was Paul when his friends wept at hearing the prophecy that Paul would be handed over to the Gentiles?
30. Who wept bitterly after denying Jesus?
31. What baby was crying when he was discovered by a princess?
32. Who wept at her husband's feet and tried to dissuade him from listening to the advice of his assistant?
33. Who was reading the words of the Law when the people began to weep?
34. To whom did Jesus say, "Weep not"?
35. What friend did Jesus mourn for?
36. What king received approval from God for weeping and tearing his clothes in repentance?
37. Who wept and said to Jesus, "I believe; help thou my unbelief"?
38. Who wept on seeing what the Amalekites had done to the people of Ziklag?
39. Who discovered the widows of Joppa weeping over the dead Tabitha?
40. Where was Jesus when the sinful woman wiped his feet with her tears?

◆Sad Rags— Sackcloth and Ashes

1. What rich man sat in a pile of ashes?
2. What pagan city wore sackcloth as a sign of repentance?
3. Who wore sackcloth when he heard Joseph had perished?
4. What prophet declared that the people of Jerusalem should put on sackcloth in view of the coming destroyer?
5. What prophet in Babylon wore sackcloth while seeking the Lord?
6. What prophet told the people to mourn in sackcloth like a young woman bewailing her lost husband?
7. What king was confronted by a prophet who had disguised himself with ashes?

27. David (2 Samuel 13:36)
28. Ephesus (Acts 20:37)
29. Caesarea (Acts 21)
30. Peter (Matthew 26:75)
31. Moses (Exodus 2:6)
32. Esther (8:3)
33. Ezra (Nehemiah 8:9)
34. The widow of Nain (Luke 7:13)
35. Lazarus (John 11:35)
36. Josiah (2 Chronicles 34:27)
37. The father of the boy with an evil spirit (Mark 9:24)
38. David (1 Samuel 30:4)
39. Peter (Acts 9:39)
40. The home of Simon the Pharisee (Luke 7:38)

Sad Rags—Sackcloth and Ashes (Answers)

1. Job (2:8)
2. Nineveh (Jonah 3:8)
3. Jacob (Genesis 37:34)
4. Jeremiah (4:8)
5. Daniel (9:3)
6. Joel (1:8)
7. Ahab (1 Kings 20:37-39)

8. What book pictures the elders of Jerusalem sitting silently on the ground and wearing sackcloth?
9. What Syrian king had his servants wear sackcloth and grovel before King Ahab?
10. Who said, "I have sewed sackcloth upon my skin, and defiled my horn in the dust"?
11. What two cities did Jesus say would have repented in sackcloth and ashes if they could have seen his miracles?
12. Who put ashes on her head after being sexually assaulted by her lecherous half brother?
13. Who put on sackcloth when he learned of a government plan to wipe out the Jews?
14. Who was Job speaking to when he said, "I abhor myself, and repent in dust and ashes"?

✦Rending the Garments

1. What kinsmen of Joseph tore their clothes when they heard he had been killed?
2. What momentous finding caused King Josiah to tear his clothes?
3. Who tore his clothes when he heard his sons and daughters had all died at once?
4. Who tore his clothes when Jesus spoke of being seated at the right hand of God?
5. Who tore his clothes when he heard of the intermarriages of Jews with foreigners?
6. Whose oration caused King Hezekiah to tear his clothes?
7. Who tore their clothes on seeing Job's pitiful condition?
8. Who tore their clothes when Joseph's cup was found in Benjamin's sack?
9. Whose death caused David to order the people to tear their clothes?
10. What queen tore her clothes when she was put out of power by Jehoiada the priest?
11. Who tore their clothes when the people of Lystra began to worship them as gods?
12. What judge tore his clothing when his hasty words came back to haunt him?

8. Lamentations (2:10)
9. Ben-Hadad (1 Kings 20:31-32)
10. Job (16:15)
11. Tyre and Sidon (Matthew 11:21)
12. Tamar (2 Samuel 13:19)
13. Mordecai (Esther 4:1-3)
14. God (Job 42:6)

Rending the Garments (Answers)

1. Reuben and Jacob (Genesis 37:29, 34)
2. The finding of the Book of the Law in the temple (2 Kings 22:11, 19)
3. Job (1:20)
4. The high priest (Matthew 26:65)
5. Ezra (9:3-5)
6. The Assyrian Rabshakeh's (2 Kings 19:1)
7. His three friends (Job 2;12)
8. Joseph's brothers (Genesis 44:13)
9. Abner's (2 Samuel 3:31)
10. Athaliah (2 Kings 11:14)
11. Paul and Barnabas (Acts 14:14)
12. Jephthah (Judges 11:35)

13. What two men tore their clothes when the Israelites murmured against the Lord about going into Canaan?
14. Who rent his clothes when he heard Absalom had taken revenge on Amnon?
15. What man's assassination caused eighty men to come to Jerusalem with torn clothes and offerings of grain and incense?
16. What leper's plea for a cure caused the king of Israel to tear his clothes?
17. What warrior's death caused David and his men to tear their clothes in grief?
18. What friend of David, loyal during Absalom's rebellion, met David with torn robe and ashes on his head?
19. Who tore his clothes when Elijah was taken to heaven?
20. What abused sister tore her clothes after being raped by Amnon?

◆Grave Matters

1. What beheaded prophet was buried by his disciples?
2. What prophet's buried bones worked a miracle?
3. Who is the only person in the Old Testament mentioned as being buried in a coffin?
4. Who was buried in the cave of Machpelah?
5. What is the first burial of a servant mentioned in the Bible?
6. Who buried Moses?
7. What prophet, after being mourned by all Israel, was buried at Ramah?
8. What rebel was buried by Joab in a great pit in the forest?
9. What king's bones were, after his body was burned, buried at Jabesh-Gilead?
10. What was placed over Achan's body after the Israelites stoned him?
11. What leader was buried "in the border of his inheritance in Timnath-serah"?
12. Who was buried with Manoah, his father?
13. What judge died at a ripe old age and was buried in the grave of Joash, his father?
14. What evil king of Judah was buried, like his father, in the garden of Uzza?

13. Joshua and Caleb (Numbers 14:6)
14. David (2 Samuel 13:31)
15. Gedaliah's (Jeremiah 41:4-5)
16. Naaman the Syrian's (2 Kings 5:7)
17. Saul's (2 Samuel 1:11)
18. Hushai the Archite (2 Samuel 15:32)
19. Elisha (2 Kings 2:12)
20. Tamar (2 Samuel 13:19)

Grave Matters (Answers)

1. John the Baptist (Matthew 14:11-12)
2. Elisha's (2 Kings 13:20-21)
3. Joseph (Genesis 50:26)
4. Abraham, Sarah, Isaac, Rebekah, Jacob, and Leah (Genesis 49:30-31; 50:13)
5. Deborah, Rebekah's nurse (Genesis 35:8)
6. The Lord (Deuteronomy 34:6)
7. Samuel (1 Samuel 25:1)
8. Absalom (2 Samuel 18:17)
9. Saul's (1 Samuel 31:12-13)
10. Heaps of stones (Joshua 8:29)
11. Joshua (24:30)
12. Samson (Judges 16:31)
13. Gideon (Judges 8:32)
14. Amon (2 Kings 21:26)

15. What wicked king, the son of a godly king, was buried in the garden of Uzza?
16. Where were Joseph's bones finally buried?
17. What king was buried by his servants in the sepulchre with his forefathers in Jerusalem?
18. What leper king was buried in a special field?
19. What did the chief priests buy with the silver Judas returned to them?
20. What did Jesus say to the man who wanted time to bury his father?
21. Who begged the Canaanites for a place to bury his dead?
22. Who begged his son to be buried somewhere else besides Egypt?
23. What book says, "Their blood have they shed like water round about Jerusalem; and there was none to bury them"?
24. Who said, "The grave is my house"?
25. What book says that in the grave there is no work, no knowledge, and no wisdom?
26. Who said, "The grave cannot praise thee, death cannot celebrate thee"?
27. What apostle said, "O grave, where is thy victory?"
28. What prophet, speaking the words of the Lord, said, "I will ransom them from the power of the grave"?
29. What figure is portrayed in these words by Isaiah: "He made his grave with the wicked, and with the rich in his death"?
30. To whom did the Israelites say, "Because there were no graves in Egypt, hast thou taken us away to die in the wilderness?"?
31. What Gospel records the graves opening after Jesus' death on the cross?
32. Who said, "The hour is coming, in which all that are in the graves shall hear his voice"?
33. What people did Jesus refer to as "graves which appear not"?
34. According to Psalm 5, what is like an open sepulchre?
35. According to Jesus, the Pharisees built tombs for whom?
36. Who gave his rock-cut tomb as a burial place for Jesus?
37. Who infuriated Isaiah by building an elaborate tomb for himself?

15. Manasseh (2 Kings 21:18)
16. At Shechem (Joshua 24:32)
17. Ahaziah (2 Kings 9:28)
18. Uzziah (2 Chronicles 26:23)
19. A field to bury strangers in (Matthew 27:6-7)
20. "Let the dead bury their dead" (Matthew 8:22)
21. Abraham (Genesis 23:4)
22. Jacob (Genesis 47:29)
23. Psalms (79:3)
24. Job (17:13)
25. Ecclesiastes (9:10)
26. Hezekiah (Isaiah 38:18)
27. Paul (1 Corinthians 15:55)
28. Hosea (13:14)
29. The Suffering Servant (Isaiah 53:9)
30. Moses (Exodus 14:11)
31. Matthew (27:52-53)
32. Jesus (John 5:28)
33. The scribes and the Pharisees (Luke 11:44)
34. The enemies' mouths (Psalm 5:9)
35. The prophets (Matthew 23:29)
36. Joseph of Arimathea (Luke 23:50-53)
37. Shebna (Isaiah 22:15-16)

38. What man who hanged himself was buried in his family tomb?
39. Whose burial at Hebron caused the grief of David?
40. According to the Law, when was a hanged man's body supposed to be buried?
41. What wicked queen did Jehu send his men to bury, though she had already been devoured by dogs?
42. Who erected a memorial pillar for himself during his own lifetime?
43. What king had his body cast at the city gate with stones heaped on it?
44. What two liars were buried by the early Christians?
45. According to Jeremiah, what king was destined to have the burial of a donkey?
46. What woman, according to Jesus, prepared him for burial?
47. Who brought myrrh and aloes for the burial of Jesus?
48. According to Revelation, whose bodies would lie in the streets for three and half days without burial?
49. What two epistles compare baptism with burial?
50. Who buried Stephen?
51. Who did God promise would be buried at a ripe old age?
52. Who buried Abraham?
53. According to Jeremiah, who would not be buried or mourned?
54. What priest did Jeremiah tell he would be buried in Babylon?
55. Who buried Isaac?
56. What prophetess died and was buried at Kadesh?
57. What priest died and was buried at Mosera?
58. What judge of Israel was buried at Shamir?
59. What king was buried in Jerusalem after being killed by Pharaoh's armies?
60. What wicked king who had sacrificed his son was refused burial in the kings' sepulchres?
61. What king of Judah, murdered by his servants, was refused burial in the kings' sepulchres?
62. What judge of Israel was buried in Gilead?
63. Who moved the bones of Saul and Jonathan to their final burial place?
64. Who was the first king to be buried in Samaria?

38. Ahithophel (2 Samuel 17:23)
39. Abner's (2 Samuel 3:31)
40. The same day as the hanging (Deuteronomy 21:23)
41. Jezebel (2 Kings 9:34-37)
42. Absalom (2 Samuel 18:18)
43. The king of Ai (Joshua 8:29)
44. Ananias and Sapphira (Acts 5:6, 10)
45. Jehoiakim (Jeremiah 22:19)
46. The woman with the ointment (Matthew 26:12)
47. Nicodemus (John 19:39)
48. The two prophets (Revelation 11:3-9)
49. Romans (6:4) and Colossians (2:12)
50. Godly men (Acts 8:2)
51. Abraham (Genesis 15:15)
52. Isaac and Ishmael (Genesis 25:9)
53. The "slain of the Lord" (Jeremiah 25:33)
54. Pashur (Jeremiah 20:6)
55. Esau and Jacob (Genesis 35:29)
56. Miriam (Numbers 20:1)
57. Aaron (Deuteronomy 10:6)
58. Tola (Judges 10:1-2)
59. Josiah (2 Chronicles 35:24)
60. Ahaz (2 Chronicles 28:27)
61. Jehoash (2 Chronicles 24:25)
62. Jephthah (Judges 12:7)
63. David (2 Samuel 21:12-13)
64. Omri (1 Kings 16:28)

65. What king was killed by Jehu and then cast into Naboth's field?
66. How long had Lazarus been in his tomb when Jesus came?
67. What king desecrated the tombs at Bethel, burning the bones on an altar?
68. What disturbed man lived among tombs?
69. What group of people told Abraham that they would not refuse him burial in their tombs?
70. In John's Gospel, who is the first person to see Jesus' empty tomb?
71. According to Matthew, who ordered the guard at Jesus' tomb?
72. What prophet referred to his unusual prison as a "grave"?
73. What prophet pictures the Lord preparing a grave for Nineveh?
74. What book compares the power of jealousy to the power of the grave?
75. What book says that the grave is one of the four things that can never be satisfied?
76. Who is the only person in the Bible pictured as wearing his grave clothes?
77. What wife of Jacob had a pillar erected upon her grave?
78. In the New Testament, what young man was raised from the dead while on his way to be buried?
79. What prophet heard God describing the armies of the heathen nations gathered around their own graves?
80. What prophet complained that his mother's womb should have been his grave?
81. In Luke's Gospel, who is the only apostle to actually investigate the empty tomb?
82. In Matthew's Gospel, who moved the stone from Jesus' tomb?

◆Death in Massive Doses

1. What nation saw 185,000 of its soldiers slaughtered by an angel of the Lord?
2. What judge and his men killed 120,000 Midianites?
3. When the Israelites lost 30,000 soldiers in the time of Samuel, who were they fighting?

65. Jehoram (2 Kings 9:25)
66. Four days (John 11:17)
67. Josiah (2 Kings 23:16)
68. The Gadarene demoniac (Mark 5:2)
69. The Hittites (Genesis 23:5-6)
70. Mary Magdalene (John 20:1)
71. Pilate (Matthew 27:65)
72. Jonah (2:2)
73. Nahum (1:14)
74. Song of Solomon (8:6)
75. Proverbs (30:16)
76. Lazarus (John 11:44)
77. Rachel (Genesis 35:19-20)
78. The son of the widow of Nain (Luke 7:14)
79. Ezekiel (32:17-31)
80. Jeremiah (20:17)
81. Peter (Luke 24:12)
82. An angel (Matthew 28:2)

Death in Massive Doses (Answers)

1. Assyria (2 Kings 19:35)
2. Gideon (Judges 8:10)
3. The Philistines (1 Samuel 4:10)

4. What king headed up the slaying of 47,000 Syrians?
5. When the Jews were allowed to defend themselves against the Persians, how many Persians were killed?
6. What king of Israel killed 20,000 men of Judah in one day because they had forsaken the Lord?
7. For what offense did the Lord kill 50,070 men of Beth Shemesh?
8. For what sin of David did the Lord kill 70,000 Israelites with a plague?
9. What king of Judah led an army that killed 500,000 soldiers of Israel?
10. What Syrian king fled when 100,000 of his soldiers were killed by the people of Israel?

◆Killed by the Beasts

1. What sinister creature came in droves and killed the people of Israel in the wilderness?
2. What son of Jacob, according to his brothers, was killed by a wild animal?
3. Which book mentions people being devoured by lions?
4. What prophet saw two female bears devour the children who had poked fun of his baldness?
5. What animals devoured the foreigners who had moved into Israel?
6. For what strange offense was a prophet killed by a lion?
7. What animal killed a man for disobeying the old prophet of Bethel?

4. David (1 Chronicles 19:18)
5. 75,000 (Esther 9:15-16)
6. Pekah (2 Chronicles 28:6)
7. For looking into the ark of the covenant (1 Samuel 6:19)
8. Taking a census (2 Samuel 24:15)
9. Abijah (2 Chronicles 13:17)
10. Ben-Hadad (1 Kings 20:29)

Killed by the Beasts (Answers)

1. Fiery serpents (Numbers 21:6)
2. Joseph (Genesis 37:33)
3. Daniel (6:24)
4. Elisha (2 Kings 2:24)
5. Lions (2 Kings 17:24-25)
6. He refused the request of another prophet to hit him (1 Kings 20:35-36)
7. A lion (1 Kings 13:20-32)

PART 14

...And Things Left Over

✦Not to Be Taken Seriously (I)

1. Why was Moses the most wicked man?
2. What book of the Bible mentions a baseball player who hit ten home runs?
3. What Old Testament character must have been as strong as steel?
4. What animal could Noah not trust?
5. How long was Noah in the belly of the whale?
6. How do we know there were newspaper reporters in Bible times?
7. What animal on the ark had the highest intelligence?
8. Which burns longer—a candle under a bushel or one on a hill?
9. Out of Gideon's seventy sons, how many were big men at birth?
10. What kind of lights did Noah use on the ark?
11. When was the rooster's crow heard by everyone on earth?
12. How does a lawyer resemble a rabbi?
13. How many animals did Noah bring into the empty ark?
14. What New Testament book has an insect in the title?
15. What are the two smallest insects in the Bible?
16. What character was the most ambitious man?
17. Who was the greatest speaker?
18. Why, according to the Bible, is it all right to be obese?
19. Who had his seat in a theater changed?
20. Who was the first canning factory run by?
21. Which book in the Old Testament is a math book?
22. Why was Noah like a hungry cat?
23. What is it that Adam never saw or had, yet left two of them for his children?
24. What Bible character may have only been a foot tall?
25. What did Joseph in the Old Testament have in common with Zacchaeus in the New?

Not to Be Taken Seriously (I) (Answers)

1. He broke all Ten Commandments at once (Exodus 32:15-19)
2. Numbers 11:32—"He that gathered least gathered ten homers."
3. Iron (Joshua 19:38)
4. The cheetah
5. Noah wasn't in the belly of the whale—Jonah was.
6. Zacchaeus couldn't see Jesus for the press (Luke 19:3)
7. The giraffe
8. Neither—both get shorter.
9. None—they were all born small, as all babies are.
10. Flood lights
11. When it crowed on the ark
12. A lawyer studies the law and the profits.
13. One—after that it was not longer empty.
14. Ti(moth)y
15. The widow's mite and the wicked flea. (See Mark 12:42 and Proverbs 28:1.)
16. Jonah—even a whale couldn't keep him down.
17. Samson—he brought the house down even though it was filled with his enemies (Judges 16:27-30)
18. Because "all the fat is the Lord's" (Leviticus 3:16)
19. Joseph—he was taken from the family circle and put in the pit (Genesis 37:3-24)
20. Noah—he had a boatful of preserved pairs.
21. Numbers
22. He went 150 days and nights without finding Ararat (e'er a rat)
23. Parents
24. Nicodemus, since he was a ruler (John 3:1)
25. Joseph was overseeing and Zacchaeus was seeing over.

26. What did Jesus have in common with the fish that swallowed Jonah?
27. How do we know Isaiah's parents were good business people?
28. What kind of fur did Adam and Eve wear?
29. If Moses had dropped his rod in the Nile, what would it have become?
30. Since Methuselah was the oldest man in the Bible, why did he die before his father?
31. During what season did Eve eat the forbidden fruit?
32. What wage does not have any deductions?
33. What king mutilated sports equipment?
34. Who was the Bible's straightest man?
35. Why couldn't they play cards on Noah's ark?
36. Why did poor Job land in bed with a cold?
37. Who was the first person to eat herself out of house and home?
38. What is the difference between Noah's ark and an archbishop?
39. How do we know David was older than Goliath?
40. What is the moral of the story of Jonah and the great fish?
41. How are roller skates like the fruit in the Garden of Eden?
42. How did Jonah feel when swallowed by the great fish?
43. Who introduced salt meat into the navy?
44. What day in human life was longest?
45. What did Adam and Eve do when driven out of Eden?
46. Why couldn't Adam and Eve gamble?
47. Who presented Adam with a walking stick?
48. Who, besides Adam and Melchizedek, had neither father nor mother?
49. Who slept five in a bed?
50. Why didn't Moses take hornets into the ark?
51. Who was the first person to have surgery performed on him?
52. Why did the people on the ark think the horses were pessimistic?
53. What is often black, brown, or white, but should always be red?
54. How do we know Abraham was smart?
55. What is the first game mentioned in the Bible?
56. What son of Noah was a real clown?

26. Jesus had dinner with a sinner, and the fish had a sinner for dinner.
27. They both raised a prophet.
28. Bareskin
29. Wet
30. Enoch, his father, never died—he was taken into heaven.
31. Early in the fall
32. The wages of sin
33. "King Ahaz cut off the borders of the bases" (2 Kings 16:17)
34. Joseph—the pharaoh made a ruler of him.
35. Because Noah sat on the deck.
36. He had poor comforters.
37. Eve
38. One was a high ark; the other is a hierarch.
39. He rocked Goliath to sleep.
40. You can't keep a good man down.
41. They come before the fall.
42. Down in the mouth
43. Noah, who took Ham into the ark
44. Adam's first day—it had no eve.
45. They raised Cain.
46. God took their Paradise (pair o' dice) away.
47. Eve—she presented him with a little Cain.
48. Joshua, the son of Nun
49. David, who slept with his forefathers
50. Moses didn't go on the ark.
51. Adam—God removed one of his ribs.
52. They were always saying neigh.
53. The Bible
54. He knew a Lot.
55. Adam and Eve played hide-and-seek with God.
56. Ham

57. What do we find in Matthew and Mark that we don't find in Luke and John?
58. Which days in Bible times passed by quickly?
59. What was the most expensive meal in the Bible?
60. Where is the first example of math in the Bible?
61. Where is the second?
62. What was the difference between the ten thousand soldiers of Israel and the three hundred Gideon chose for battle?
63. Why couldn't Cain please God with his offering?
64. Why wouldn't the rooster fight on the ark?
65. How were the disciples cruel to corn?
66. How did God keep the oceans clean?
67. What minor affliction brought about Samson's death?
68. Who was the Bible's first financial wizard?
69. What was the Bible's first theatrical performance?
70. Where does the Bible talk about smoking?
71. What did Noah say as he was loading the ark?
72. When was tennis played in the Bible?
73. How did Adam and Eve feel when they left the garden?
74. Who is the first king in the Bible?
75. Who is the first man in the Bible?
76. Who is the first woman in the Bible?
77. Is the Book of Josiah in the Old or New Testament?
78. Who was the shortest man in the Bible?
79. Who was the first electrician in the Bible?
80. Who was the smallest man in the Bible?
81. Why was building the tower of Babel such a sad project?
82. What came first—the chicken or the egg?
83. What book mentions a righteous baseball pitcher?

◆Across the Biblical Spectrum

1. What color was the hideous seven-headed dragon in Revelation?
2. What is the first color mentioned in the Bible?
3. What doting father gave his favorite son a coat of many colors?
4. What New Testament woman was a seller of purple cloth?
5. What book describes a handsome man whose hair is black like a raven?

57. The letter a.
58. Fast days
59. Esau's—it cost him his birthright.
60. God divided the light from the darkness.
61. God told Adam to go forth and multiply.
62. 9,700
63. He just wasn't Abel.
64. He was chicken.
65. They pulled its ears.
66. With Tide
67. Fallen arches
68. Noah—he floated his stock while the whole world was in liquidation.
69. Eve's appearance for Adam's benefit
70. Genesis—Rebecca lighted off her camel.
71. "Now I herd everything."
72. Joseph served in Pharaoh's court.
73. A little put out
74. King James, if you have the King James Version—he's mentioned in the dedication.
75. Chap. 1
76. Genesis (Jenny's sis)
77. Neither—there is no such book.
78. Nehemiah (Knee-high-miah) or Bildad the Shuhite (Shoe-height)
79. Noah—he unloaded his family and the animals and made the ark light (arc light)
80. Peter, who slept on his watch (Matthew 26:40)
81. There were so many tiers.
82. The chicken—God doesn't lay any eggs.
83. Psalm 26:1—"Judge me, O Lord; for I have walked in mine integrity."

Across the Biblical Spectrum (Answers)

1. Red (Revelation 12:3)
2. Green (Genesis 1:30—"I have given every green herb")
3. Jacob (Genesis 37:3)
4. Lydia (Acts 16:14)
5. Song of Solomon (5:11)

6. What prophet had a vision of four chariots pulled by different colored horses?
7. According to Isaiah, what color does the Lord wear?
8. According to Isaiah, what color are sins?
9. What color was the sun in Revelation when it became like sackcloth?
10. What fabulous animal is mentioned as churning up white foam in the sea?
11. Who, according to 2 Peter, had a place of deep blackness reserved for them?
12. What evil woman was dressed in purple and scarlet and covered with jewels?
13. According to Joel, what fateful day would be a day of blackness?
14. Which Old Testament book contains the most references to the color blue?
15. According to Psalms, what color is the sinner after being washed by God?
16. What color was the cloth draped over the ark of the covenant?
17. Who sang a victory song that mentions white donkeys?
18. What Gospel mentions Jesus commenting on the red sky as a weather omen?
19. In Mark's Gospel, what color was the robe Jesus wore when the soldiers mocked him?
20. What three colors was the curtain for the Holy of Holies in the temple?
21. What Jew wore the royal purple garments in a foreign court?
22. What prophet talked about idols dressed in blue and purple garments?
23. Who had a vision of a heavenly being with white hair and white clothing?
24. What people defeated by Gideon wore purple garments?
25. What book speaks of an industrious wife who wears clothes of fine purple linen?
26. What prophet saw a drought end when the sky grew black?
27. What book mentions people who had worn purple pawing through the garbage of Jerusalem?

6. Zechariah (6:1-3)
7. Red (Isaiah 63:2)
8. Scarlet (Isaiah 1:18)
9. Black (Revelation 6:12)
10. Leviathan (Job 41:32)
11. False teachers (2 Peter 2:17)
12. Babylon, the great harlot (Revelation 17:4)
13. The day of the Lord (Joel 2:2)
14. Exodus (because of the many references to the tabernacle furnishings)
15. Whiter than snow (Psalm 51:7)
16. Blue (Numbers 4:6)
17. Deborah and Barak (Judges 5:10)
18. Matthew (16:2)
19. Purple (Mark 15:17)
20. Blue, red, and purple (2 Chronicles 3:14)
21. Mordecai (Esther 8:15) or Daniel (5:29)
22. Jeremiah (10:9)
23. Daniel (7:9)
24. The Midianites (Judges 8:26)
25. Proverbs (31:22)
26. Elijah (1 Kings 18:45)
27. Lamentations (4:5)

28. What servant of a prophet had his skin turned white as snow?
29. What colors were the fabrics used inside Solomon's temple?
30. Which of Jesus' parables mentions a rich man dressed in purple robes?
31. What insect invasion made the Egyptian ground black?
32. Who prayed that the day he was born would be covered with blackness?
33. Who had a vision of horsemen with breastplates that were yellow like sulfur?
34. How many times does the Bible mention brown?
35. What book mentions an immoral woman covering her bed with colored sheets from Egypt?
36. What prophet saw a multicolored eagle carrying off the top of a cedar tree?
37. What disease was considered to be healed if healthy black hair was growing on the skin?
38. What creature eliminated every green thing from the land of Egypt?
39. In Revelation, what did the rider on the red horse bring to the earth?
40. What kind of pastures are mentioned in Psalm 23?
41. According to Proverbs, what kind of person thrives like a green leaf?
42. What prophet says that God is like a green tree giving shelter to those who trust him?
43. In Revelation, what caused the green grass on earth to be burned up?
44. What color do the armies of heaven, in Revelation, wear?
45. What color cord was the harlot Rahab supposed to tie to her window so the Israelites would recognize her home?
46. In Revelation, what did the rider on the black horse bring to the earth?
47. What book mentions a woman with lips like a scarlet ribbon?
48. What color was the horse in Revelation that carried a rider with a pair of scales in his hands?
49. According to Job, what animal searches for green things to eat in the mountains?

---

28. Gehazi, Elisha's servant (2 Kings 5:27)
29. Blue, red, and purple (2 Chronicles 2:14)
30. The parable of the rich man and Lazarus (Luke 16:19)
31. Locusts (Exodus 10:15)
32. Job (3:5)
33. John (Revelation 9:17)
34. Once (the color of a horse) (Zechariah 1:8)
35. Proverbs (7:16)
36. Ezekiel (17:3)
37. Leprosy (Leviticus 11:31, 37)
38. The locusts (Exodus 10:15)
39. War (Revelation 6:4)
40. Green pastures
41. A righteous person (Proverbs 11:28)
42. Hosea (14:8)
43. Hail, fire, and blood poured on the earth (Revelation 8:7)
44. White (Revelation 19:14)
45. Scarlet (Genesis 2:18)
46. Famine (Revelation 6:6)
47. Song of Solomon (4:3)
48. Black (Revelation 6:5)
49. Wild donkeys (Job 39:8)

50. According to Matthew's Gospel, what color was the robe the Roman soldiers put on Christ when they mocked him?
51. What evil woman in Revelation rode on a scarlet beast?
52. In Revelation, what fallen city is noted as having dressed itself in scarlet and purple?
53. Where are black sheep mentioned in Bible?
54. Who practiced genetic engineering by using green and white branches in his flocks' drinking water?
55. What color were the clothes of the person who held seven stars in his hand?
56. What color hair was considered a symptom of leprosy?
57. What color was the cloth over the altar in the tabernacle?
58. What king promised purple robes for the man who could explain a strange inscription?
59. Who raised the question about whether there was flavor in the white of an egg?
60. Who, according to Lamentations, had their skin blackened after the fall of Jerusalem?
61. What book advises people always to wear white clothing?
62. According to Isaiah, what color would God change the scarlet sins to?
63. What prophet mentioned a harlot cavorting with soldiers in purple uniforms?
64. Who had a vision of ravenous locusts that devoured foliage and made the trees' branches white?
65. Where was Jesus when his clothes became radiantly white?
66. What color were the clothes of the angel that stood by Jesus' tomb?
67. What sweet food was white like coriander seed?
68. What color stone was promised to the faithful people at the church of Pergamum?
69. What church was told to buy white clothes to cover its nakedness?
70. What color clothes were the twenty-four elders in Revelation wearing?
71. According to David, which leader had clothed the women of Israel in fine scarlet robes?
72. What color cow was to be burned so that its ashes could be used in removing uncleanness?
73. What color thread was tied around the arm of the firstborn of Tamar's twins?

50. Scarlet (Matthew 27:28)
51. The great harlot (Revelation 17:3)
52. Babylon (Revelation 18:16)
53. Genesis 30:35—Laban had them in his flock.
54. Jacob (Genesis 30:37-42)
55. White (Revelation 1:14)
56. White (Leviticus 13:3)
57. Blue (Numbers 4:11)
58. Belshazzar (Daniel 5:7)
59. Job (6:6)
60. The princes (Lamentation 4:8)
61. Ecclesiastes (9:8)
62. White (Isaiah 1:18)
63. Ezekiel (23:6)
64. Joel (1:7)
65. The Mount of Transfiguration (Matthew 17:2)
66. White (Matthew 28:3)
67. Manna (Exodus 16:31)
68. White (Revelation 2:17)
69. Laodicea (Revelation 3:18)
70. White (Revelation 4:4)
71. Saul (2 Samuel 1:24)
72. Red (Numbers 19:2)
73. Scarlet (Genesis 38:28)

74. Who complained that his skin had turned black?
75. What color were the pomegranates around the hem of the high priest's robes?
76. What people did Jesus compare to whitewashed tombs?
77. What person did Paul call a "whitewashed wall"?
78. Whose name means "red"?
79. What color were the cords on the tassels the Israelites were commanded to put on their garments?
80. What sea was parted by a wind from God?
81. In the Law, what color ram's skin was acceptable as an offering?
82. What color horse did Faithful and True ride?
83. According to Moses, what color is a grape's blood?
84. What people were frightened away when they mistook the redness of the morning sun on water for blood?
85. Whose face turned red with weeping?
86. What color was the first of the four horses in Revelation?
87. Who warned his followers that they could not change the color of their hair by worrying?
88. What color was the stew Esau begged Jacob to give him?
89. According to Nahum, what city was attacked by soldiers in scarlet uniforms and carrying scarlet shields?
90. In Revelation, what did the rider on the white horse bring to the earth?
91. According to Proverbs, we should avoid looking at wine when it is what color?
92. What color horse did Death ride?
93. What color did the moon become when the sixth seal was broken open?
94. Which of Jacob's sons was described as having teeth whiter than milk?
95. What prophet mentions multicolored carpets?
96. Who had a throne with purple cushions?
97. What prophet said that prophets had whitewashed a pile of loose stones?
98. What Gospel says that the transfigured Jesus wore clothes whiter than anyone could ever wash them?
99. What book mentions making robes white by washing them in blood?
100. What curious object was in the hand of the person sitting on the white cloud in Revelation?

74. Job (30:30)
75. Blue, red, and purple (Exodus 28:33)
76. The scribes and Pharisees (Matthew 23:27)
77. Ananias the high priest (Acts 23:3)
78. Edom (Esau's other name) (Genesis 25:30)
79. Blue (Numbers 15:38)
80. The Red Sea (Exodus 13:18)
81. Red (Exodus 25:5)
82. White (Revelation 19:11)
83. Red (Deuteronomy 32:14)
84. Moabites (2 Kings 3:22)
85. Job's (16:16)
86. White (Revelation 6:2)
87. Jesus (Matthew 5:36)
88. Red (Genesis 25:30)
89. Nineveh (Nahum 2:3)
90. Conquest (Revelation 6:2)
91. Red (Proverbs 23:31)
92. Pale (or pale green, depending on your translation) (Revelation 6:8)
93. Blood red (Revelation 6:12)
94. Judah (Genesis 49:12)
95. Ezekiel (27:24)
96. Solomon (Song of Solomon (3:10)
97. Ezekiel (13:10)
98. Mark (9:3)
99. Revelation 7:14—the blood of the Lamb makes them clean.
100. A sickle (Revelation 14:14)

NOTE: Answers may vary because the names of colors differ in different translations.

✦Going to Extremes

1. Who was the youngest king mentioned in the Bible?
2. What was the largest army assembled?
3. What king of Judah had the longest reign?
4. What king of Israel had the shortest reign?
5. What is the shortest prayer in the Bible?
6. What are the two shortest verses in the Bible?
7. What is the longest verse in the Bible?
8. What is the longest prayer in the Bible?
9. What is the biggest animal mentioned in the Bible?
10. What is the smallest animal mentioned in the Bible?
11. What is the longest book in the Bible?
12. What is the longest book in the New Testament?
13. What word, the name of Isaiah's son, is the longest word in the Bible?
14. What is the longest chapter in the Bible?

✦Hairsbreadth Escapes

1. Paul, newly converted to Christianity, enraged the Jewish leaders in a certain city, so they decided to murder him. His friends let him down in a basket through the city wall. What city was it?
2. The judge Ehud stabbed the fat Moabite king Eglon while they were alone together. What simple maneuver did Ehud use to evade the king's guards?
3. Nebuchadnezzar breached the walls of Jerusalem, but the king and many others escaped. How?
4. The king of Sodom escaped his attackers by hiding where?
5. In Mark's Gospel, a young man who was following Jesus on the night of his betrayal just barely escaped from being apprehended himself. What was the sole garment the young man was wearing, and how did he escape?
6. Where did Joseph take Mary and the infant Jesus in order to escape the wrath of King Herod?
7. After Moses, still living in the royal household of Egypt, killed an Egyptian, where did he take refuge?

Going to Extremes (Answers)

1. Joash (or Jehoash), who began his reign at the age of seven (2 Chronicles 24:1)
2. One million men, brought by Zerah the Ethiopian against Asa of Judah (2 Chronicles 14:9)
3. Manasseh, who ruled for 55 years (2 Kings 21:1)
4. Zimri, who ruled for seven days after usurping the throne (1 Kings 16:15)
5. "Lord, save me," uttered by Peter while sinking (Matthew 14:30)
6. "Jesus wept" (John 11:35) and "Eber, Peleg, Reu" (1 Chronicles 1:25)
7. Esther 8:9—90 words in the King James Version
8. Probably Nehemiah 9:5-38
9. The whale (Genesis 1:21)
10. The gnat (Matthew 23:24)
11. Psalms
12. Luke
13. Maher-shalal-hash-baz (Isaiah 8:1)
14. Psalm 119, with 176 verses

Hairsbreadth Escapes (Answers)

1. Damascus (Acts 9:19-25)
2. He locked the door to the king's chamber and escaped through an upstairs porch (Judges 3:25-26)
3. There was a secret gate next to the king's garden (2 Kings 25:1-5)
4. In slime pits (Genesis 14:9-11)
5. The garment was a linen cloth. When the men grabbed him by the cloth, he fled away naked (Mark 14:51-52)
6. To Egypt (Matthew 2:13)
7. In Midian (Exodus 2)

8. When a violent storm caused the death of all of Job's children, how many people in the household escaped the tragedy?
9. Jesus was threatened with stoning by people gathering in Jerusalem for the Feast of Dedication. How did he escape?
10. Of the many times Saul tried to kill David, one of the closest calls was when he threw a spear at David. What did David do?
11. How did Michal, David's wife, fool the messengers who came to fetch the runaway David?
12. Running from Saul, David took refuge in Gath, where the king was worried about having a popular folk hero in town. How did David keep himself from being a victim of the king's anger?
13. When Absalom was trying to usurp the crown from his father, David, a woman helped David by hiding two of his messengers from Absalom's men. How did she hide them?

◆Hugs and Kisses

1. What two hostile brothers met and kissed each other, weeping all the way?
2. What soldier murdered a man while kissing him?
3. What prophet talked about kissing calves?
4. Who kissed Barzillai, an old man who had provided supplies for the army?
5. Who kissed Absalom after his two years in exile?
6. Who poured oil on Saul's head and kissed him?
7. What aged father kissed one son, mistaking him for the other?
8. Who met Moses in the wilderness and kissed him?
9. When Jacob died, who wept over him and kissed him?
10. What bereaved woman kissed her daughters-in-law good-bye as she left to return to her own country?
11. What rebel was so magnetic in personality that the men of Israel couldn't help kissing him?
12. Who kissed David when he was fleeing from Saul?
13. Who met Moses by the mount of God and kissed him?
14. Who kissed his brothers in a tearful family reunion?

---

8. One (Job 1:14-19)
9. We don't know—the Gospel account gives no explanation (John 10:22-39)
10. He merely sidestepped the spear so it went into a wall (1 Samuel 19:10)
11. She placed an idol (presumably human-sized) in David's bed and told the messengers he was sick (1 Samuel 19:11-18)
12. He pretended to be crazy (1 Samuel 21:10-15)
13. She hid them in a well, spread a covering over the well, and spread grain over the covering to hide it (2 Samuel 17:17-21)

Hugs and Kisses (Answers)

1. Jacob and Esau (Genesis 33:4)
2. Joab (2 Samuel 20:9-10)
3. Hosea (13:2), who was referring to calf idols
4. David (2 Samuel 19:39)
5. David (2 Samuel 14:33)
6. Samuel (1 Samuel 10:1)
7. Isaac, who kissed Jacob instead of Esau (Genesis 27:27)
8. Jethro, his father-in-law (Exodus 18:5, 7)
9. Joseph (Genesis 50:1)
10. Naomi (Ruth 1:9)
11. Absalom (2 Samuel 15:5-6)
12. Jonathan (1 Samuel 20:41)
13. Aaron (Exodus 4:27)
14. Joseph (Genesis 45:15)

15. Who kissed and blessed Ephraim and Manasseh, Joseph's sons?
16. Who kissed his nephew the first time they met?
17. Who returned home after making peace with his son-in-law and kissing his grandchildren good-bye?
18. What book begins, "Let him kiss me with the kisses of his mouth: for thy love is better than wine"?
19. What book says, "Every man shall kiss his lips that giveth a right answer"?
20. Who had a tearful farewell, with many kisses, at the city of Miletus?
21. Which epistle says, "Greet with a kiss of charity"?
22. According to Proverbs, whose kisses are deceitful?
23. Where was Jesus when the sinful woman kissed his feet and anointed him?
24. Which epistles end with Paul's admonition to greet fellow Christians with a "holy kiss"?
25. Where is a kiss described as lustful?
26. Who kissed Jesus as a supposed sign of friendship?
27. Who kissed the prodigal son?
28. Which book says, "Kiss the Son, lest he be angry"?
29. Who kissed Rachel almost as soon as he met her?
30. What prophet protested men kissing the image of Baal?
31. To whom did Job speak about kissing the hand as an act of homage?

✦Foot Coverings

1. Who was told by God to take his shoes off because he was standing on holy ground?
2. Who told people that he was not worthy to carry the Messiah's sandals?
3. Who told a king that he would not accept a gift of shoelaces?
4. What book mentions the custom of giving a person one's shoe as a sign of transferring property?
5. What nation did God toss his shoes upon?
6. During what historic event were the Hebrews instructed to keep their shoes on and be ready to travel?

15. Jacob (Genesis 48:10, 20)
16. Laban, Jacob's uncle and future father-in-law (Genesis 29:13)
17. Laban (Genesis 31:55)
18. Song of Solomon (1:2)
19. Proverbs (24:26)
20. Paul (Acts 20:36-38)
21. 1 Peter (5:14)
22. An enemy's (Proverbs 27:6)
23. The home of Simon the Pharisee (Luke 7:36-43)
24. Romans (16:16), 1 Corinthians (16:20), 2 Corinthians (13:12), and 1 Thessalonians (5:26)
25. Proverbs 7:13
26. Judas (Matthew 26:48)›
27. His father (Luke 15:20)
28. Psalms (2:12)
29. Jacob (Genesis 29:11)
30. Elijah (1 Kings 19:18)
31. Eliphaz, Bildad, and Zophar (Job 31:27)

Foot Coverings (Answers)

1. Moses (Exodus 3:5)
2. John the Baptist (Matthew 3:11)
3. Abram told this to the king of Sodom (Genesis 14:23)
4. Ruth (4:7)
5. Edom—"Over Edom will I cast out my shoe" (Psalm 60:8)
6. Passover (Exodus 12:11)

7. For what crime could a man have his shoe taken away and his face spit in?
8. What were the best-made shoes in the Bible?
9. Who did Jesus tell not to carry sandals with them on their journey?
10. What town's people tricked Joshua by putting on worn-out shoes when they went to meet him?
11. What sea, according to Isaiah, would be dried up by the Lord so that men could walk over it in their shoes?
12. What prophet, once he had taken his shoes off, walked around barefoot for years?
13. According to Ezekiel, what city did God put leather sandals on?
14. Who was told not to take his shoes off after his wife died?
15. Which prophet accused the people of Israel of selling the poor people for a pair of sandals?
16. What book has a devoted lover praising a woman's sandaled feet?
17. Who was told by the commander of the heavenly army to take off his shoes?
18. Who ordered a pair of sandals for his son's feet?
19. Who was told by an angel to put on his clothes and shoes?
20. Who prophesied that soldiers' boots would be used as fuel for burning?

✦Stones, Rolling and Nonrolling

1. Who suggested that stones could be turned to bread?
2. Who used a stone for a pillow?
3. What enemies of Joshua were pelted by stones from the Lord?
4. In what humiliating way was Abimelech murdered?
5. Who had a vision of an angel casting an enormous stone into the sea?
6. Who erected a large pillar stone and called it Ebenezer?
7. What shepherd boy went into battle with a bag of stones?
8. Who built an altar of stone that was consumed by fire from heaven?

7. Refusing to marry the widow of his deceased brother (Deuteronomy 25:9)
8. The shoes of the Hebrews who left Egypt, since they lasted for forty years (Deuteronomy 29:5)
9. The disciples (Matthew 10:10)
10. The people of Gibeon (Joshua 9:5)
11. The Egyptian sea (Isaiah 11:15)
12. Isaiah (20:2)
13. Jerusalem (Ezekiel 16:10)
14. Ezekiel (24:17)
15. Amos (2:6)
16. Song of Solomon (7:1)
17. Joshua (5:15)
18. The father of prodigal son (Luke 15:22)
19. Peter (Acts 12:8)
20. Isaiah (9:5)

Stones, Rolling and Nonrolling (Answers)

1. Satan (Luke 4:3)
2. Jacob (Genesis 28:11-22)
3. The Amorites (Joshua 10:11)
4. A woman dropped a millstone on his head (Judges 9:53)
5. John (Revelation 2:17)
6. Samuel (1 Samuel 7:12)
7. David (1 Samuel 17:49)
8. Elijah (1 Kings 18:31-38)

9. What patriarch and his father-in-law heaped up stones as a sign of their covenant together?
10. Who sat on a stone while the Amalekites fought the Israelites?
11. Who had a dream about a giant statue struck by a stone?
12. Which disciple was called a rock?
13. In Revelation, what did the Spirit promise to the churches that would overcome?
14. Who set up a commemorative stone after the Israelites covenanted to serve the Lord?
15. Which of Paul's epistles speaks about a "spiritual rock" that was Christ?
16. Who rolled the stone across the tomb when Jesus was buried?
17. Who spoke of a rejected stone becoming the chief cornerstone?
18. What friend of Jesus had a stone rolled over the front of his tomb?
19. Who rolled a stone from off a well so that Laban's flocks could be watered?
20. Who sealed up five Amorite chieftains in a cave by rolling large stones across the entrance?
21. Who was thrown into a den of wild animals that was sealed with a stone?
22. Who brought costly stones for the foundation of the temple in Jerusalem?
23. Who did Jesus tell that the stones would cry out if the people were silenced?
24. Who set up a commemorative pillar of stone at Paddan-Aram?
25. Who struck a rock and brought water from it?
26. Who prophesied that there would not be one stone of the temple that would not be thrown down?
27. Who picked up twelve souvenir stones from the dry path across the Jordan River?
28. Who had a garment with two onyx stones engraved with the names of the children of Israel?
29. Who wrote on tablets of stone for Moses?
30. Who had a breastplate with twelve precious stones in it?
31. What precious jewel is mentioned by Jesus in a parable about the kingdom?

9. Jacob and Laban (Genesis 31:44-52)
10. Moses (Exodus 17:8-12)
11. Nebuchadnezzar (Daniel 2:34-35)
12. Peter (Matthew 16:18)
13. A white stone (Revelation 2:17)
14. Joshua (24:27)
15. 1 Corinthians (10:4)
16. Joseph of Arimathea (Matthew 27:59-60)
17. Jesus (Matthew 21:42)
18. Lazarus (John 11:38-40)
19. Jacob (Genesis 29:10-11)
20. Joshua (10:16-18)
21. Daniel (6:17)
22. Solomon (1 Kings 5:17)
23. The Pharisees (Luke 19:40)
24. Jacob (Genesis 35:9, 14)
25. Moses (Exodus 17:6)
26. Jesus (Mark 13:1-2)
27. Joshua (4:4-8)
28. Aaron (Exodus 28:9-12)
29. God (Exodus 24:12)
30. The high priest (Exodus 28:17-20)
31. The pearl (Matthew 13:45-46)

32. What city is decorated with twelve precious stones?
33. What did Jesus say should not be cast before swine?
34. What did Job say was so precious it could not be purchased with gems?
35. What, according to Proverbs, is more precious than rubies?
36. What prophet said that Jerusalem would have walls made of jewels?
37. What city has gates made of pearl?
38. What epistle says that Christian women should not wear pearls?
39. What prophet talks about nine precious stones adorning the king of Tyre?
40. Which psalm says that the stone rejected by the builders becomes the chief stone?
41. Who questioned Job about the cornerstone of the earth?
42. Who spoke about God laying a precious cornerstone for Jerusalem?
43. Which epistle refers to Christ as a living stone?
44. Which epistle says that the apostles and prophets are a foundation and Christ is the chief cornerstone?
45. Who was Peter addressing when he spoke of Jesus as the cornerstone?

✦Boats and Other Floating Things

1. What king's household was carried in the only ferry boat mentioned in the Bible?
2. What was the material used in making the basket the infant Moses was floating in?
3. Who joined with wicked King Ahaziah of Israel in building a navy to go to Tarshish?
4. What nervous prophet actually requested that he be thrown off a storm-tossed ship at sea?
5. What king of Israel had two navies?
6. What was Jesus doing when a storm struck the boat carrying him and his disciples?
7. What was the only ship in the Bible mentioned by name?

32. The New Jerusalem (Revelation 21:19-20)
33. Pearls (Matthew 7:6)
34. Wisdom (Job 28:16)
35. Wisdom (Proverbs 3:15)
36. Isaiah (54:12)
37. The New Jerusalem (Revelation 21:21)
38. 1 Timothy (2:9)
39. Ezekiel (28:11-13)
40. Psalm 118:22
41. God (Job 38:6)
42. Isaiah (28:16)
43. 1 Peter (2:4-8)
44. Ephesians (2:20-22)
45. The Sanhedrin (Acts 4:11)

Boats and Other Floating Things (Answers)

1. David's (2 Samuel 19:16-18)
2. Bulrushes daubed with slime and pitch (Exodus 2:3)
3. King Jehoshaphat of Judah (2 Chronicles 20:35-57)
4. Jonah (1:4-16)
5. Solomon (1 Kings 9:26-28; 10:22)
6. Sleeping (Luke 8:22-24)
7. Castor and Pollux (Acts 28:11)

8. What was the name of the island where Paul and his companions landed after the shipwreck?
9. Who used a ship as a pulpit?
10. What two prophets predicted attacks from the war ships of Chittim?
11. What New Testament author uses the symbol of a ship's rudder to describe the power of the human tongue?
12. Who sent timber, in the form of rafts, to King Solomon?
13. What prophet predicted a glorious day when God's people would not be threatened with attacking ships?
14. What was Noah's ark made of?

✦Them Bones, Them Bones

1. What weapon did Samson use to kill a thousand men?
2. Whose bones were buried under a tree at Jabesh?
3. Who was made from a single bone?
4. Who was spared having his bones broken because he had already died?
5. Who had a vision of a valley filled with men's dry bones?
6. What saintly king desecrated a pagan altar by burning human bones on it?
7. What prophet's bones had sufficient power to raise another man from the dead?
8. What leader, carefully buried in an Egyptian coffin, had his bones transported out during the exodus and was buried at Shechem?
9. Which psalm contains a lament that passersby can count the psalmist's bones?

✦Things in Baskets

1. What king received seventy human heads in baskets?
2. What apostle owed his life to a basket?
3. What ill-fated servant had a dream of three bread baskets?
4. How many basketsful of food were collected after the feeding of the five thousand?

8. Malta (or Melita) (Acts 28:1)
9. Jesus (Luke 5:3)
10. Balaam (Number 24:24) and Daniel (11:30)
11. James (3:4)
12. Hiram of Tyre (1 Kings 5:8-9)
13. Isaiah (33:21)
14. Gopherwood (Genesis 6:13-16)

Them Bones, Them Bones (Answers)

1. The jawbone of an ass (Judges 15:15)
2. Saul's and his sons' (1 Samuel 31:11-13)
3. Eve (Genesis 2:21-22)
4. Jesus (John 19:33, 36)
5. Ezekiel (37:1-14)
6. Josiah (2 Kings 23:16)
7. Elisha's (2 Kings 13:20-21)
8. Joseph (Joshua 24:32)
9. Psalm 22 (v. 17)

Things in Baskets (Answers)

1. Jehu (2 Kings 10:7)
2. Paul (Acts 9:25)
3. Pharaoh's baker (Genesis 40:16-17)
4. Twelve (Matthew 14:20)

5. Who had a vision of two baskets of figs in front of the temple?
6. What prophet had a vision of a basket of summer fruits?
7. Who had a vision of a wicked woman rising up out of a basket?
8. What future liberator was found floating in a basket in the river?
9. Who served an angel a young goat in a basket?
10. How many basketsful of food were collected after the feeding of the four thousand?

◆As a Reminder

1. What was given as a reminder that the world would never again be destroyed by a flood?
2. What ritual was to be a reminder of Christ's body and blood?
3. What day of the week is a reminder of God's completed creation?
4. What was the manna put into the ark of the covenant a reminder of?
5. What festival was to be a memorial of the Jews' salvation from the wicked Persian Haman?
6. What feast was to be a reminder of the simple homes the Israelites had in Egypt?
7. What feast was a reminder of the death angel killing the Egyptian firstborn?
8. Who made brazen lights to remind the people of Israel that no one except Aaron's descendants should serve as priests?
9. What woman did Jesus say would have her story remembered for doing a kindness to him?
10. Who set up twelve stones to remind the people of God's power in bringing them across the Jordan?

◆A Sign unto You

1. What was given as a sign that the shepherds had found the baby Jesus?

5. Jeremiah (24:1)
6. Amos (8:1)
7. Zechariah (5:7)
8. Moses (Exodus 2:3-5)
9. Gideon (Judges 6:19)
10. Seven (Matthew 15:37)

As a Reminder (Answers)

1. The rainbow (Genesis 9:13-16)
2. The Lord's Supper (Luke 22:19)
3. The Sabbath (Deuteronomy 5:15)
4. God's supernatural provision in the desert (Exodus 16:32)
5. Purim (Esther 9:28)
6. The Feast of Tabernacles (Leviticus 23:39-43)
7. Passover (Exodus 12:11-14)
8. Eleazar (Numbers 16:39-40)
9. The woman who anointed his feet at Bethany (Matthew 26:6-13)
10. Joshua (4:7)

A Sign unto You (Answers)

1. The swaddling clothes and the manger (Luke 2:12)

2. What was given as a sign that God would not flood the earth again?
3. What gift was given to Christians as a sign of God's power to unbelievers?
4. What day was a sign of completion and rest?
5. According to Jesus, what prophet's sign would be given to the unbelieving Jews?
6. Who received a wet fleece as a sign of God's approval?
7. Who prophesied a virgin conceiving a child as a sign of God's presence?
8. Who saw a "slow" sundial as a sign of Hezekiah's recovery from illness?
9. Who set up twelve stones as a sign of God's parting of the Jordan?
10. What nation suffered ten plagues that were signs of God's power?
11. What food was a sign of the deliverance from Egypt?
12. What king saw an altar broken as a sign that God was speaking through a prophet?
13. What prophet advised building a signal fire as a sign of the coming invasion of Babylon?

◆Lamps, Candles, Etc.

1. Who had a vision of Jesus walking among seven gold candlesticks?
2. Who told a story about ten women lighting their lamps to meet a bridegroom?
3. Who saw a torch from God pass between the animals he had brought to sacrifice?
4. Which psalm says, "Thy word is a lamp unto my feet, and a light unto my path"?
5. Who was told to make a seven-branched candlestick to place inside the tabernacle?
6. According to Jesus, where do we never put our light?
7. What king sang, "For thou art my lamp, O Lord, and the Lord will lighten my darkness"?
8. What man, seeing his headquarters collapse, called for a light to check on Paul and Silas?

2. A rainbow (Genesis 9:13-17)
3. Tongues (1 Corinthians 14:22)
4. The Sabbath (Exodus 31:13)
5. Jonah's (Matthew 16:4)
6. Gideon (Judges 6:36-38)
7. Isaiah (7:14)
8. Isaiah (2 Kings 20:8-11)
9. Joshua (4:6)
10. Egypt (Exodus 10:2)
11. Unleavened bread (Exodus 13:7-9)
12. Jeroboam (1 Kings 13:5)
13. Jeremiah (6:1)

Lamps, Candles, Etc. (Answers)

1. John (Revelation 1:12)
2. Jesus (Matthew 25:1)
3. Abraham (Genesis 15:17)
4. Psalm 119 (verse 105)
5. Moses (Exodus 25:31-37)
6. Under a bushel (Matthew 5:15)
7. David (2 Samuel 22:29)
8. The Philippian jailor (Acts 16:29)

9. What judge confused the Midianite army by having his men break the jars they were using as lanterns?
10. According to the New Testament, what city has no need of lamps or candles?
11. In Jesus' parable, what was the woman who searched her house with a lantern looking for?

◆Threads and Ropes and Chains

1. What hyperactive person broke all the chains that had been used to bind him?
2. Who dropped a scarlet cord from her window to aid the Israelite spies?
3. Who made chains strung with pomegranates to decorate the temple?
4. Who put a chain of gold around Daniel's neck?
5. What people had golden chains around their camels' necks?
6. What apostle had his chains removed by an angel?
7. Who bound King Zedekiah in chains and blinded him?
8. Who gave birth to twins, one of which had a scarlet thread tied around it by the midwife?
9. Who put a golden chain around Joseph's neck?
10. What judge was bound up in cords by the Philistines?
11. What prophet was bound up in chains, along with the others who were carried away as captives?
12. What figure in the New Testament is bound up for a thousand years by a chain?
13. Who arrived in Rome bound by a chain?
14. Who wore an ephod with gold chains on it?
15. Whose servants put ropes on their heads and begged Ahab for mercy?
16. What apostle was on a ship where the ropes holding the lifeboat were deliberately cut?

9. Gideon (Judges 7:16-21)
10. The New Jerusalem (Revelation 22:5)
11. A lost coin (Luke 15:8)

Threads and Ropes and Chains (Answers)

1. The Gadarene demoniac (Mark 5:3-4)
2. Rahab the harlot (Joshua 2:15-19)
3. Solomon (2 Chronicles 3:16)
4. Belshazzar (Daniel 5:29)
5. Midianites (Judges 8:26)
6. Peter (Acts 12:6-7)
7. Nebuchadnezzar (Jeremiah 39:7)
8. Tamar (Genesis 38:28)
9. Pharaoh (Genesis 41:42)
10. Samson (Judges 16:6-9)
11. Jeremiah (40:1)
12. Satan (Revelation 20:1-2)
13. Paul (Acts 28:20)
14. Aaron (Exodus 28:14)
15. The servants of Ben-Hadad (1 Kings 20:31)
16. Paul (Acts 27:30-32)

✦Things on Wheels

1. What prophet's exit is associated with chariots of fire?
2. Who sent back the ark of the covenant on a cart pulled by two cows?
3. What king had 1400 chariots and 12,000 horses?
4. What foreign official was in his chariot when Philip came to him?
5. Who had a vision of four chariots driven by angels?
6. What king burned the idolatrous chariots of the sun?
7. Who took off in his chariot when his tax collector was stoned by the people?
8. Who got to ride in Pharaoh's second chariot?
9. What tribe was given six covered wagons in which to haul the tabernacle and its furnishings?
10. What mighty nation had its chariots ruined in the Red Sea?
11. What king rode into battle in a chariot but was fatally wounded by an Assyrian arrow?
12. Who sent wagons to Canaan to carry his father and his in-laws to Egypt?
13. What Syrian leper rode up to Elijah's house in a chariot?
14. What king of Israel was noted as a fast and furious chariot driver?
15. What king, fatally wounded while fighting the Egyptians, was brought back to Jerusalem in a chariot?
16. Who had a servant that saw a hillside covered with chariots of fire?

✦The Bible on Screen

1. What controversial 1985 movie starred actor Richard Gere as a king of Israel?
2. Cecil B. DeMille's *The Ten Commandments* (1956), which starred Charlton Heston as Moses, was a remake of a 1923 silent film of the same title. What famous director made the earlier film?
3. What 1966 epic featured director John Huston both as Noah and the voice of God?

Things on Wheels (Answers)

1. Elijah (2 Kings 2:11)
2. The Philistines (1 Samuel 6:7-14)
3. Solomon (1 Kings 10:26)
4. The Ethiopian eunuch (Acts 8:27-28)
5. Zechariah (6:1-8)
6. Josiah (2 Kings 23:11)
7. Rehoboam (1 Kings 12:18)
8. Joseph (Genesis 41:41, 43)
9. The Levites (Numbers 7:1-9)
10. Egypt (Exodus 14:27-28)
11. Ahab (1 Kings 22:34-38)
12. Joseph (Genesis 45:17-21)
13. Naaman (2 Kings 5:9)
14. Jehu (2 Kings 9:20)
15. Josiah (2 Chronicles 35:23-24)
16. Elisha (2 Kings 6:14-17)

The Bible on Screen (Answers)

1. *King David*
2. Cecil B. DeMille
3. *The Bible*

4. What much-loved TV movie was directed by Franco Zefferelli, an Italian best known for his work with Shakespeare and opera?
5. In the 1949 film *Samson and Delilah*, directed by Cecil B. DeMille, who played the leading roles?
6. The popular 1943 film *Song of Bernadette* featured actress Linda Darnell in the role of a biblical character. Who did she play?
7. What bald actor, famous for his role in another biblical film, played Solomon (with hair!) in the 1959 film *Solomon and Sheba?*
8. Italian Communist director Pier Paolo Pasolini shocked the world with his 1964 film based on the life of Christ. What was the film's title?
9. What 1981 TV movie starred Anthony Hopkins and Robert Foxworth as two apostles?
10. What 1953 film starred Charles Laughton as a lecherous Herod and Rita Hayworth as the title character?
11. What heartwarming 1963 film with Sidney Poitier took its title from Jesus' statement about "Solomon in all his glory"?
12. What 1932 film showed the declining Roman Empire and the growth of the church, and featured Charles Laughton as the despised Emperor Nero?
13. What popular 1953 film, based on a novel by Lloyd Douglas, told the story of Peter and featured such actors as Richard Burton, Jean Simmons, and Victor Mature?
14. This gaudy 1951 film was based on a popular novel by Polish author Henryk Sienkiewicz. It told the story of the early Christians and their persecution under Nero, played by Peter Ustinov. What was the film?
15. This MGM film, made in 1961, was criticized as being "too reverent" in its portrayal of Jesus, played by Jeffrey Hunter. What was the title?
16. Based on a popular stage play, this off-beat 1936 film showed Southern blacks acting out the roles of Old Testament characters. What was the film?
17. In the immensely popular *The Greatest Story Ever Told* (1965), practically every star in Hollywood had a small role. What role, with only one line of dialogue, did John Wayne play in this movie about Jesus?

4. *Jesus of Nazareth*
5. Victor Mature and Hedy Lamarr
6. The Virgin Mary
7. Yul Brynner
8. *The Gospel According to St. Matthew*
9. *Peter and Paul*
10. *Salome*
11. *Lilies of the Field*
12. *The Sign of the Cross*
13. *The Robe*
14. *Quo Vadis?*
15. *King of Kings*
16. *The Green Pastures*
17. The centurion at Jesus' crucifixion (who said, "Truly, this was the son of God")

18. *Ben-Hur*, made in 1959, won 11 of the 12 Academy Awards it was nominated for. What biblical character appeared in the film but did not speak?
19. What 1973 movie, filmed on location in Israel, featured young actors in a musical based on a popular (and controversial) play?
20. Two films—*The Omen* (1976) and *Damien* (1978)—were loosely based on biblical predictions about the Antichrist. What was the title of the third film in the trilogy, in which Christ actually confronts Satan in the final battle?
21. Who played the leading roles in *David and Bathsheba* (1951)?
22. What 1973 musical, based on a stage play taken from the Gospel of Matthew and using old hymns set to new music, was filmed in locations across Manhattan?
23. Director Frank Capra caused controversy when he stated that he wanted to cast a popular singer-actor as the lead in his proposed film about the life of Paul. What unlikely star did Capra want?
24. What Paul Newman film about the establishment of the State of Israel has the title of a book of the Bible?
25. What blond Swedish actor played the role of Jesus in *The Greatest Story Ever Told*?
26. What characters from the early years of Jesus' life appear as characters in the film *Ben-Hur*?
27. In the 1956 film *Moby Dick*, which two of the main characters have biblical names?
28. The movie *The Little Foxes* takes its title from which Old Testament book?
29. What actor, familiar to audiences for his portrayals of gangsters, played the quarrelsome Dathan in *The Ten Commandments*?
30. What 1957 film, based on an Ernest Hemingway novel, took its title from the Book of Ecclesiastes?

18. Jesus
19. *Jesus Christ Superstar*
20. *The Final Conflict* (1981)
21. Gregory Peck and Susan Hayward
22. *Godspell*
23. Frank Sinatra
24. *Exodus*
25. Max von Sydow
26. The three wise men
27. Ahab and Ishmael
28. The Song of Solomon 2:15 ("The little foxes that spoil the vines")
29. Edward G. Robinson
30. *The Sun Also Rises*

✦Not to Be Taken Seriously (II)

1. What did God say when Noah told him he wanted to build the ark out of bricks?
2. What book of the Bible mentions a lousy baseball player?
3. What did Paul do besides preach, teach, and make tents?
4. Who spoke when he was just a baby?
5. Where did Noah strike the first nail on the ark?
6. What is the first medicine mentioned in the Bible?
7. How do we know there was deviled ham in Bible times?
8. What was the name of Isaiah's horse?
9. Where in the Bible does it say people had a Honda auto?
10. Why didn't the last dove return to the ark?
11. What book of the New Testament contains a fruit in its title?
12. Why was Moses buried in the land of Moab?
13. What would have happened to Israel if all the women had left?
14. How many books in the Old Testament were named after Esther?
15. Which Old Testament prophets were blind?
16. What dishonest musical instrument did David play?
17. What age were the goats when Adam named them in the garden?
18. Who were the twin boys in the Old Testament?
19. In the New Testament?
20. Why was there no alcohol drunk when the Israelites were crossing the Red Sea?
21. Why did Moses cross the Red Sea?
22. Did Noah have a pig in the ark?
23. Who was the fastest runner in the Bible?
24. Where was Solomon's temple?
25. How did Ruth treat Boaz badly?
26. Who rang the first bell?
27. For how long did Cain hate his brother?
28. Who was the most successful doctor in the Bible?
29. Who in the Bible was a very lazy person?
30. Why was a woman in the Old Testament turned into a pillar of salt?
31. As strong as Samson was, what was the one thing he couldn't hold for long?

Not to Be Taken Seriously (II) (Answers)

1. He said, "No, Noah—go for wood [gopherwood]."
2. Psalm 19:12: "Who can understand his errors?"
3. He was a baker because he went to Philippi (fill a pie).
4. Job—he cursed the day he was born.
5. On the head
6. The two tablets God gave to Moses
7. Devils went into a herd of swine.
8. Is Me—because Isaiah said, "Whoa, is me!"
9. Acts 1:14—"They all continued with one accord."
10. She had found sufficient grounds to stay away.
11. Phi(lemon)
12. He was dead.
13. It would have been a stagnation.
14. Twenty-two—the rest were named before Esther.
15. Hosea, Joel, Amos, Jonah, Nahum, Habbakuk—none of them has i's.
16. The lyre
17. They were just kids.
18. First and Second Samuel
19. First and Second Timothy
20. It was dry land.
21. To avoid Egyptian traffic
22. Yes—there was Ham.
23. Adam—he was first in the human race.
24. On the side of his head
25. She pulled his ears and walked on his corn.
26. Cain hit Abel
27. As long as he was Abel
28. Job—he had the most patience.
29. The boy that loafs and fishes
30. She was dissatisfied with her Lot.
31. His breath

32. To be baptized by John the Baptist, what did a person have to do?
33. What two things could Samson never have for breakfast?
34. When the ark landed on Ararat, was Noah the first one out?
35. What city was named after something you find on a car?
36. What do you have that Cain and Abel never had?
37. What prophet was a space traveler?
38. Why was the kangaroo the most miserable animal on the ark?
39. Where did the Israelites keep their money?
40. How do we know Cain took a nap after he killed Abel?
41. What time was it when the elephant sat on Noah's chair?
42. How do we know God has a sense of humor?
43. What vegetable did Noah refuse to take on the ark?
44. Why was the Red Sea angry?
45. Why didn't Jonah trust the ocean?
46. What was the rudest animal on the ark?
47. What did the skunks have that no other animals on the ark had?
48. During the days of creation, what weighed less—the days or the nights?
49. What is the sleepiest land in the Bible?
50. Where were freeways first mentioned in the Bible?
51. How long did Samson love Delilah?
52. Who killed a fourth of the people in the world?
53. What was Eve's formal name?
54. Where does the Bible talk about the power of TV and radio?
55. Which bird on the ark was a thief?
56. When a camel without a hump was born on the ark, what did Noah's wife name him?
57. What was Adam and Eve's phone number?
58. Why did Moses have to be hidden quickly as a baby?
59. Why did the tower of Babel stand in the land of Shinar?
60. What did Samson eat to become strong?
61. What was in the wall of Jerusalem that the Israelites did not put there?
62. Where is baseball first mentioned in the Bible?
63. Where is the second mention?
64. And the third?

---

32. To go from bad to immerse
33. Lunch and dinner
34. No—he came fourth out of the ark.
35. Tyre
36. Grandparents
37. Elijah—he went up in a fiery chariot.
38. Her children had to play inside on rainy days.
39. The banks of the Jordan
40. He went to the land of Nod.
41. Time to get a new chair
42. He can take a rib.
43. Leeks
44. The children of Israel crossed it.
45. He knew there was something fishy in it.
46. The mockingbird
47. Baby skunks
48. The days—they were light.
49. The land of Nod
50. Genesis 1:30—"The Lord made every creeping thing."
51. Until she bald him out
52. Cain, when he killed Abel
53. Madam Adam
54. Esther 1:3—"The power of Persia and Media."
55. The robin
56. Humphrey
57. Adam 8-1-2
58. Because it was a rush job
59. It would have looked funny lying on its side.
60. Mussels
61. Cracks
62. Genesis 3:6—Eve stole first; Adam stole second.
63. Judges 7:20—Gideon and his men rattled their pitchers.
64. Psalm 26:1—"I shall not slide."

65. If Solomon were alive today, why would he be considered a remarkable man?
66. Who was named after a chicken?
67. How many species of animals did Noah take into the ark?
68. Why was the queen of Sheba so impressed by Solomon?
69. What book of the Old Testament has an ugly old woman in its name?
70. Who was the most popular actor in the Bible?
71. What aviator is mentioned in the Bible?
72. When Joseph was in prison in Egypt, what were the names of his cell-mates?
73. When was Adam born?
74. Was there money on Noah's ark?
75. What book mentions a bad pitcher in baseball?

◆A Few Bits of Potpourri

1. Which Gospel was, according to tradition, written first?
2. Which epistle was called "an epistle of straw" by Martin Luther, who disliked it because he thought it taught salvation by works?
3. What New Testament book had the most difficulty being accepted as Scripture by the early Christians?
4. What Egyptian bishop was the first person to list the 27 New Testament books that we now have?
5. What American president published an edition of the Gospels which left out all the supernatural elements?
6. Who printed the first Bible?
7. What year did that occur?
8. What conqueror said, "The Bible is no mere book, but a Living Creature, with a power that conquers all that oppose it"?
9. What world-famous author said, "The New Testament is the very best book that ever was or ever will be known in the world"?
10. What was the name of the Jewish scholars who first inserted vowels into the text of the Hebrew Old Testament?
11. What is the oldest known manuscript of the New Testament, written in Greek, produced in Israel, and discovered by a Russian?

65. He would be almost three thousand years old.
66. Hen (Zechariah 6:14)
67. All of them
68. She was amazed that a man with so many wives had the time to write books.
69. (Hag)gai
70. Samson—he brought the house down.
71. Pilate
72. Butler and Baker
73. A little before Eve
74. Yes—the duck had a bill, the skunk had a scent, and the frog had a greenback.
75. Ezekiel 36:12—"Yea, I will cause them to walk."

A Few Bits of Potpourri (Answers)

1. Mark
2. James
3. Revelation
4. Athanasius of Alexandria. This occurred in A.D. 367.
5. Thomas Jefferson
6. Johann Gutenberg
7. 1456
8. Napoleon
9. Charles Dickens
10. The Masoretes
11. Codex Sinaiticus

12. What year was the first American Bible printed?
13. Who was the first person to use the term *New Testament* to refer to the Christian scriptures?
14. What three languages was the Bible originally written in?
15. What form of Greek was the New Testament written in?
16. What material were the first manuscripts of the New Testament written on?
17. What president, speaking of the Bible, said, "That book is the rock on which our republic rests"?

12. 1752, in Boston
13. Tertullian of Carthage, around A.D. 200. Writing in Latin, Tertullian actually called the Scriptures *Novum Testamentum*.
14. Hebrew and Aramaic (Old Testament) and Greek (New Testament)
15. Koine, the common Greek of the Roman Empire
16. Papyrus, a material made from strips of reeds
17. Andrew Jackson